PREPARING FOR AN
AGING WORLD

THE CASE FOR CROSS-NATIONAL RESEARCH

Panel on a Research Agenda and New Data
for an Aging World

Committee on Population
and
Committee on National Statistics

Division of Behavioral and Social Sciences and Education

National Research Council

NATIONAL ACADEMY PRESS
Washington, D.C.

NATIONAL ACADEMY PRESS • 2101 Constitution Avenue, NW • Washington, DC 20418

Notice: The project that is the subject of this report was approved by the Governing Board of the National Research Council, whose members are drawn from the councils of the National Academy of Sciences, the National Academy of Engineering, and the Institute of Medicine. The members of the committee responsible for the report were chosen for their special competences and with regard for appropriate balance.

This study was funded primarily by NIH Contract No. N01-OD-4-2139 between the National Academy of Sciences and the National Institute on Aging, National Institutes of Health, U.S. Department of Health and Human Services. Additional funding was provided by the Andrew W. Mellon Foundation and the Rockefeller Foundation. Any opinions, findings, conclusions, or recommendations expressed in this publication are those of the author(s) and do not necessarily reflect the views of the organizations or agencies that provided support for the project.

Suggested citation: National Research Council (2001) *Preparing for an Aging World: The Case for Cross-National Research*, Panel on a Research Agenda and New Data for an Aging World, Committee on Population and Committee on National Statistics, Division of Behavioral and Social Sciences and Education. Washington, DC: National Academy Press.

Library of Congress Cataloging-in-Publication Data

Preparing for an aging world : the case for cross-national research /
Panel on a Research Agenda and New Data for an Aging World, Committee on
Population and Committee on National Statistics, Division of Behavioral
and Social Sciences and Education, National Research Council.
    p. cm.
Includes bibliographical references and index.
  ISBN 0-309-07421-5 (pbk.)
  1. Aging—Research. 2. Aged—Economic conditions. 3. Aged—Health
and hygiene. I. National Research Council (U.S.). Panel on a Research
Agenda and New Data for an Aging World.
  HQ1061 .D317 2001
  305.23'072—dc21
                                        2001002008

Additional copies of this report are available from the National Academy Press, 2101 Constitution Avenue, NW, Lockbox 285, Washington, DC 20055; (800) 624-6242 or (202) 334-3313 (in the Washington metropolitan area); Internet, http://www.nap.edu

Printed in the United States of America

THE NATIONAL ACADEMIES

National Academy of Sciences
National Academy of Engineering
Institute of Medicine
National Research Council

The **National Academy of Sciences** is a private, nonprofit, self-perpetuating society of distinguished scholars engaged in scientific and engineering research, dedicated to the furtherance of science and technology and to their use for the general welfare. Upon the authority of the charter granted to it by the Congress in 1863, the Academy has a mandate that requires it to advise the federal government on scientific and technical matters. Dr. Bruce M. Alberts is president of the National Academy of Sciences.

The **National Academy of Engineering** was established in 1964, under the charter of the National Academy of Sciences, as a parallel organization of outstanding engineers. It is autonomous in its administration and in the selection of its members, sharing with the National Academy of Sciences the responsibility for advising the federal government. The National Academy of Engineering also sponsors engineering programs aimed at meeting national needs, encourages education and research, and recognizes the superior achievements of engineers. Dr. William A. Wulf is president of the National Academy of Engineering.

The **Institute of Medicine** was established in 1970 by the National Academy of Sciences to secure the services of eminent members of appropriate professions in the examination of policy matters pertaining to the health of the public. The Institute acts under the responsibility given to the National Academy of Sciences by its congressional charter to be an adviser to the federal government and, upon its own initiative, to identify issues of medical care, research, and education. Dr. Kenneth I. Shine is president of the Institute of Medicine.

The **National Research Council** was organized by the National Academy of Sciences in 1916 to associate the broad community of science and technology with the Academy's purposes of furthering knowledge and advising the federal government. Functioning in accordance with general policies determined by the Academy, the Council has become the principal operating agency of both the National Academy of Sciences and the National Academy of Engineering in providing services to the government, the public, and the scientific and engineering communities. The Council is administered jointly by both Academies and the Institute of Medicine. Dr. Bruce M. Alberts and Dr. William A. Wulf are chairman and vice chairman, respectively, of the National Research Council.

PANEL ON A RESEARCH AGENDA
AND NEW DATA FOR AN AGING WORLD

F. THOMAS JUSTER *(Chair)*, Institute for Social Research, University of Michigan

RICHARD BLUNDELL, Department of Economics, University College London, United Kingdom

RICHARD V. BURKHAUSER, Department of Policy Analysis and Management, Cornell University

GRAZIELLA CASELLI, Dipartimento di Scienze Demografiche, Università di Roma "La Sapienza," Italy

LINDA P. FRIED, Welch Center for Prevention, The Johns Hopkins University

ALBERT I. HERMALIN, Institute for Social Research, University of Michigan

ROBERT L. KAHN, Institute for Social Research, University of Michigan

ARIE KAPTEYN, Center for Economic Research, Tilburg University, the Netherlands

MICHAEL MARMOT, Department of Epidemiology and Public Health, University College, London, United Kingdom

LINDA G. MARTIN, The Population Council, New York City

DAVID MECHANIC, Institute for Health, Health Care Policy and Aging Research, Rutgers University

JAMES P. SMITH, RAND, Santa Monica, California

BETH J. SOLDO, Population Studies Center, University of Pennsylvania

ROBERT WALLACE, Department of Preventive Medicine, University of Iowa

ROBERT J. WILLIS, Institute for Social Research, University of Michigan

DAVID WISE, John F. Kennedy School of Government, Harvard University, and National Bureau of Economic Research, Cambridge, Massachusetts

ZENG YI, Center for Demographic Studies, Duke University, and Institute of Population Research, Peking University

NIKOLAI BOTEV, *Liaison*, Population Activities Unit, United Nations Economic Commission for Europe, Geneva

Staff

KEVIN KINSELLA, *Study Director*
ELIZABETH WALLACE, *Project Assistant*
BRIAN TOBACHNICK, *Project Assistant*
BARNEY COHEN, *Director, Committee on Population*

Consultants

ROB ALESSIE, Department of Economics, Free University of
    Amsterdam
JAMES BANKS, Institute for Fiscal Studies, London
AXEL BÖRSCH-SUPAN, Department of Economics, University of
    Mannheim, Germany
DAVID CUTLER, Department of Economics, Harvard University
TULLIO JAPPELLI, University of Salerno, Italy
YUKINOBU KITAMURA, Institute of Economic Research, Hitotsubashi
    University, Tokyo
FRANCO PERACCHI, Tor Vergata University, Rome
LUIGI PISTAFERRI, Stanford University
NORIYUKI TAKAYAMA, Institute of Economic Research, Hitotsubashi
    University, Tokyo
SARAH TANNER, Institute for Fiscal Studies, London
ELIANA VIVIANO, Bank of Italy, Milan

COMMITTEE ON POPULATION

Preface

Nearly two decades have elapsed since the United Nations convened the First World Assembly on Aging (Vienna, 1982). During that period, researchers have made enormous progress toward understanding various dimensions of the human aging process, from the molecular level upwards to the global population level. As our knowledge has expanded, we have come to better appreciate the dynamic nature of the aging process and to recognize the many unanswered questions that urgently need attention. On the eve of the Second World Assembly on Aging (Madrid, 2002), we hope this volume helps focus ongoing and future research in several important arenas.

I would like to thank, first and foremost, my fellow panelists. Drawn from a variety of academic disciplines, most have studied one or more aspects of aging for the bulk of their careers. Each member contributed to the study by providing background readings, leading discussions, making presentations, and critically commenting on the various report drafts. The different perspectives that members brought to the table were instrumental in synthesizing ideas and forging agreement on overarching recommendations.

Drafting the final report was a uniquely collaborative enterprise. The panel divided itself into five working groups, corresponding to the major substantive content areas—labor force participation; income, wealth and saving; family structure and intergenerational transfers; health and disability; and subjective well being. Each of the panel members made significant contributions to the report in at least one of these areas, and many contributed comments in a number of areas.

This report reflects the efforts of many organizations and individuals beyond those represented on the panel. The panel itself was established under the auspices of the Committee on Population, directed by Barney Cohen, and the Committee on National Statistics, currently directed by Andy White. Both directors were instrumental in developing and guiding the study. The impetus and funding for this project came primarily from the Behavioral and Social Research Program of the U.S. National Institute on Aging, and we are grateful to Richard Suzman for his motivation and suggestions. We also are grateful to the Andrew W. Mellon Foundation and the Rockefeller Foundation for additional project funding.

A set of papers was commissioned to survey extant data and knowledge in several areas and to assist the panel in its deliberations. We benefited greatly from the work of these consultants: by Rob Alessie and Arie Kapteyn on wealth and savings in the Netherlands; by James Banks and Sarah Tanner on household wealth in the United Kingdom; by Richard Blundell and Sarah Tanner on work and retirement in the United Kingdom; by Axel Börsch-Supan on savings and retirement in Germany; by David Cutler on data needs for studying health care systems; by Tullio Jappelli and Luigi Pistaferri on household wealth accumulation in Italy; by Yukinobu Kitamura and Noriyuki Takayama on household wealth in Japan; and by Franco Peracchi and Eliana Viviano on work and retirement in Italy.

The panel met six times over the course of 16 months. To ensure that the panel was attuned to the latest information on key topics covered in this volume, one meeting was arranged in London in September of 1999 to bring together researchers from countries other than the U.S. as well as from international organizations involved with aging research and policy. For their presentations and/or insightful comments, we are indebted to Gary Andrews (Center for Ageing Studies, Flinders University, Australia), Arpo Aromaa (National Public Health Institute, Helsinki, Finland), Alessandro Cigno (Dipartimento di Studi sullo Stato, University of Firenze, Italy), J. Edward Dowd (Ageing and Health Program, World Health Organization, Geneva), Catherine Fallon (Directorate of Employment and Social Affairs, European Commission, Brussels), Luigi Ferrucci (Istituto Ortopedico Toscano, Firenze, Italy), Emily Grundy (Centre for Population Studies, London School of Hygiene and Tropical Medicine), Gunhild Hagestad (Northwestern University), Peter Hicks (Social Policy Division, Organization for Economic Co-Operation and Development, Paris), Felicia Huppert (Department of Psychiatry, University of Cambridge), Stephane Jacobzone (Social Policy Division, Organization for Economic Co-Operation and Development, Paris), Alan Lopez (Epidemiology and Burden of Disease Program, World Health Organization, Geneva), James Nazroo (Department of Epidemiology and Public Health, University College London), Jean-Marie Robine (INSERM Demography and Health, Montpellier, France), Richard Wall (Cambridge Group for the History of Population Social Structure, University of Cambridge), Mary Beth Weinberger (Population Division, United Nations, New York), and several of the commissioned paper authors mentioned above.

This report was reviewed in draft form by individuals chosen for their diverse perspectives and technical expertise, in accordance with procedures approved by the Report Review Committee of the National Research Council (NRC). The purpose of this independent review is to provide candid and critical comments that will assist the institution in making the published report as sound as possible and to ensure that the report meets institutional standards for objectivity, evidence, and responsiveness to the study charge. The review comments and draft manuscript remain confidential to protect the integrity of the deliberative process.

We thank the following individuals for their participation in the review of this report: Joseph G. Altonji, Institute for Research on Poverty and Department of Economics, Northwestern University; Gary Andrews, Center for Ageing Studies, Flinders University, Australia; Arpo Aromaa, National Public Health Institute, Helsinki, Finland; Axel Borsch-Supan, Department of Economics, University of Mannheim, Germany; Jonathan Gruber, Department of Economics, Massachusetts Institute of Technology; Michael Hurd, Center for the Study of Aging, RAND, Santa Monica, California; James H. Schulz, Florence Heller Graduate School, Brandeis University (emeritus); and Linda Waite, Center on Aging, National Opinion Research Center, University of Chicago.

Although the reviewers listed above have provided many constructive comments and suggestions, they were not asked to endorse the conclusions or recommendations nor did they see the final draft of the report before its release. The review of this report was overseen by T. Paul Schultz, Department of Economics, Yale University. Appointed by the National Research Council, he was responsible for making certain that an independent examination of this report was carried out in accordance with institutional procedures and that all review comments were carefully considered. Responsibility for the final content of this report rests entirely with the authoring panel and the institution.

Lastly, we must acknowledge the efforts of two individuals as well as the staff of the NRC's Committee on Population and the National Academy Press. Julia Hum, University College, provided valuable assistance with the logistical aspects of the panel meeting in London. Heather Hewett, research secretary at the Institute of Social Research, University of Michigan, expertly facilitated communication and the transfer of data, and test files between myself, the panel members, and the NRC staff. Within the NRC, we are indebted to Elizabeth Wallace and Brian Tobachnick, project assistants, for providing the essential infrastructure that facilitates such a project. Elizabeth skillfully and cheerfully handled a plethora of administrative matters during most of the panel's tenure, and Brian later took the reins and assured the orderly and efficient completion of the report and its subsequent preparation for publication. Special thanks go to Rona Briere, who edited the volume and made numerous suggestions for its improvement, and to Alisa Decatur for implementing the editorial changes. Kevin Kinsella, the NRC study director, not only helped to manage the overall work of the panel, along with Barney Cohen, Director of the Committee on Population, but also played a major role in drafting the panel report. Kevin wrote most of Chapter 2 (the demographic background of the problem), the initial draft of Chapter 1 (Introduction), and played a major role in the drafting of Chapter 5 (Intergenerational Transfers).

F. Thomas Juster, *Chair*
Panel on a Research Agenda
and New Data for an Aging World

Contents

PREPARING FOR AN
AGING WORLD

Executive Summary

Dramatic changes in fertility and mortality rates during the 20th century ensure that the world will age rapidly during the 21st century. The speed and pattern of population aging are determined by three principal factors. First and historically most important is the secular decline in fertility rates, which has the effect of producing a gradual but sustained increase in the ratio of older to younger people in a population. Second is the decline in mortality rates, which have fallen substantially in many countries over the past century as the result of a combination of advances in public health (e.g., water purification, antismoking campaigns), medical technology (e.g., the treatment of heart disease), and standards of living (e.g., better nutrition). The final factor is the pronounced but transitory rise in post-World War II fertility rates, usually called the "baby boom," which appeared with varying intensity and duration in a subset of developed countries. This increase in fertility rates contributed temporarily to younger age distributions, but the aging of the baby boom cohorts will soon accelerate population aging in these countries.

The projected growth in the numbers and proportions of the world's older population poses an array of challenges to policy makers. How do changes in the ratio of workers to retirees affect the ability of societies to fund old-age security systems? Are we living healthier as well as longer lives, or are our added years accompanied by disabilities and generally poor health? In what ways can the structure and the delivery mechanisms of health systems best adapt to the needs of older populations with a higher prevalence of chronic disease? How do changing family structures affect the demand for public transfers of money, time, and living space? Will population aging lead to lower levels of aggregate saving, investment, and productivity growth? Will health care costs rise or decline relative to other costs?

Three other important features of population aging are also noteworthy. First, there are uncertainties about how some of the demographic forces will play out. For example, will increases in life expectancy accelerate with the development of new technology? Will persistent below-replacement fertility levels compel societies to alter immigration policies? How might the socioeconomic characteristics of tomorrow's elderly population differ from those of today? Second, because population aging generally is a gradual phenomenon, its socioeconomic consequences tend to appear gradually as well, and in some cases with a fair degree of predictability. Thus if policy makers recognize and appreciate the import of the coming changes, they will have a window of opportunity in which to develop policies and programs for coping with the stresses induced by changing population age structures. And third, most statements about aged individuals tend to reflect averages and mask a great deal of diversity in the population. For example, while a greater proportion of the elderly[1] than the nonelderly have some degree of disability, most of the elderly are not disabled. Likewise, there are prominent socioeconomic gradients among older populations in most countries that require explication and policy response.

As we move through the 21st century, countries around the world are apt to face slower growth (or even contraction) of the workforce, rapid increases in the over-65 and especially the over-80 population, potentially larger numbers of disabled persons and greater demand on health care systems, and the increase in poverty likely to accompany rising numbers of widows. Many countries are now in the early stages of adapting to their changing population age structures. Since current and prospective policy responses are likely to differ among countries, a number of natural experiments are, or shortly will be, under way, enabling countries to learn from each other's experience. To take advantage of this opportunity, the U.S. National Institute on Aging asked the National Academies, through its National Research Council, to convene a panel that would provide recommendations for an international research agenda and for the types of data needed to implement that agenda in the context of rapid demographic change.

---

[1]There is a growing awareness that the category "elderly" is an inadequate generalization that conceals the diversity of a broad age group spanning more than 40 years of life. For cross-national comparative purposes, however, some chronological demarcation of age categories is required. In this report, the term "elderly" refers to persons aged 65 and over, and the term "oldest old" to persons aged 80 and over.

MAJOR RECOMMENDATIONS

This study focuses on five domains of research: work and retirement, savings and wealth, family structure and intergenerational transfers, health and disability, and well-being. Recommendations specific to each of these topics are included in the respective report chapters. The panel also developed six major, overarching recommendations that it believes are essential to effective cross-national research and to the generation of policy-relevant data.

I. The development and use of multidisciplinary research designs are crucial to the production of data on aging populations that can best inform public policies.

The range of topics addressed in this volume illustrates the need for multidisciplinary work that cuts across research domains. Recent demonstrations of the importance of cross-domain relationships—between health and retirement decisions, between economic status and health, between family structure and well-being in older age—amplify the contention that public policy must be guided by an understanding of the interplay of multiple factors. Initiatives in Europe, the United States and Asia that integrate several salient domains of people's lives into single survey instruments have proven to be successful prototype data collection efforts. Study domains include income and wealth, labor force activity and retirement, health status and utilization of health care facilities, cognition, and intergenerational transfers. The panel believes these models can serve as building blocks for research in many countries, including countries that are less developed as well as those more developed.

It is the panel's conviction that the optimum way to develop both the research agenda and the data needed to deal with the economic and social issues associated with an aging world is through the ongoing interaction of multidisciplinary national scientific communities. Extended interaction among demographers, economists, epidemiologists, social psychologists, sociologists, and statisticians is absolutely essential to (1) the creation and refinement of harmonized measures (conceptually comparable across societies) that are necessary to understand outcomes such as labor force participation, health and disability status, complex family relationships, and economic status; and (2) the development of databases that can be used to maximize the potential of cross-national and cross-temporal research for identifying the determinants of critical outcome variables.

It is important to stress that potential gains will not be realized unless there is a continuing and effective dialogue between the policy community and researchers that results in the design of a program of data collection that can properly inform policy makers. This dialogue must be ongoing since many of the key dimensions of population aging can be expected to change as socioeconomic circumstances evolve.

II. Longitudinal research should be undertaken to disentangle and illuminate the complex interrelationships among work, health, economic status, and family structure.

There is a pressing need in most countries for longitudinal microdata that include extensive measures of economic status, financial incentives to retire, various aspects of health status, and intergenerational relations and transfers. Such data are needed to better understand patterns of age-related transition along these dimensions, interrelationships among the dimensions, and ultimately the ways in which these domains contribute to overall well-being. One can anticipate with some degree of certainty the demographic parameters and trends that give rise to broad policy issues. Much less is known about individual responses to policy interventions, for example, the labor supply response of 60-year-old men and women to a restructuring of public pension plans that raise the early retirement age from 62 to 65. Ultimately, policy options are grounded in understanding individual and family behaviors and their responsiveness to changing life circumstances.

From a research standpoint, the variation in response patterns associated with changing circumstances implies the need for panel studies that trace cohorts over time. Studies can be repeated cross sections, single-cohort panel studies, or panel studies that continue to add new cohorts at the bottom end of the age range and are thus continually representative of the study population. If affordable, panel studies that add new cohorts are clearly best, since they not only capture the dynamics of change over time for individuals, but also continue to describe the broader population and not just a single cohort. Because the world is dealing with a phenomenon (population aging) that is likely to require the careful attention of policy makers for at least the next five decades, neither repeated cross sections nor single-cohort designs are very attractive. Interestingly, panel studies that add new cohorts may be less expensive than repeated cross sections with the same frequency, sample size, and length, simply because the cost of reinterviews is much lower than that of initial interviews. (The reason reinterviews are less expensive is that contact costs are lower; for example, telephone calls can be made to set up appointments.)

It is crucial to note that the focus of panel studies on aging should not be restricted to the upper ends of the age spectrum. We know that the characteristics of tomorrow's cohorts of elderly will be very different from those of today and will be determined by lifelong experiences. Within the bounds of practicality, surveys need to capture as much of the life-course experience as possible.

III. National and international funding agencies should establish mechanisms that facilitate the harmonization (and in some cases standardization) of data collected in different countries.

The panel believes major scientific and policy gains would be possible if a number of countries could be induced to embark on data design and collection activities that would provide a rich set of comparable (i.e., harmonized) data. Advantages would arise from the confluence of several factors: the differential rates of population aging throughout the world that result from differences in fertility and mortality histories and thus provide a unique opportunity for countries to learn from each other's experiences; the concomitant economic and social changes (e.g., in pension reform, marriage and divorce rates, schooling levels, adoption of innovative medical technology) that are occurring differentially throughout the world; and the growing awareness among policy makers that problems resulting from global aging pose what is arguably the most important set of economic and social challenges they will face over the next half-century. To benefit from the possibility of exploiting institutional differences to understand the effects of policy measures, data collection efforts in different countries must be harmonized in the sense that conceptually comparable information is collected, and procedures (e.g., for sampling and quality control) are synchronized to the extent possible. Much of this harmonization can probably be achieved through extensive exchange of information among scientific groups working on new data collection efforts.

This emphasis on harmonization does not imply that survey protocols need be identical in all countries. The track record of prior attempts to impose standardized data collection approaches across countries is mixed at best. Each country has unique institutional features and policy priorities that shape data collection and research. To illustrate, while all countries are likely to regard estimates of household wealth as an important element of their data collection activity, they are unlikely to measure the same components; for example, only the United States has 401(k) plans in household wealth portfolios. On the other hand, disability, disease, and functional health need to be measured in a standardized way to enable accurate cross-national analysis. The objective is to enable researchers to estimate accurate models of the incentives to work, to retire, and to save, and make it possible to link these patterns to other important domains of older peoples' lives.

IV. Cross-national research, organized as a cooperative venture, should be emphasized as a powerful tool that can enhance the ability of policy makers to evaluate institutional and programmatic features of policy related to aging in light of international experi-

ence, and to assess more accurately the impact of potential modifications to existing programs.

Cross-national studies conducted within a framework of comparable measurement can be a substantially more useful tool for the analysis of policy impact than studies of single countries. A cross-national perspective provides a broader and richer set of institutional arrangements within which to understand policy initiatives, and offers opportunities to relate variations in institutional arrangements to the distribution of attributes that determine program eligibility, benefit levels, and ultimately individual and household behaviors.

Sophisticated comparative analyses can exploit differences and changes in policy rules across countries by isolating their impacts from those of other macroeconomic and social changes. One penetrating example of cross-national research on 11 developed countries revealed three important features that could not easily have been discerned from single-country studies. First, the data showed a strong correspondence between early and normal retirement ages and the probability of departure from the labor force. Second, public pension provisions in many countries were found to place a heavy tax burden on work past the age of early retirement eligibility, and therefore to provide a strong incentive for early withdrawal from the labor force. Third, this implicit tax—and hence the incentive to leave the labor force—varied substantially among countries, as did retirement behavior. Thus, considering comparisons across the countries made it possible to draw several general conclusions about the relationship between retirement incentives and retirement behavior.

More generally, at least three conditions must be met to provide an accurate assessment of policy impacts on behavior. Thinking of the policy as a treatment, (1) there must be a sizable comparison (untreated) group with observable characteristics similar to those of the treatment group; (2) the comparison group must be unaffected by the policy (no spillover effects); and (3) the treatment and comparison groups must be subject to the same socioeconomic trends over time. Cross-national comparisons can help on all three counts. Policy interventions typically occur in one country but not elsewhere, meaning that valid comparison groups generally exist across but not within countries. Comparison groups in other countries are unlikely to be affected by a policy intervention in one country, so that spillover effects within countries do not necessarily distort the estimated impact of the intervention. Finally, comparison groups can be selected on the basis of characteristics that suggest relatively similar life experiences; for example, individuals with high incomes and education levels can be compared across countries. And even when within-country variation is informative, cross-country comparisons can add substantially to the variability in the data and thereby improve the precision of a policy intervention's estimated impact.

V. Countries should aggressively pursue the consolidation of information from multiple sources to generate linked databases.

The integration of different types of information (e.g., survey, census, administrative, medical) produces a dataset whose depth and explanatory power exceed what is possible for any single source. The advantage of linking survey data with administrative records is that the latter are likely to contain extended histories that could not be obtained from a survey, or if obtainable, would be associated with significantly higher measurement error. Under ideal conditions, therefore, administrative records can provide unbiased measures of change over time for a standard set of concepts. The ability to merge data of this sort with data tailored to the analytic issues addressed by surveys clearly has major advantages.

Beyond the scientific advantages, the linking of administrative and other information with survey data reduces respondent burden, a not-insignificant factor given the complexities of survey research instruments and the sometimes strong cultural reluctance to participate in survey endeavors. And finally, close attention must be paid to novel and potentially revolutionary ways of gathering data. The likelihood that a large majority of households in many countries will soon be connected to the Internet, for example, opens up promising new methods of data collection.

VI. The scientific community, broadly construed, should have widespread and unconstrained access to the data obtained through the methods and activities recommended in this report.

Good data are public goods for both policy and research. Scientific advances and policy insights that may emerge from the development of a dataset are greatly enhanced if a broad community of scientific users with different interests, theoretical perspectives, and models have ready access to the information. Moreover, the best way to identify errors in data is through the user community. The Health and Retirement Survey (HRS) in the United States, begun in the early 1990s and soon to be entering its second decade, is a prominent example of how data should be made available to the research community at large. Perhaps the most important reason for the widespread use of HRS data is that they are made available in a timely fashion on the Internet to scientists and policy makers alike. More than 300 scientific papers, many by non-U.S. researchers, have been written using these data.

The track record and protocols for access to data in many countries tend to discourage use of the data. In various European and Asian countries, researchers' access to data is severely limited or unnecessarily costly in terms of time and/or money. Because of restricted access and the limited role of scientists in the design of surveys, scientific innovation in the collection of data is hampered. Moreover, many of the best scientists in these countries often choose to use data from other countries to test their ideas since it is too difficult to use their own national data. The panel recognizes that all surveys involve legitimate and thorny issues of privacy and confidentiality that must be explicitly addressed and resolved. There are, however, statistical and legal methods for preserving confidentiality that can be used without unduly limiting scientific access to data.

FIVE RESEARCH DOMAINS

As noted, an inexorable demographic momentum will produce increasingly aged populations in most if not all nations of the world. There is, however, ample reason to believe that nations will be able to cope with the current and projected demographic changes provided policy makers have access to information about the emerging economic and social forces that will shape future societal well-being. The panel focused on five interrelated research domains in which new international data are required to inform policy making in the coming decades. Their relative importance is likely to differ by society and may change within a society over time. But if countries want to use current natural experiments throughout the world to improve their own adaptations to population aging, these are the five essential domains that must be addressed by international data and research.

Work, Retirement, and Pensions

The declining labor force participation of older persons in many parts of the world is one of the most dramatic economic trends of the past four decades. While the decline appears to have leveled off or even reversed in the last decade in some Organization for Economic Co-Operation and Development (OECD) countries, it has done so at historically low rates. Moreover, the decline has continued to occur in other, quite similar OECD countries. The increasing financial pressure faced by public pension systems around the world is often attributed to demographic trends that have led to aging populations. But decreasing labor force participation rates for a given age structure also contribute to financial imbalances within pension programs, further increasing the number of retired persons relative to those in the workforce. Ironically, public pension schemes in some countries, while providing protection against income loss in retirement, have themselves offered incentives to leave the labor force early, thus by their very structure exacerbating the financial problems countries face.

Two central features of public pension plans have an important effect on work incentives. The first is the age at which benefits are initially available, called the early retirement age. The extent to which people continue to work after they reach early retirement age is closely related to the second important feature of plan provisions, the pattern of benefit accrual. The most important determinant of benefit accrual is the adjustment to benefits if a person works for another year. In some countries, there is an "actuarial" adjustment such that benefits are increased to offset the fact that they are received for fewer years. In other countries, however, there is no such adjustment. If there is no adjustment, or if the adjustment is not large enough to offset the fewer years of receipt of benefits, the result is an incentive to leave the labor force.

In many countries, disability and unemployment insurance programs effectively provide for early retirement before the explicit early retirement age. Such programs must be considered in conjunction with the public pension program itself when social security reform is contemplated. One must be able to calculate accrual under various programs, in addition to accrual under the public program. Ideally, one should also know which paths to retirement are available to each person. A person who is eligible for disability benefits, for example, typically experiences much stronger early retirement incentives than one not eligible for these benefits. Eligibility usually depends on program provisions and individual circumstances that are often difficult to determine solely from administrative or survey data.

While the public pension system is the principal source of retirement benefits in many countries, in other countries it is only one of several important sources. In the United Kingdom, the Netherlands, the United States, and elsewhere, employer-provided pension plans are a key source of benefits; some retirees receive defined benefits in the form of annuities from employers in addition to payments from the public pension system. Indeed, in some countries (e.g., the United States), employer-provided benefits are often integrated with publicly provided benefits. The incentive effects of these private defined-benefit plans are quite similar to those of public pension programs. For many developing countries that are just designing pension programs with private as well as public components, there are opportunities to learn from the trials and errors of wealthier nations.

Private Wealth and Income Security

Income security during retirement, coupled with an increase in post-retirement years during which individuals can enjoy family and leisure, is one of the primary social achievements of the 20th century in most industrialized nations. At the same time, this accomplishment has introduced some fundamental public policy challenges associated with population aging. The two most basic challenges are (1) that individuals will have sufficient income security during their retirement years so that retirement does not necessarily imply a substantial decline in living standards, and (2) that individuals will have protection against the increasing risk of experiencing periods of poor health. From a policy viewpoint, these challenges involve a number of critical interrelationships, including those between health and economic status (i.e., income and wealth), between public policy and individual behavior (in particular, the extent to which public income support discourages private savings), and between demography and the stock market. The latter interaction is particularly important for countries that rely heavily on individual choices to provide for old age.

Although economists have gained a better understanding of individual saving and investment decisions and how these decisions interact with policy, numerous questions remain. Some are fundamental, such as whether the elderly dissave in old age (they should, according to economic theory) and whether consumption levels change at retirement (by and large they should not, according to economic theory). Others are directly related to policy, such as whether generous public or private pension provisions seriously attenuate individual incentives to save for retirement (they appear to); whether we can explain the current low savings rate in the United States (capital gains appear to be an important part of the explanation); and whether the recent runup of the stock market was driven by demography (there is some evidence that it may have been, and if so, this has important consequences for the wealth position of the baby boomers when they retire).

Clearly, such questions can be answered only if adequate data are available. Partly on the basis of research commissioned for five countries (Japan, the United Kingdom, the Netherlands, Italy, and Germany), we provide an overall assessment of datasets available in various countries and their potential to support investigation of important research and policy questions such as those posed above. In none of the countries except the United States is there substantial information about health in combination with wealth. Given the important interaction among health status, work status, and the amount of wealth accumulated over the life course, this is a serious omission. Although quality problems, including substantial underreporting of several asset categories (in particular, stocks and bonds) and selective nonresponse, are associated with many surveys, our general verdict is that the quality of the existing wealth surveys is surprisingly good. Thus careful cross-national comparisons using the data from these surveys are warranted. In many other countries, however, such data for addressing key policy issues do not currently exist and will have to be developed. We have identified strategies for dealing with these limitations.

Transfer Systems

The well-being of older persons depends to a large extent on the content and volume of an intricate set of transfer systems in which they are engaged over their lifetimes. In industrialized countries, the most salient of these systems are associated with individual savings behavior (representing transfers over individual life cycles), exchanges with family members, and intergenerational transfers from current workers to non-workers through many types of social security and pension programs. Individuals usually participate in a variety of transfer systems concurrently, with the mix varying across individuals and societies, as well as over the life course. The older generation in many countries is particularly likely to be involved in a complex series of exchanges involving public programs, employers, and family members, with significant shifts in salience and magnitude often occurring with age.

Although considerable progress has been made in understanding the volume, content, and implications of each major transfer system, many gaps remain. Particularly deserving of attention are interrelationships across systems and how changes in one system (for example, public pensions) affect another (for example, the level and direction of family support). Insofar as different transfer systems overlap and compete, sound policy and program development requires the best possible knowledge of how this marketplace operates, how responsive its different elements are, and what efficiencies and inefficiencies exist.

Many of the key transfer systems can be understood and measured at both the individual and family levels, as well as at the societal or macro level. This complexity poses further challenges to the tracing of interrelationships across systems. A microbehavioral approach is the major perspective for studying family exchanges, while macroeconomic analysis is the dominant strategy for studying public and employer transfer arrangements. The mix of transfer programs and their salience varies considerably between the more and less developed economies and within each group as well. This variation in approaches, incentives, and reactions to new programs and societal changes provides a continuum of experience whose study can greatly illuminate understanding of the dynamics of each system and the interrelationships across systems.

The Health of Aging Populations

Health plays an important role in the social outcomes associated with the other substantive research areas discussed in this report: retirement, wealth accumulation, transfer systems, and well-being. Hence it is critical that appropriate health data be collected to populate models that can be used to explain differences in these substantive outcomes within and across countries. At the same time, health is a critical policy variable in its own right. Although population aging may or may not result in increasing proportions of elderly persons in poor health, the numbers experiencing that condition are almost certain to increase. Thus as the populations of all industrialized countries and most developing countries age, the social and economic demands on individuals, families, communities, and nations will grow, with a substantial impact on formal and informal medical and social care systems and on the financing of medical services in general.

In conjunction with growing numbers of older persons, most nations face secular changes in health status, as reflected in rates and outcomes of various conditions and disabilities. For example, rates of heart attack and stroke are decreasing in many cases, while such trends may not be obvious for cancers. Some countries are experiencing rising rates of acquired immune deficiency syndrome (AIDS) at older ages. Research increasingly suggests declines in rates of severe physical disability among older persons in developed nations, although the cross-national comparability of such findings remains problematic. Trends in cognitive impairment and dementia have enormous policy implications, but our time-series knowledge base is lacking. Whether changes in disease and disability rates alter the rates of long-term institutionalization within and among nations is uncertain as well.

While all countries must address the changing health needs of their older citizens, their approaches are surprisingly diverse in terms of health system organization, administration, and financing. At the same time, national health systems themselves are in transition. Administratively centralized national health systems are being decentralized. Quality-of-care assurance mechanisms are increasingly in vogue. The diversity among nations in approaches to health system structure, program content, and financing argues for the value and utility of cross-national research for those attempting to improve the levels and quality of both preventive and therapeutic health services while maintaining budget discipline and responsiveness to cultural and social expectations.

However, effective cross-national and cross-cultural research demands suitably comparable data on health status and outcomes, informal and alternative sources of medical and social services, and health system administration and financing. These data must come from a variety of sources, including vital statistics and administrative records; research studies; population censuses; health outcome evaluations; and geographically defined longitudinal population surveys that assess the trajectories of the health, social, and economic status of families with older persons. Such information frequently is nonexistent, inaccessible, or nonstandardized, making it difficult if not impossible to conduct high-quality, informative cross-national research on health.

Well-Being

The supreme criterion by which the success of a government can be judged is the quality of life its citizens experience from birth to death. Questions of well-being are particularly important during major life transitions, both because such transitions provide a specific frame of reference for the assessment of well-being and because they involve significant changes in activity patterns. Proposals for the continuing assessment of well-being have been put forth for at least a half-century. Despite these proposals and a wide range of research efforts by academics, there is no consensus on the conceptual definition, conceptual levels, or measurement of well-being. Thus there is a pressing need for review and integration in this critical area.

The economic distinction between stocks and flows suggests a framework for helping to meet this need. Stocks reflect the cumulative impact of past history on a current state; a person's total assets or wealth is thus a stock. The change in that person's assets or wealth during some specific time period represents the corresponding flow. The analogy to subjective well-being is obvious. A person's satisfaction with his or her job, marriage, or life as a whole is a stock; a change in any of those satisfactions during a specific time period, or a change that results from a particular activity, is a flow.

Employment is a major source of well-being, for both extrinsic and intrinsic reasons. Remuneration determines access to most of the resources society offers—from housing, to clothing, to transportation, to entertainment, to higher education, and on through the long list of goods and services for sale. But one's job is also a source of more intrinsic satisfactions (or dissatisfactions)—the opportunity to use valued skills and abilities and to acquire additional ones, the sense of involvement in a larger productive process, and the cooperative and friendly relationships that may develop in the workplace. For all these reasons, the transition from paid employment to retirement or from full-time paid employment to part-time or temporary postretirement work is of great importance for individual well-being. The process of aging is in most respects gradual; in contrast, retirement for many people is an abrupt transition. Whether it comes as welcome or unwelcome, retirement signals significant changes in an individual's (or couple's) pattern of activity, use of time, and network of social relations. It is a life event of major importance with implications for both the stock and flow of well-being.

Cross-national research on aging should include the development of overall measures of subjective well-being (life satisfaction), as well as further development and assessment of measures of emotional states and moods. Cross-national comparisons should also include the experience of major life events, especially those stressful events that are increasingly likely in old age, such as illness, bereavement, retirement (complete or partial), and changes in activity patterns.

1

Introduction

Changing population age structures are compelling governments to create or revamp policies and programs that affect many facets of life. In Japan, the parliament voted in early 2000 to cut public pension benefits and raise the retirement age, mirroring the private pension reductions announced by the country's largest employers. Throughout Europe, persistent levels of below-replacement fertility have led to projected (and in some countries current) declines in total population size, prompting nations once opposed to large-scale immigration to rethink such policies in light of likely future shortages of workers and growing numbers of pensioners. In parts of sub-Saharan Africa, grandparents have become the principal caregivers for large numbers of children who have lost their parents to the HIV/AIDS epidemic. In the United States, the Congressional Budget Office projects that the proportion of gross domestic product (GDP) now devoted to social security, Medicare, and Medicaid will more than double (to 17 percent) by the year 2040, with most of the change occurring in the health arena.

The global population is aging at an accelerated rate. While the size of the world's elderly population has been growing for centuries, what is new in the 21st century is the rapid pace of aging and the graying of populations at very different levels of socioeconomic development. Long-term trends toward lowered fertility and improved health and longevity have generated growing proportions and numbers of older population throughout most of the world. Fertility decline and urbanization arguably were the dominant global demographic trends during the second half of the 20th century, much as rapid improvements in life expectancy characterized many nations during the first half of the century. Today, population aging is poised to emerge as a preeminent worldwide demographic phenomenon.

From a historical perspective, population aging represents a human success story. As education and income levels and access to safe, effective contraception have risen, increasing numbers of individuals have been able to achieve their lower reproductive goals. Moreover, most people live much longer lives, in better health, and with different personal expectations than their forebears. For example, people now expect to live for many years after leaving full-time work.

At the same time, the sustained shift in population age structure poses an array of challenges to policy makers. Questions such as the following are rising to the top of many political agendas: How do changes in the ratio of workers to retirees affect the ability of societies to fund old-age security systems? Are we living healthier as well as longer lives, or are our added years accompanied by disabilities and poor health status? In what ways can the structure and the delivery mechanisms of health systems best adapt to the needs of older populations that have a higher prevalence of chronic disease? How do changes in family structure affect the demand for public transfers of money, time, and space? Will shifting age distributions result in increased or decreased national saving and investment? Social scientists have already spent a good deal of time trying to find answers to such questions. The purpose of this report is to inform policy makers about the current state of knowledge, as well as to identify the types of data that, if collected, could assist in policy decisions necessitated by the transition to a more-aged society.

Research conducted during the last decade suggests that efforts to answer questions such as those posed above can benefit substantially from a multidisciplinary approach. Recent empirical work on the importance of cross-domain relationships—between health and retirement decisions, between economic status and health, between family structure and well-being in older age—supports the contention that public policy should be guided by an understanding of the interplay of multiple factors. Policies to address changing worker/retiree ratios, for example, must be informed not only by demographic considerations, but also by examination of incentive structures for retirement, the changing health profile of older workers, and an understanding of household decision making with regard to work and retirement patterns.

Planning for an aging society thus requires innovative research programs that can yield data on interrelated domains of life, a theme to which we return below and throughout this report. Moreover, policies and programs need to be informed by both macro and micro perspectives on aging. At the macro level, we need a clearer picture of the impact of existing policies and programs on decisions with regard to workforce transitions, health care utilization, and a variety of intergenerational transfers. At the micro level, we need to understand the various dimensions of well-being (e.g., physical and emotional health, economic status, family and interpersonal relationships), patterns of age-related transition along these dimensions, and their interrelationships. We can anticipate with some degree of certainty the demographic parameters and trends that give rise to broad policy issues. More elusive is the extent to which individual transitions within various statuses are policy responsive. Ultimately, policy options must be grounded in an understanding of individual and family behaviors and their responsiveness to changing circumstances.

IS THERE A "CRISIS OF AGING"?

In the year 2000, the net balance of the world's elderly population increased more than 750,000 each month. Two decades hence, the net increase likely will be on the order of 2 million per month (U.S. Bureau of the Census, 2000). The magnitude of the increase in the absolute number of the world's elderly has led to popular perceptions that population aging may overwhelm or radically alter important social institutions. Warnings have been sounded about the likely collapse of public pension systems; about rampant health care costs that may result in age-based rationing of care; about intergenerational conflict as the economics of old age siphon resources away from education, day care, and youth training programs; and about the ability of society's most basic institution, the family, to continue caring for its older members.

There is, however, ample reason to believe that nations will be able to cope with current and projected demographic changes provided policy makers have access to information about the emerging economic and social forces that will shape future societal well-being. Indeed, an overarching theme of this report is that both aging and policy responses to the phenomenon are highly malleable. Not long ago, the stereotypical view of individual aging was one of overall decline and certain inevitable outcomes: cessation of work, increasing disability, deteriorating social networks, and often a descent into poverty. We now know, however, that no single formula describes old age and that older individuals are as heterogeneous as younger ones along many dimensions. Yet there may be a structural lag in attitudes, policies, and practices regarding older persons (Riley et al., 1999). One policy challenge is to recast aging populations as a natural resource rather than a societal drain, and to exploit opportunities to use these growing reservoirs of human capital.

This report rejects both an alarmist and a complacent view of aging, noting that there is time for nations to design and implement the research tools and protocols that will make it possible for future policies to address ongoing structural age change. However, considerable lead time is required to develop the types of data that the scientific community now recognizes as crucial to understanding the aging process. The temporal window of opportunity is shrinking, and nations need to implement clear strategies for generating a stream of continuous information that can guide policy making in this crucial arena in the 21st century. Delayed action could have serious consequences and could indeed result in an "aging crisis" in terms of sharp overall tax increases and reductions in individual health and income benefits during retirement years.

THE VALUE AND CHALLENGES OF
CROSS-NATIONAL RESEARCH

While each country's approach to social policy is a function of unique historical and cultural developments, a primary motivation for undertaking the present study was the belief that nations can learn from each other. In an increasingly interdependent world, the rationale for cross-national research on aging is becoming stronger. A basic function of such research is to allow countries to compare performance. Why, for example, might poverty rates among the elderly differ substantially among neighboring countries? Why do estimates of healthy life expectancy vary widely among countries with similar levels of gross national product (GNP) per capita and well-developed health care systems? What lessons might be transferred from one setting to another? When done well and presented effectively, cross-national comparisons can be powerful motivators for change. The highlighting of differences among nations raises questions about whether national trends are unique and culture-specific or more universal and more fundamental to the human aging process. Comparisons prompt researchers and policy makers to reevaluate existing data, help them identify best practices for similar programs, and facilitate consideration of appropriate interventions.

One theme of this report is that countries fall along a continuum in the process of population aging. Despite the historical and cultural differences that may bedevil comparative research, policy makers should be able to learn from the experiences of their colleagues in other countries. In the West, population aging varies among countries, reflecting differing patterns of long-term fertility and mortality decline, as well as the appearance of unexpected demographic changes, such as the post-World War II baby boom in a number of nations. Countries with relatively prolonged baby booms will experience the aging of their populations later, and may be in a position to evaluate the successes and failures of policies adopted in nations with higher proportions of older populations. In some Asian countries, governments provide tax incentives for children to live with or near their parents, and parents can take advantage of children's health insurance. Variants of these programs may be useful elsewhere in the world. Further, the evolution of new political arrangements (such as the European Union) should in theory enhance the desirability of and opportunities for collecting comparable data.

Comparative research also enhances understanding of variations in the underlying dynamics of population aging and the effectiveness of similar policies and programs in different national settings. Countries and programs are frequently classified into broad categories that may obscure important variations. For instance, elderly people in Western nations are often portrayed as distanced from their children as compared with less industrialized regions where the elderly tend to live with their children. This simple dichotomy ignores the fact that while levels of elderly-child coresidence are much lower in the West than elsewhere, considerable contact, exchange, and personal care assistance takes place between parents and children. Similarly, variations in the cost of public pension systems and in labor force participation rates across industrialized nations often go unmentioned in sweeping pronouncements about the implications of aging for social security coffers. One penetrating and powerful example of cross-national research suggests that the trend toward early retirement in industrialized nations may have been induced in part by public pension systems themselves (Gruber and Wise, 1999). That is, the benefit structure intended to provide earnings replacement at older ages also offers strong incentives for early retirement, thereby intensifying the financial pressures on the system. This finding implies a causal relationship between policies designed to insure against substantial loss of income at older ages and retirement behavior, highlights the importance of research on system design features that can provide such protection in ways that have the least impact on behavior, and offers a framework within which countries can contrast their experiences and modify policies accordingly.

Cost is another consideration that argues for comparative study. Most of the data used in international comparisons today have come from cross-sectional studies of aging populations. Aging is a highly dynamic process, and cross-sectional surveys can capture only a single moment of the dynamic. The bulk of the process must be inferred from sequential cross-sectional surveys or through the creation of hypothetical cohorts to simulate the total experience across the life cycle. Panel studies involving longitudinal data collection are much better suited to capturing the dynamics of individual and group aging. These studies are relatively expensive, and may appear prohibitively so in many nations. At the same time, it can be argued that the cost of a well-designed longitudinal investigation is less than that of a series of cross-sectional studies of equivalent sample size and frequency, while the payoff in terms of benefits to policy making is far greater. In any case, an obvious strategy is for countries to coordinate their research on population aging in order to cross-fertilize the scientific knowledge base and to obtain maximum leverage from relatively modest public investments.

Another way to envision the advantages of cross-national research is to consider policy evaluation. One common method of assessing policy interventions is to measure differences between a treatment group (persons targeted by the policy intervention) and a control group (persons unaffected by the intervention). To essentially eliminate bias in estimating policy effects, three conditions are required: (1) there is a sizable comparison group with observable characteristics similar to those of the treatment group; (2) the comparison group is completely unaffected by the intervention; and (3) the treatment and comparison groups are subject to the exact same trends over time. Suppose that researchers and policy makers have only national samples available. Where treatments are universal but only for a specific subpopulation (such as in a medical screening), the first condition fails to be met immediately; that is, no suitable comparison group exists. The second condition fails to be met when there are spillover effects on the rest of the community. Finally, even if a comparison group can be chosen within a community or country, the third condition fails to be met when the two groups are sufficiently different (for example, in terms of health experiences over time).

Cross-national comparisons can help on all three counts (see Appendix A for a more formal exposition). Interventions or broader policies often are seen in one country and not another; a prime example is a universal health insurance scheme. Even if the policy is universal within a country, there is international variation, and the before-and-after contrasts can be drawn across countries. Alternatively, different countries may introduce similar interventions or treatments but with different timing, so that the contrast can still be drawn. Second, any spillover effects usually are contained within national boundaries, so that the contrast across countries remains valid. Finally, similar comparison groups can be chosen across countries—for instance, high-income and high-education individuals who are likely to have experienced and to continue to experience similar overall trends. We also note that, even in cases where within-country variation is informative, cross-country comparisons can add substantially to the informative variability of the data and thereby considerably improve the precision with which the impact of interventions is estimated.

While the theoretical benefits of comparative international research for policy making are increasingly clear, the conduct of such research poses a number of challenges. The basic challenges for cross-national research are the development of research questions and designs that can be readily adapted to different social and cultural settings, the harmonization of concepts and measures that provide a reasonably acceptable level of cross-national comparison, and the coordination of data collection and analysis across countries. Each of these challenges represents a major undertaking. Recent decades have seen heightened sensitivity to and substantial technical advances in the validation of measures in different cultural settings, yet many problems remain. Data on the same variable or process may differ in myriad small ways. A prime example is the measurement of activity restriction among older adults using a set of indicators commonly called "activities of daily living" (ADLs). The World Health Organization has recommended the use of a particular ADL instrument. However, a recent analysis of surveys in nine European nations showed that while the use of a set of ADL questions is widespread, there are significant differences among the surveys in both wording and the items included (Robine et al., 2000). These differences preclude comparison of the prevalence of ADL restrictions among countries.

In some cases, cross-national measurement problems are trivially easy to correct. For example, temperature measured in Fahrenheit in the United States can be converted to centigrade to conform to the European standard. In other cases, the theoretical idea is well understood but not trivial to implement. Consider the conversion of monetary measures to a common value. Current foreign exchange rates may convert French francs into U.S. dollars, but this conversion may not reflect purchasing power parity, a concept that attempts to equate the true purchasing power of given incomes in France and the United States. For many variables used in studies of health, psychology, and economics, methods for obtaining common measurements are not well understood, in part because they have received inadequate systematic attention from the scientific community.

Progress is being made on a number of fronts; for example, there is a continuing large-scale cross-national effort to create instruments that produce valid measures of depression that are comparable across countries, cultures, and language groups. To continue making progress along these lines, active collaboration of scientists from different disciplines and countries is essential. The analysis of data without shared protocols can lead to misleading conclusions. Careful planning of the collection and exchange of comparable data would have long-term benefits that would accumulate over time, benefits that could be shared by countries that may not have the near-term infrastructural capability to implement major country-specific data initiatives.

CHARGE TO THE PANEL

Given the crucial implications of burgeoning numbers of older people and the need for a scientific basis for policies addressing the opportunities and problems associated with major shifts in population age structures, the U.S. National Institute on Aging requested that the National Academies convene a panel of experts to explore the scientific opportunities for conducting policy-relevant comparative research on aging. The panel was asked to provide recommendations for an international research agenda and for the kinds of data needed to carry out that agenda in the context of rapid demographic aging. Specifically, the panel was asked to address the following statement of task:

• To identify the scientific opportunities for conducting policy-relevant cross-national research on aging.
• To review existing sources of socioeconomic, demographic, and health data on aging populations and to analyze the strengths and weaknesses of current international data collection efforts for addressing the priorities of various countries in aging research.
• To outline data collection efforts that, if undertaken internationally, would advance understanding of the aging process around the world.
• To identify potential obstacles to comparative work on aging, such as national variations in common definitions or differences among countries in laws governing privacy and access to data.

STUDY APPROACH AND SCOPE

The panel's ultimate charge was to produce a set of recommendations regarding issues in research on aging and to identify the data needed to help policy makers better understand the economic and social problems likely to arise with changes in population age structure. The panel's mandate was not to recommend specific policies for dealing with these issues, but rather to identify the types of data and research paradigms that would enable policy makers to make better-informed decisions. In this spirit, the panel:

• Examined the advantages of multidisciplinary involvement in data development.
• Highlighted areas in which cross-country analysis is critical.
• Considered the process by which the scientific community could develop and implement a data-driven research agenda.
• Examined the advantages that would ensue from combinations of survey and administrative data.

• Considered privacy and confidentiality issues relating to the dissemination and use of basic data.

The study's core concern was with the behavioral, socioeconomic, and health aspects of human population aging. Therefore, research in the important realms of molecular and cellular aging in various species fell outside the panel's purview. The panel also recognized that related studies on aging by the National Academies and others are currently under way and that it would be largely redundant to focus on topics that are covered thoroughly in existing or forthcoming reports. For example, a considerable amount of work has been done in the field of the biodemography of aging (National Research Council, 1997) and in the emerging area of how to integrate the collection of biological (including genetic) data into population-based surveys (National Research Council, 2001). Likewise, an evaluation of population projection methodology has been completed (National Research Council, 2000a), and current opportunities in cognitive research on the aging human mind have been delineated (National Research Council, 2000b). The United Nations (2000) Population Division recently convened a technical meeting on the living arrangements of older persons. Increasing attention also is being given to macroeconomic effects that may accompany shifting population age structures (see, for example, Peterson, 1999; MacKellar, 2000). While these areas are touched upon at least briefly in this report, relevant discussions may be found in other publications and are not detailed here.

The panel debated the important substantive areas in which international comparisons would potentially be most useful, and eventually focused on five interrelated research domains that require new international data to inform policy making in the coming decades: (1) labor force participation and the transition to retirement; (2) patterns and distributions of income, savings, and wealth; (3) changes in family structure and intergenerational transfers; (4) health and disability trends; and (5) subjective assessments of well-being that may be related to, but are largely independent of, conventional financial status and health measures. The panel formed five working groups to address these areas. The relative importance of these domains is likely to differ by society and may change within a society over time. However, if countries want to take advantage of natural experiments currently ongoing throughout the world to improve their own adaptations to population aging, these are the five essential domains that must be addressed by international research.

CROSS-CUTTING ISSUES

Several cross-cutting issues emerged during the panel's working group and plenary deliberations. Six such issues implicitly underlie the entire report and are discussed explicitly to some degree in each chapter. These issues also played a major role in shaping the panel's recommendations.

International applicability. One major obstacle the panel faced was formulating international research recommendations that would be pertinent to countries with diverse patterns of aging and stark differences in research infrastructure. For example, a detailed inventory of stock market holdings, private retirement annuities, fungible wealth, and so on may be crucial to understanding the well-being of older persons in highly industrialized nations, but may be much less important if not irrelevant in predominantly agricultural societies. The terms "developed" and "developing" are still used when grouping countries and making broad generalizations about modernization and economic development, but these categories are increasingly antiquated and may be misleading. While some policy issues regarding aging may be very different in parts of Latin America versus Europe, others may be quite similar.

Given the relatively advanced levels of population aging in industrialized nations, this report concentrates primarily, though by no means exclusively, on data issues in these countries. At the same time, the panel believes its recommendations should be viewed in light of a continuum of national research capabilities and needs. In some nations, population aging is just beginning to be acknowledged as a policy concern, and an appropriate first step in research might be simply to mine existing census data and anthropological studies to create a descriptive national profile of the elderly population. In other countries where little research has been conducted on aging per se, there may be valuable troves of existing data (e.g., hospital, clinical, and other administrative records) that could be used in developing an international comparative perspective as a means of stimulating policy debate. And cutting-edge research questions that have relevance in some less industrialized nations may be salient in more industrialized nations as well. As described in Chapter 5, for instance, the complexity of kin networks and the implications for family transfer patterns may be far greater in parts of Africa and Asia than in countries characterized by nuclear family units that have been declining in average size for generations.

The interrelated nature of this report's subject matter. As noted earlier, it is essential to recognize that the topics covered in this report are highly interrelated. For example, a large body of research demonstrates a significant relationship between income and wealth on the one hand and health outcomes such as morbidity and mortality on the other (Smith, 1999). Economic status in older age correlates with living arrangements and family transfers of money, time, and space. Health obviously affects the ability to work and the retirement decision, but mounting evidence suggests that the reverse also is true. Ultimately, the quality of life at older ages is affected by all these realms. Understanding and accounting for these functional linkages is crucial to successful policy development. The overriding need for complex data becomes clear given that policy initiatives in one arena may have unexpected and confounding effects in other areas.

The value of data linkage. Two potentially conflicting trends in many societies today are the expansion of available data on the one hand and growing concerns about individual protections and confidentiality on the other. The tension between the two is heightened by technological and methodological advances that allow microdata (i.e., at the individual level) from different sources to be linked. Researchers and policy makers find this to be an exciting and extremely useful development, a way to broaden knowledge of aging populations at relatively low cost and without additional survey intrusions (Woodbury et al., 1999). At the same time, they must appreciate the ethical and legal issues that arise. In the United States, the balance between private rights and the public interest in scientific databases constitutes an ongoing debate (see, for example, National Research Council, 1999; National Research Council, 2000c). National policies and laws governing privacy and access to data vary widely and represent significant potential obstacles to comparative research on aging. Finding ways to better exploit and develop data linkages while recognizing the necessity of protecting individual and group rights is a central emphasis of this report.

The diversity of the older population. As noted earlier, the term "elderly" conceals the diversity of individuals within an age range that spans more than 40 years. Like younger age groups, persons aged 65 and over have very different personal and social resources, health, living arrangements, and degrees of integration into social life. Underlying this diversity at older ages is the fact that different birth cohorts often have had very different life experiences. Man-made and natural disasters, major health breakthroughs, sudden economic changes, and landmark political decisions may, for example, shape a single 5-year birth cohort in ways that make its members behave in significantly different ways from persons born just before or just after that 5-year period. More gradual processes, such as changes in family structure, improvements in educational attainment, and higher vaccination rates, also cause future cohorts to enter the ranks of the elderly with very different characteristics than those of the current elderly population.

One characteristic that elderly populations do not share with younger age groups is their gender balance. Women make up the majority of the elderly population in nearly every country of the world, and their share of the older population increases with age. This numerical imbalance in favor of women is reflected in many of the topics considered in this report, ranging from disability to marital status to living arrangements. Given that gender differences in such areas as life expectancy, work history, asset accumulation, and care giving pervade most societies, it is imperative that policies regarding the well-being of older individuals account carefully for differential gender impacts.

The importance of socioeconomic differences. Related to diversity is the fact that the health of elderly populations in all countries varies according to socioeconomic position. The magnitude of these differences, as well as their causes, varies over time within and among societies. To develop policies effectively, one must have an understanding of these causes, which in turn requires a fuller understanding of the determinants of socioeconomic differences in health and functioning. Policy responses to such differences will ideally cover a wide range of determinants, including the provision of, access to, and response to medical care and social services. Therefore, an underlying need in any research agenda is to include a link to socioeconomic position in the collection of population and health data on elderly individuals.

The need to deal with uncertainty. The panel recognizes that aging in the future may be quite different from what we understand it to be today. We can only surmise, for instance, about the impact of new patterns of family dissolution and formation on elders' future support systems and well-being. Will changes in transnational capital flows interact with shifting age structures to produce new patterns of savings and wealth accumulation for old age? Will demographic pressures eventually outweigh ingrained cultural norms and result in political realignments and decisions that substantially affect older persons? Even the underlying process of aging itself may be radically altered by the deciphering of the human genetic code and resultant developments in gene therapy. One major challenge to any research agenda, then, is how to account for such future uncertainty. Can the research designs we propose accommodate, or even anticipate, the unexpected?

ORGANIZATION OF THIS REPORT

The following chapter reviews the current and projected demographic dimensions of population aging in the global context, with emphasis on the dynamics and worldwide variability of the process. Attention is given to changes in mortality and morbidity and the especially rapid growth of the oldest portions of elderly populations, changes that are likely to have pronounced ramifications for future policy development.

Chapters 3 through 7 address in turn the five principal research domains identified earlier; recommendations in each area are provided at the end of the respective chapter. At the same time, given the necessity of studying interrelationships among the five domains as discussed above, an attempt is made in each chapter to cast its main points in the light of linkages to the other domains.

Chapter 3 examines patterns of work, retirement, and pension arrangements across countries, as well as pension reforms and their likely impact on retirement behavior. The discussion centers on retirement incentives as key system variables in understanding the transition from work to retirement, and concludes with a delineation of the most important data and methods needed to model retirement behavior and hence inform policy making in this arena.

Chapter 4, which deals primarily with issues of savings and wealth, proceeds from a recognition that income security systems, despite their successes in providing generally adequate standards of living in industrialized nations, may have to be substantially revised if those achievements are to be maintained during the next century. One policy that many if not most countries (including those in the developing world) will consider involves some reliance on individual savings and wealth accumulation as a means of supplementing public-tier support. To date, however, we know relatively little about the motivations and propensities for households to save for retirement and about actual wealth levels within and among countries. This chapter highlights the main theoretical issues that arise with regard to household savings and wealth accumulation. It then compares data from six nations with an eye toward salient patterns, quality, and comparability, as well as how our stock of knowledge in this area can be improved.

In Chapter 5, the text moves to a discussion of family structure and intergenerational transfers, noting that the well-being of older persons depends to a great extent on the content and volume of an intricate set of transfer systems in which they are engaged throughout their lives. The mix of transfer programs and their salience varies considerably between the more and less developed economies and within each group as well. Many of the key transfer systems can be understood and measured at both the individual and family levels, as well as at the societal or macro level, a fact that presents further challenges to attempts to trace interrelationships across systems. A microbehavioral approach is the major perspective for studying family exchanges, while macroeconomic analysis is the dominant strategy for studying public and employer transfer arrangements.

Chapter 6 begins with an overview of the linkages between health and other subjects addressed in this report, and presents a conceptual framework that incorporates many of those linkages. The chapter reviews quantitative approaches to characterization of the health status of older persons, with particular attention to concepts and measurements of functional status. It then turns to the assessment of national heath care systems and their utilization. The quality and availability of extant national and international health data on older persons are considered in light of possibilities for cross-national studies. The chapter concludes with a discussion of the strengths of and obstacles to comparative research on health.

The penultimate chapter addresses a common policy goal shared by all countries, the well-being of their elderly constituents. The supreme criterion by which a government can be judged successful is the quality of life its citizens experience from birth to death. Questions of well-being are particularly important during major life transitions, both because such transitions provide a specific frame of reference for the assessment of well-being and because they involve significant changes in activity patterns. Despite a wide range of research efforts over the past half-century, there is little or no consensus on either the conceptual definition or measurement of well-being. Recent research in these areas has proceeded along various lines, and the chapter suggests a need for integration of at least five conceptual levels of well-being: external conditions, subjective well-being, persistent mood level, transient emotional states, and the biochemical/neural basis of behavior. The distinction between stocks and flows is offered as a promising basis for resolving the differences among concepts and measurements.

Finally, Chapter 8 puts several of the report's cross-cutting themes into sharper focus. In addition, six overarching recommendations for future research are presented.

REFERENCES

Gruber, J., and D. Wise, eds.
  1999 *International Comparison of Social Security Systems.* Chicago: University of Chicago
        Press.
MacKellar, F.L.
  2000 The predicament of population aging: A review essay. *Population and Develop-
        ment Review* 26(2):365-397.
National Research Council
  1997 *Between Zeus and the Salmon: The Biodemography of Longevity.* Committee on Popu-
        lation. K.W. Wachter and C.E. Finch, eds. Commission on Behavioral and Social
        Sciences and Education. Washington, DC: National Academy Press.
  1999 *A Question of Balance: Private Rights and the Public Interest in Scientific and Technical
        Databases.* Committee for a Study on Promoting Access to Scientific and Techni-
        cal Data for the Public Interest, Commission on Physical Sciences, Mathematics,
        and Applications. Washington, DC: National Academy Press.

2000a *The Aging Mind: Opportunities in Cognitive Research.* Committee on Future Directions for Cognitive Research on Aging. P.C. Stern and L.L. Carstensen, eds. Commission on Behavioral and Social Sciences and Education. Washington, DC: National Academy Press.

2000b *Beyond Six Billion: Forecasting the World's Population.* Committee on Population. J. Bongaarts and R.A. Bulatao, eds. Commission on Behavioral and Social Sciences and Education. Washington, DC: National Academy Press.

2000c *Improving Access to and Confidentiality of Research Data: Report of a Workshop.* Committee on National Statistics. C. Mackie and N. Bradburn, eds. Commission on Behavioral and Social Sciences and Education. Washington, DC: National Academy Press.

2001 *Cells and Surveys: Should Biological Measures Be Included in Social Science Research?* Committee on Population. C.E. Finch, J.W. Vaupel, and K. Kinsella, eds. Commission on Behavioral and Social Sciences and Education. Washington, DC: National Academy Press.

Peterson, P.G.

1999 Gray dawn: The global aging crisis. *Foreign Affairs* 78(1):42-55.

Riley, M.W., J. Riley, and A. Foner

1999 The aging and society paradigm. In *Handbook of Theories of Aging: In Honor of Jim Birren*, V.L. Bengston and K.W. Schaie, eds. New York: Springer.

Robine, J-M., C. Jagger, and V. Egidi

2000 *Selection of a Coherent Set of Health Indicators.* Montpellier, France: Equipe INSERM Demographie et Sante.

Smith, J.P.

1999 Healthy bodies and thick wallets: The dual relationship between health and economic status. *Journal of Economic Perspectives* 13:145-166.

United Nations

2000 United Nations Technical Meeting on Population Aging and Living Arrangements of Older Americans. Available: http://www.undp.org/popin/popdiv/untech/untech.htm [February 27, 2001].

U.S. Bureau of the Census

2000 International Data Base. Available: http://www.census.gov/ipc/www/idbnew.html [February 28, 2001].

Woodbury, R., A. Gustman, L. Lillard, O. Mitchell, and R. Willis

1999 The Value of Linked Data in Aging Research. Paper prepared for April 17-18, 2000 meeting of the Panel on a Research Agenda and New Data for an Aging World, Washington, DC.

2

Our Aging World

One prominent demographic outcome of the 20th century is the extent of population aging that has resulted from reduced fertility and increased survival. For the first time in history, many societies have the opportunity to age. Accompanying this broad demographic process, however, are other changes—shifting disease profiles, macroeconomic strains, emergent technologies, changing work patterns and social norms—that are difficult for societies to anticipate and plan for. The intersection of such changes with an evolving demographic context may generate unforeseen issues that become the socioeconomic problems of current and future generations.

Although virtually all of the world's populations are becoming older on average, the extent and pace of aging can vary enormously from society to society. Likewise, as noted in Chapter 1, the meaning of the term "elderly" varies as a result of broad national differences in culture, institutions, and health. Indeed, any chronological demarcation of age boundaries is arbitrary and open to dispute on the grounds that it poorly represents the biological, physiological, or even psychological dimensions of the human experience. Attainment of age 85 may be as extraordinary in one nation as it is commonplace in another. Nevertheless, such demarcation is necessary for a descriptive comparison of international aging. In the following pages, therefore, the term "elderly" refers to persons aged 65 and over, and the term "oldest old" refers to those at least 80 years old.[1]

---

[1]The chronological demarcation of "oldest old" is an arbitrary one. In industrialized nations, the term usually refers to people aged 85 and over, while in less industrialized nations, where life expectancy on average is lower, the term commonly refers to people aged 80 and over.

As a backdrop for subsequent chapters, this chapter describes the current demographic situation of the world's elderly and considers how the future situation might evolve. In addition to reviewing numbers and proportions of elderly people around the world, the discussion provides an overview of the dynamics of population aging, the increasingly important influence of changes in mortality at older ages on overall population aging, and the uncertainty such changes may introduce into our best efforts to project the size and composition of tomorrow's older population.

NUMBERS AND PROPORTIONS OF ELDERLY

Estimates for the year 2000 indicate an aggregate global total of 419 million persons aged 65 and over, 6.9 percent of the earth's total population. As noted in Chapter 1, the net balance of the world's elderly population is currently increasing by more than 750,000 people each month; two decades from now, the increase will likely be 2 million per month. The number of persons aged 65 and over has increased by 289 million since 1950 and by 99 million just since 1990.[2] In 1995, 30 countries had elderly populations of at least 2 million; projections to the year 2030 indicate that more than 60 countries will reach this level.[3]

Population aging refers most commonly to an increase in the percentage of all extant persons who have lived to or beyond a certain age. While the size of the world's elderly population has been increasing for centuries, it is only in recent decades that the proportion has caught the attention of researchers and policy makers. Italy was the demographically oldest of the world's major[4] nations in 2000, with more than 18 percent of

---

[2]The demographic estimates and projections in this chapter are taken from two sources. Unless otherwise noted, estimates prior to 1990 are from the latest revision of *World Population Prospects* (United Nations, 1999). Estimates and projections from 1990 onward are from the International Data Base maintained by the International Programs Center, U.S. Bureau of the Census, and supported by the Office of the Demography of Aging, U.S. National Institute on Aging.

[3]Though these and other projected figures are by no means certain, they may be more accurate than demographic projections of total population because the latter must incorporate assumptions about the future course of human fertility. Short- and medium-term projections of tomorrow's elderly are not contingent upon fertility because anyone who will be aged 65 or over in 2030 has already been born. When projecting the size and composition of the world's future elderly population, human mortality is the key demographic component. As discussed later in this chapter, current and future uncertainties about changing mortality, particularly at the oldest old ages, may produce widely divergent projections of the size of tomorrow's elderly population.

[4]Some small nations or areas of special sovereignty, such as Monaco, San Marino, and the Isle of Man, have high percentages of elderly among their populations. Monaco's percentage is higher than that of Italy.

its population aged 65 and over (compared with 8 percent in 1950). Other notably high levels (17 percent or more) are seen in Sweden, Greece, Belgium, and Japan. The elderly share of total population will increase only modestly in most industrialized nations between 2000 and 2010, and may even dip slightly as a function of the relatively small cohorts born prior to and during World War II. After 2010, the numbers of and percents of elderly should increase rapidly in some countries as the large post-war birth cohorts (the baby boom) begin to reach age 65.

Europe has had the highest proportions of population aged 65 and over among major world regions for many decades and should remain the global leader in this regard well into the 21st century (see Table 2-1).

TABLE 2-1 Percent Elderly, by Age and Region: 2000 to 2050

Region	Year	65 Years and Over	75 Years and Over	80 Years and Over
Europe	2000	14.0	5.6	2.8
	2015	16.3	7.7	4.3
	2030	23.1	10.8	6.3
	2050	28.6	15.7	10.2
North America	2000	12.6	6.0	3.3
	2015	14.8	6.3	3.8
	2030	20.3	9.4	5.4
	2050	20.7	11.6	8.0
Oceania	2000	10.2	4.5	2.4
	2015	12.7	5.4	3.2
	2030	16.3	7.5	4.4
	2050	20.0	10.6	6.6
Asia	2000	5.9	1.9	0.8
	2015	7.7	2.7	1.3
	2030	11.9	4.5	2.2
	2050	18.0	8.5	4.9
Latin America/Caribbean	2000	5.5	1.9	0.9
	2015	7.4	2.8	1.5
	2030	11.6	4.5	2.4
	2050	18.1	8.4	4.9
Near East/North Africa	2000	4.3	1.4	0.6
	2015	5.2	1.8	0.9
	2030	8.1	2.8	1.3
	2050	13.3	5.4	2.9
Sub-Saharan Africa	2000	2.9	0.8	0.3
	2015	3.1	1.0	0.4
	2030	3.7	1.3	0.6
	2050	5.3	1.8	0.9

SOURCE: U.S. Bureau of the Census (2000).

Of the 30 nations with populations at least 13 percent elderly in 2000, only 2 (Japan and Uruguay) are non-European. Until recently, Europe also had the highest proportions of population in the most advanced age categories. But by 1995, percentages of population aged 75 and over and 80 and over in North America had surpassed those in Europe as a whole, largely as a result of small European birth cohorts around the time of World War I. By 2015, however, these percents are again expected to be highest in Europe, and in the year 2050, nearly one of every six Europeans is projected to be aged 75 or older.

North America and Oceania also have relatively high aggregate percentages of elderly, and these are projected to increase substantially in the coming decades. Levels for 2000 in Asia and Latin America/Caribbean are expected to more than double by 2030, while aggregate proportions of elderly population in sub-Saharan Africa will grow rather modestly as a result of continued high fertility in many nations.

Two important factors bear mention when considering aggregate elderly proportions of regional populations. The first is that regional averages often mask great diversity (see Figure 2-1). Bangladesh and Thailand may be close geographically, but they have divergent paths of expected population aging. Likewise, many Caribbean nations have high proportions of elderly population (the Caribbean is the oldest of all developing world regions) in comparison with their Central American neighbors. By the middle of the 21st century, the elderly share of the total population in Italy is projected to exceed 36 percent, significantly higher than the European average in Table 2-1. Second and more important, percentages by themselves may not give a sense of the growth of absolute numbers. Although the change in percent elderly in sub-Saharan Africa from 2000 to 2015 in Table 2-1 is barely perceptible, the size of the elderly population is expected to increase by 50 percent, from 19.3 to 28.9 million people.

Sometimes lost amid the attention paid to population aging in Europe and North America is the fact that older populations in developing countries typically are growing more rapidly than those in the industrialized world.[5] As noted earlier, the net balance of the world's elderly population was increasing by more than 750,000 persons each month at the end of the 1990s; 80 percent of this change was occurring in the developing world. Projections to the year 2050 suggest that the growth rate of the elderly in

---

[5]The country classification used in this chapter corresponds to that of the United Nations, wherein "more developed" (and its synonyms "industrialized" and "developed") comprises all nations in Europe (including seven of the former republics of the Soviet Union) and North America, plus Japan, Australia, and New Zealand. The remaining nations of the world are classified as "less developed" (also referred to as "developing").

34

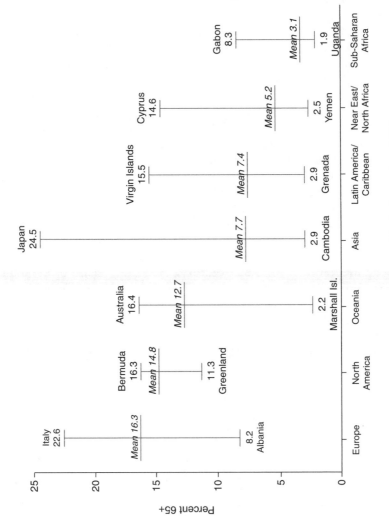

FIGURE 2-1 Mean and range of variation in percent elderly, by region: 2015.
SOURCE: U.S. Bureau of the Census (2000).

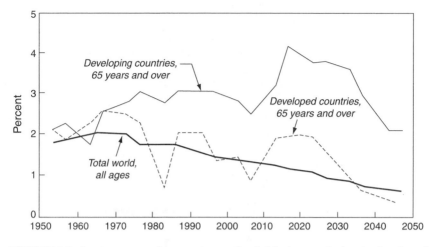

FIGURE 2-2 Average annual percent growth of elderly population in developed and developing countries.
SOURCE: United Nations (1999).

the developing world will remain significantly higher than in today's industrialized countries (see Figure 2-2). Between 2000 and 2050, countries as diverse as Colombia, Liberia, and Malaysia may expect more than a quadrupling of their elderly populations.

GROWTH OF THE OLDEST OLD

As a result of past fluctuations in fertility and current trends in mortality, age categories within the elderly aggregate may grow at different rates. An increasingly important feature of societal aging is the progressive aging of the elderly population itself. The fastest-growing age segment in many countries is the oldest old. This group currently constitutes more than 20 percent of the aggregate elderly population in industrialized countries (as opposed to about 13 percent in 1950). In the year 2000, nine industrialized nations had oldest old populations in excess of 1 million. While the proportions of oldest old are lower in developing countries, absolute numbers may be quite high. China, for example, was home to approximately 11.5 million oldest old in 2000, more than in any other country of the world. Figure 2-3 shows the estimated percent distribution of the world's population aged 80 and over at the turn of the century.

There is substantial international variation in the projected age components of elderly populations. The share of oldest old among all elderly in the United States was 26 percent in 2000 and is expected to be the same by 2030; the flow of baby boom cohorts into the ranks of the elderly after

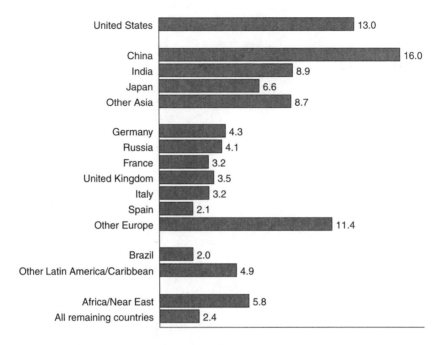

FIGURE 2-3 Percent distribution of world population aged 80 and over: 2000.
NOTE: Data represent the share of the world's total oldest old in each country or region. Individual countries with 2 percent or more of the total are shown separately.
SOURCE: U.S. Bureau of the Census (2000).

2010 will keep the overall elderly population relatively young. Because of differences in past fertility and mortality trends, some European nations will experience a sustained rise in the share of the oldest old among their elderly populations, while others will see an increase during the next two decades and then a subsequent decline. The most striking global increase is likely to occur in Japan; by 2030, nearly 40 percent of all elderly Japanese are expected to be at least 80 years old. Most developing countries should experience modest long-term increases in this ratio.

The share of oldest old among the elderly population may not change significantly in some societies, but burgeoning absolute numbers merit attention. In the United States, the oldest old increased from 374,000 in 1900 to more than 9 million today. The static proportion noted above for the United States masks a projected absolute increase of more than 9 million oldest old (see Figure 2-4). Four-generation families are becoming

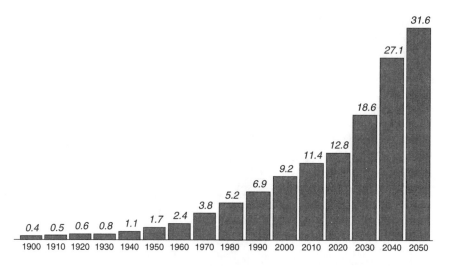

FIGURE 2-4 Population aged 80 and over in the United States: 1900 to 2050 (in millions).
SOURCES: U.S. Bureau of the Census for 1900-1990, decennial census data; for 2000-2050, "Population Projections of the United States by Age, Sex, Race, Hispanic Origin, and Nativity: 1999 to 2100" (published January 2000) <http:// www.census.gov/population/www/projections/natproj.html>.

increasingly common (Soldo, 1996; Grundy et al., 1999), and the aging of baby boom cohorts may result in a great-grandparent boom.

The demands of the oldest old vis-à-vis policy making should increase markedly in the 21st century as a result of levels of illness and disability much higher than those of other age groups. The numerical growth and increasing heterogeneity of the oldest old compel social planners to seek further health and socioeconomic information about this group. While it may be simplistic to equate the growth of the oldest old with spiraling health care costs (Binstock, 1993), the fact remains that this group consumes disproportionate amounts of health and long-term care services (Suzman et al., 1992).

METRICS OF AGING

Speed of Aging

The transition from a youthful to a more aged society has occurred gradually in some nations, but will be compressed in many others. For instance, it took only a quarter of a century for the proportion of population aged 65 and over in Japan to increase from 7 to 14 percent (see Figure

2-5). A similarly short transition period is projected for China beginning in the year 2000, and for several other East Asian nations, such as South Korea and Thailand, beginning slightly later in the 21st century. These rapid gains will be driven by sharp drops in fertility in recent decades. In

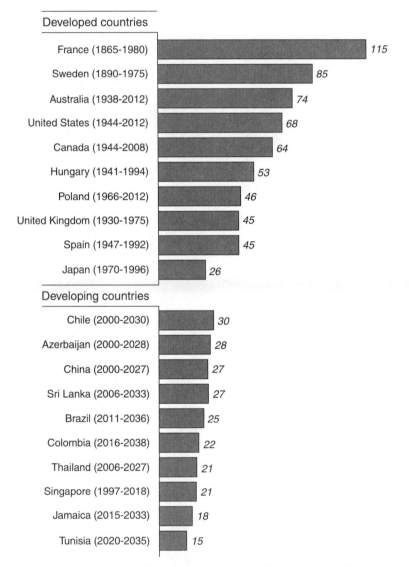

FIGURE 2-5 Speed of population aging (number of years required or expected for percent of population aged 65 and over to rise from 7% to 14%). SOURCE: Kinsella and Gist (1995).

South Korea, for example, the total fertility rate[6] plummeted from 5 children per woman in the late 1960s to less than 1.8 today. The pace of aging in parts of Asia stands in stark contrast to that in some European countries, where the comparable change occurred over a much longer period. The percent elderly among France's population was higher in the mid-1800s than the current percent elderly in a large majority of the world's developing countries. However, today's rapidly aging societies are likely to face the contentious issues related to health care costs, social security, and intergenerational equity that have sparked public debate in Europe and North America. The speed of population aging may even prompt governments to rethink their overall population policies. Singapore, once a prime advocate of fertility reduction, achieved such success in this arena that the declining birth rate became a cause for political and economic concern. Consequently, Singapore's "Stop at 2" (children) policy was modified in 1987 to provide incentives for higher fertility, particularly among better-educated segments of the population (Phillips and Bartlett, 1995).

Median Age

Another way to look at population aging is to consider a society's median age, the age that divides a population into numerically equal parts of younger and older persons. While nearly all industrialized countries are above the 31-year level, most developing nations have median ages under 25. In some African and South Asian countries in the mid-1990s, half of the entire population was younger than 15, and high numbers of annual births are likely to keep these countries relatively young in the near future. Yet in developing countries such as China, South Korea, and Thailand, where fertility rates have fallen precipitously, median ages are rising rapidly and should exceed 40 by the year 2025.

The concept of median age encourages a broader view of population aging that focuses less on the elderly population per se. In many developing countries, the initial effects of population aging will be seen in the relative growth of young and middle-aged adult populations. This implies a shift in overall population age structure, with accompanying changes in labor force characteristics, household/family structure, and disease patterns. On the one hand, the movement of large birth cohorts into the prime working ages represents an opportunity from a business or government planning perspective. As the working-age population swells, it provides a large potential labor force that may serve as a social and tax

---

[6]The total fertility rate is defined as the average number of children that would be born per woman if all women lived to the end of their childbearing years and bore children according to a given set of age-specific fertility rates.

base for dependents at both ends of the age continuum. Large numbers of workers relative to elderly persons also may provide the incentive to introduce or expand defined-benefit (pay-as-you-go) pension programs. The latter, however, often become unsustainable in the long run as declines in fertility eventually produce shrinking cohorts of new workers (see Chapter 3). And the potential opportunity presented by a large labor force may be confounded by unstable economic growth and job availability. For example, dramatic percentage increases in labor force size are likely to occur in Africa and the Near East during the period 1990-2020, and the aggregate number of potential job seekers will more than double. The percentage increase will be less in other developing regions, but the absolute growth will be enormous. In Asia alone, economies will need to generate more than a billion additional jobs during the next three decades simply to maintain current rates of employment.

Head-Count Ratios

A second common set of aging indicators includes the aging index and the elderly support ratio, both of which relate the size of one broad age group (or groups) to another. The aging index is usually defined as the number of people aged 65 and over per 100 youths under the age of 15. Changes in this ratio over time simply indicate the shifting balance of children versus elderly within a society. By the year 2030, most developed countries have a projected aging index of at least 100, and several European countries and Japan likely will have indexes in excess of 200.[7] The elderly support ratio typically is construed as the number of people aged 65 and over per 100 persons aged 20-64, the so-called working-age population. This ratio is often combined with a youth support ratio (persons aged 0-19 per 100 persons aged 20-64) to form a total support ratio that provides a rough indication of the number of non-economically active versus economically active persons in a given society. Such aggregate "head count" measures may be broadly useful in thinking about evolving population age structures, and the shifting weight of youth versus elderly in a country such as China can be remarkable (see Figure 2-6). However, measures such as the elderly support ratio also embody questionable assumptions that make them of limited analytical use (see Box 2-1).

---

[7]Given its aggregate nature, the aging index may be more useful for examining within-country differences in the level of population aging than for tracking national-level changes. For example, there can be significant differences in the extent of aging between urban and rural areas and among broader regions, especially in large nations such as Brazil. Based on 1991 census data, the overall aging index in Brazil was 14. However, this measure ranged from less than 6 in several northern states of the country to 21 in the state of Rio de Janeiro.

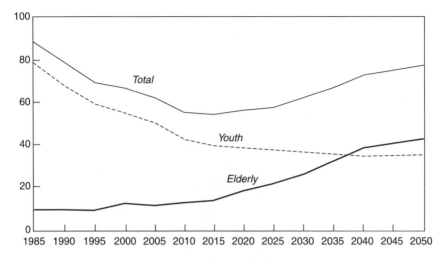

FIGURE 2-6 Support ratios in China: 1985 to 2050.
NOTE: Total ratio = persons 0 to 19 and 65 years and over per 100 persons 20 to 64 years; youth ratio = persons 0 to 19 years per 100 persons 20 to 64 years; elderly ratio = persons 65 years and over per 100 persons 20 to 64 years.
SOURCE: U.S. Bureau of the Census (2000).

DYNAMICS OF POPULATION AGING

More sophisticated models and analyses of aging have been developed to partition population growth into different categories (Lee, 1994) and to consider factors such as generation length (Preston, 1986), fertility and mortality "echo" effects (Stolnitz, 1992), population momentum (Kim and Schoen, 1997), and changes in age distribution within age categories (Chu, 1997). Regardless of how one conceptualizes population aging, the process involves primarily change over time in levels of fertility and mortality. Populations with high fertility tend to have low proportions of older persons and vice versa. Current total fertility rates in excess of 6 children per woman usually correlate with elderly population shares of less than 3 percent.

Demographers use the term "demographic transition" to refer to the gradual process whereby a society shifts from having high to having low rates of fertility and mortality.[8] This transition is characterized first by declines in infant and child mortality as infectious and parasitic diseases

---

[8]The concept of demographic transition is broad, and some would argue that it has many permutations and/or that there is more than one form of demographic transition; see, for example, the discussions in Coale and Watkins (1986) and Jones et al. (1997).

BOX 2-1
Usefulness of Elderly Support Ratios

Implicit in the standard definition of an elderly support ratio is the notion that all people aged 65 and over are in some sense dependent on the population at the working ages, 20 to 64. The latter often provide direct support to the elderly, as well as indirect support through taxes and contributions to social welfare programs. We know, of course, that elderly populations are extremely diverse in terms of resources, needs, and abilities, and that many elderly are not dependent in either a financial or a physical (health) sense. Older people pay taxes, possess wealth that fuels economic growth, and provide support to younger generations. Likewise, substantial portions of the working-age population may not be financial earners because of unemployment, inability to work, pursuit of education, and so on.

While it is empirically difficult to incorporate factors such as intrafamily financial assistance and child care activities into an aggregate social support measure, it is feasible to take account of the employment characteristics of both the working-age and elderly populations. In Figure 2-7, the topmost bar for each country represents the standard elderly support ratio as defined above. The second bar includes only the economically active population aged 20 to 64 in the denominator, thereby excluding those who choose not to work, unpaid household workers, nonworking students, and perhaps those individuals whose health status keeps them out of the labor force. The third bar represents a calculation similar to the second, but removes economically active people aged 65 and over from the numerator on the assumption that they are not economically dependent. The fourth bar builds on the third by adding these economically active elderly to the ratio denominator of other economically active individuals, on the assumption that these working elderly continue to contribute tax revenue to national coffers.

The alternative ratios are higher than the standard elderly support ratio in industrialized countries except in Japan, where the elderly have a relatively high rate of labor force participation (often as part-time workers). To the extent that policy and program agencies use support ratio calculations, the impact of including versus excluding labor force participation rates appears considerable in most countries. Data permitting, other adjustments might be made to these ratios to account for such factors as (1) workers under age 20, (2) unemployment rates, (3) average retirement ages, (4) levels of pension receipt and institutionalization among the elderly, and (5) the prevalence of disabilities. The implications of some of these factors are considered in more detail in subsequent chapters. And it may be argued that an intergenerational accounting method such as that discussed in Chapter 5 provides a more useful summary of the state of balance in an age distribution than do population support ratios.

are controlled. The resulting improvement in life expectancy at birth occurs while fertility tends to remain high, thereby producing large birth cohorts and an expanding proportion of children relative to adults. Other things being equal, this initial decline in mortality produces a younger population age structure as more babies and young children survive the

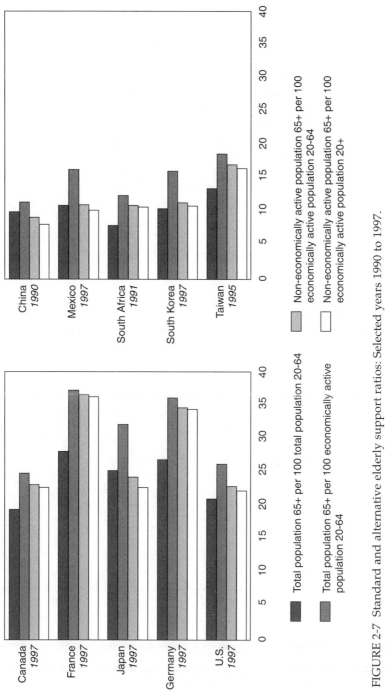

FIGURE 2-7 Standard and alternative elderly support ratios: Selected years 1990 to 1997.
SOURCE: U.S. Bureau of the Census (2000).

initial high-risk years (Lee, 1994). Generally, whole populations begin to age when fertility rates decline and mortality improvements occur at older ages. Successive birth cohorts may eventually become smaller and smaller, although some countries experience a "baby boom echo" when women from large birth cohorts reach childbearing age.

International migration usually does not play a major role in the demography of aging. One might expect that a steady stream of migration from one country to another would result in additional aging in the sending country, given that most migrants tend to be under the age of 65, and a corresponding rejuvenation of the receiving country. However, numerous studies have shown that the numbers of migrants must be very large to have an appreciable effect on population aging (see, e.g., Lesthaeghe et al., 1988; Le Bras, 1991; Lesthaeghe, 2000). In a major receiving country such as the United States, it has been shown that an annual immigration of 1.4 million persons a year has a very small effect on the projected future percentage of elderly (Day, 1996). Sustained immigration has little impact on overall age composition because immigrants themselves age (Espenshade, 1994), and because initial labor migration often becomes family migration as relatives join family members who have become established in a new country.

International migration can, however, be significant in smaller populations. Certain Caribbean nations, for example, have experienced a combination of emigration among working-age adults, immigration of elderly retirees from other countries, and return migration of former emigrants who are above the average population age; all three factors contribute to population aging. And, as noted below, international migration may come to assume a more prominent role in the aging process, particularly in graying countries where persistently low fertility has led to stable or even declining total population size. Eventual shortages of workers could generate demand for immigrant labor (Peterson, 1999) and could force nations to choose between relaxed immigration policies and pronatalist strategies designed to raise birth rates (Kojima, 1996). Debate on these issues has recently heated up in Europe (United Nations, 2000b).

The most prominent historical factor in population aging has been fertility decline. The generally sustained decrease in total fertility rates in industrialized nations since at least 1900 has resulted in current levels below the population replacement rate of 2.1 live births per woman in most such nations. Persistent low fertility since the late 1970s has led to a decline in the size of successive birth cohorts and a corresponding increase in the proportion of older relative to younger persons. The Population Division of the United Nations (1999) projects that the populations of Japan and most of Europe will decrease in size over the next 50 years, a projection that has resulted in increased attention to "replacement migration" as a possible solution to declining populations and rapid aging (Eberstadt, 2000; United Nations, 2000a, b). This concern is increasingly discussed in popular as well as scholarly literature, although some demographers (see Bongaarts, 2000) have emphasized that delayed childbearing and expressed preference for larger family sizes may well raise the currently low levels of European fertility.

Fertility change in the developing world has been more recent and more rapid, with most regions having achieved major reductions in fertility rates over the last 30 years. Although the aggregate total fertility rate remains in excess of 5 children per woman in Africa, overall levels in Asia and Latin America decreased by about 50 percent (from approximately 6 to 3 children per woman) from 1965 to 1995. Total fertility in many developing countries—notably Chile, China, South Korea, Thailand, and at least a dozen Caribbean nations—is now at or below replacement level.

Figure 2-8 illustrates the historical and projected transition in population age structure in developed and developing countries. At one time, most if not all countries had a youthful age structure similar to that of developing countries as a whole in 1950. A large percentage of the entire population was under the age of 15. Given the relatively high rates of fertility that prevailed in most developing countries from 1950 through

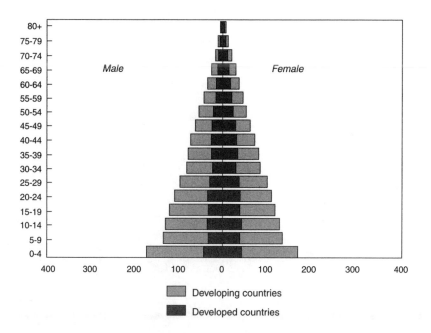

FIGURE 2-8a Population, by age and sex: 1950 (in millions).
SOURCE: United Nations (1999).

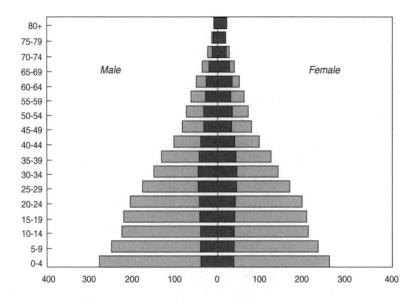

FIGURE 2-8b Population, by age and sex: 1990 (in millions).
SOURCE: United Nations (1997).

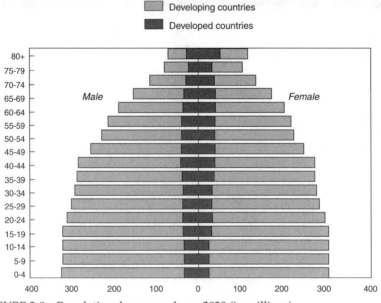

FIGURE 2-8c Population, by age and sex: 2030 (in millions).
SOURCE: U.S. Bureau of the Census (2000).

the early 1970s, the overall pyramid shape had changed very little by 1990. However, the effects of fertility and mortality decline can be seen in the projected pyramid for 2030, which loses its strictly triangular shape as the elderly portion of the total population increases.

The picture in developed countries has been and will be quite different. In 1950, there was relatively little variation in the size of 5-year groups between the ages of 5 and 24. The beginnings of the post-World War II baby boom can be seen in the 0-to-4-year age group. By 1990, the baby boom cohorts were 25 to 44 years old, and the cohorts under age 25 were becoming successively smaller. If fertility rates continue as projected through 2030, the aggregate pyramid will start to invert, with more weight on the top than on the bottom. The prominence of the oldest old (especially women) will increase, and persons aged 80 and over will outnumber any younger 5-year age group.

Life Expectancy at Birth

The stunning gains in human life expectancy that accelerated in the mid-1800s and continued during the following century often are attributed primarily to improvements in medicine. However, the major impact of improvements in both medicine and public health did not occur until the late 19th century (McKeown, 1979). Earlier and more important factors in lowering mortality were innovations in industrial and agricultural production and distribution, which enabled nutritional diversity and consistency for large numbers of people (Thomlinson, 1976). A growing research consensus attributes the gain in human longevity since the early 1800s to a complex interplay of advances in medicine and public health coupled with new modes of familial, social, economic, and political organization, as well as related behavioral changes (Preston and Haines, 1991; Moore, 1993).

Although the effect of fertility decline is usually the driving force behind changing population age structures, changes in mortality assume much more importance as countries reach lower levels of fertility (Caselli and Vallin, 1990; Gjonca et al., 1999). Since the beginning of the 20th century, industrialized countries have made great progress in extending life expectancy at birth (see Table 2-2).[9] Japan enjoys the highest life

---

[9]Measurement of mortality trends and magnitudes of change requires the selection of an appropriate index that represents the level of mortality and a decision about how to measure relative change. Life expectancy at birth is the most widely used index for representing the level of mortality in a population, but there are two measurement problems that should be recognized when comparing changes in life expectancy. The first is that life expectancy at birth is a highly summarized index of mortality at all ages. It is useful to monitor change over time in life expectancy at birth, but it may be more instructive to

TABLE 2-2 Life Expectancy at Birth for Selected Countries, 1900 to 2000 (in years)

Region/Country	Circa 1900		Circa 1950		2000	
	Male	Female	Male	Female	Male	Female
Developed Countries						
Western Europe						
Austria	37.8	39.9	62.0	67.0	74.5	81.0
Belgium	45.4	48.9	62.1	67.4	74.5	81.3
Denmark	51.6	54.8	68.9	71.5	74.0	79.3
France	45.3	48.7	63.7	69.4	74.9	82.9
Germany[a]	43.8	46.6	64.6	68.5	74.3	80.8
Norway	52.3	55.8	70.3	73.8	75.7	81.8
Sweden	52.8	55.3	69.9	72.6	77.0	82.4
United Kingdom	46.4	50.1	66.2	71.1	75.0	80.5
Southern and Eastern Europe						
Czech Republic[a]	38.9	41.7	60.9	65.5	71.0	78.2
Greece	38.1	39.7	63.4	66.7	75.9	81.2
Hungary	36.6	38.2	59.3	63.4	67.0	76.1
Italy	42.9	43.2	63.7	67.2	75.9	82.4
Spain	33.9	35.7	59.8	64.3	75.3	82.5
Other						
Australia	53.2	56.8	66.7	71.8	76.9	82.7
Japan	42.8	44.3	59.6	63.1	77.5	84.1
United States	48.3	51.1	66.0	71.7	74.2	79.9
Developing Countries[b]						
Africa						
Egypt			41.2	43.6	61.3	65.5
Ghana			40.4	43.6	56.1	58.8
Mali			31.1	34.0	45.5	47.9
South Africa			44.0	46.0	50.4	51.8
Uganda			38.5	41.6	42.2	43.7
Congo (Brazzaville)			37.5	40.6	44.5	50.5
Asia						
China			39.3	42.3	69.6	73.3
India			39.4	38.0	61.9	63.1
Kazakhstan			51.6	61.9	57.7	68.9
South Korea			46.0	49.0	70.8	78.5
Syria			44.8	47.2	67.4	69.6
Thailand			45.0	49.1	65.3	72.0
Latin America						
Argentina			60.4	65.1	71.7	78.6
Brazil			49.3	52.8	58.5	67.6
Costa Rica			56.0	58.6	73.3	78.5
Chile			57.8	61.3	72.4	79.2
Mexico			49.2	52.4	68.5	74.7
Venezuela			53.8	56.6	70.1	76.3

[a]Figures for Germany and Czech Republic prior to 1999 refer to the former West Germany and Czechoslovakia, respectively.

[b]Reliable estimates for 1900 for most developing countries are unavailable.

SOURCES: United Nations (1988); Siampos (1990); U.S. Bureau of the Census (2000).

expectancy of the world's major countries; according to current mortality schedules, the average Japanese born today can expect to live 80 years. The level in various European nations approaches or exceeds 79 years. Three important observations can be made concerning the trends shown in Table 2-2. First, the relative difference among countries has narrowed with time. Second, the pace of improvement has not been linear, especially for males. From the early 1950s to the early 1970s, for example, there was little or no change in male life expectancy in Australia, the Netherlands, Norway, and the United States; in Eastern Europe and much of the former Soviet Union, male life expectancy declined in the 1970s and early 1980s, and again in some countries in the early 1990s. Third, the difference in female versus male longevity, which universally has been in favor of women in this century, has widened with time.

Reliable estimates of life expectancy in most developing countries prior to 1950 are lacking. Since the middle of the 20th century, estimated changes in the progress of life expectancy in developing regions have been more uniform than in the industrialized world. Most nations have experienced continued improvement, with some exceptions in Latin America and more recently in Africa. The most dramatic gains have been achieved in East Asia, where regional life expectancy at birth increased from less than 43 years in 1950 to more than 70 years in 1995. Extreme variations exist throughout the developing world, however. While Costa Rica, Taiwan, and numerous Caribbean island nations enjoy levels that match or exceed those of many European nations, the normal lifetime in other countries spans fewer than 45 years. Aggregate life expectancy at birth in Latin America (69 years) is 20 years higher than in sub-Saharan Africa. On average, individuals born in an industrialized country will outlive their counterparts in the developing world by 13 years according to mortality schedules for the late 1990s.

Moreover, while global reductions in overall mortality levels have been the norm in recent decades, the HIV/AIDS epidemic has had a devastating impact on life expectancy in parts of Africa and Asia. The impact of the epidemic on life expectancy at birth can be considerable, given that AIDS deaths often are concentrated in the childhood and

---

consider change over time in mortality in different age groups. In other words, very different mortality trends may be occurring at different ages in a single population, trends that would not be well represented by an overall measure of life expectancy at birth.

A second important point regarding life expectancy at birth is the reliability of mortality information at older ages, especially in developing countries. In a large majority of such nations, there simply are no reliable, representative statistics on older-age mortality. Hence, life-table estimates of older-age mortality typically represent an assumption based on a model.

middle adult (30 to 45) ages. Projections to the year 2010 suggest that AIDS will continue to reduce average life expectancy at birth by more than 25 years from otherwise-expected levels in countries such as Botswana, Kenya, and Zimbabwe (Stanecki and Way, 1999). The impact on future population age structure and overall population aging is less striking insofar as the effects of a long-term epidemic become more evenly distributed across age groups.

The Feminization of Old Age

As noted earlier, the female advantage in life expectancy at birth is nearly universal. At the end of the 20th century, the average gap between the sexes in developed countries was roughly 7 years, but as great as 13 years in parts of the former Soviet Union as a result of unusually high levels of adult male mortality. The gender differential usually is smaller in developing countries, commonly in the 3-to-6-year range. Moreover, women's share of the older population increases with age. In some nations the sex ratio at older ages can be pronounced. As a result of the lingering effects of heavy male mortality during World War II, for example, women account for 80 percent of the oldest old in Russia and nearly 75 percent in Germany.

Gender-specific differences in mortality play an important role in determining factors such as marital status and living arrangements in older age. Because women tend to marry men who are older and to remarry less frequently upon divorce or the death of a spouse, percents widowed are much higher for women than men until extreme old age. The typical age/gender pattern is illustrated in Figure 2-9 with data from Belgium, where percents widowed for women are 2 to 4 times higher than for men between the ages of 60 and 85. Many older widows in industrialized nations live alone. These realities combine with a host of other gender differences (e.g., in educational attainment, poverty, and functional status) to present special problems for women as they age.

Life Expectancy and Mortality at Age 65

Where infant mortality rates are still relatively high but declining, as in many developing countries, most of the improvement in life expectancy at birth results from infants surviving the high-risk initial years of life. But when infant and childhood mortality reaches low levels, as in developed countries, improvements in average life expectancy are achieved primarily through declines in mortality among older segments of the population.

Any discussion of changes in death rates and life expectancy at older

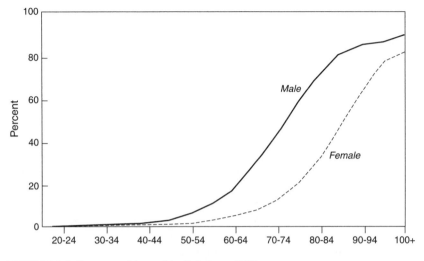

FIGURE 2-9 Percent widowed in Belgium: 1995.
SOURCE: U.S. Bureau of the Census (2000).

ages is hampered by the fact that the relevant data are suspect in quality
at best and nonexistent at worst. Even in many industrialized nations
with good vital registration systems, it is widely recognized that there
may be problems with data at older ages (Condran et al., 1991; Kestenbaum, 1992; Murray and Lopez, 1996; see also Chapter 6). In general,
mortality among older adults is inherently more difficult to study than
that among children and youth. Data on child mortality usually can be
collected from mothers, whereas there is no single universally suitable
informant to provide data about adult deaths. Likewise, while characteristics of parents are among the more crucial determinants of the risk of
death in childhood, it is less reliable to use the socioeconomic characteristics of respondents as proxies for those of deceased individuals when
studying adult mortality differentials (Timaeus, 1993).

A more onerous problem in measuring older-age mortality, of course,
is age misreporting. Particularly in developing countries, older persons
are often unlikely to have birth certificates and health documentation.
Actual age and age at death both tend to be exaggerated, which may
introduce large biases into the estimation of mortality rates at older ages
(Dechter and Preston, 1991). Where feasible, the assessment of age misreporting and the quality of mortality estimates at older ages can be
greatly enhanced by linking data from different sources to investigate
distortions and systematic biases in particular datasets. One innovative
approach used in the United States (Hill et al., 2000) involves linking a

sample of death certificates for native-born whites aged 85 and over to both census data from the early 1900s and Social Security Administration records. The results show surprising consistency among sources and suggest that (at least for U.S. whites) the effect of age misreporting on old-age mortality estimates is very small.

Old-Age Mortality in Developed Countries

Reliable data for Japan shown in Table 2-3 illustrate the rapid declines in old-age mortality that characterize many industrialized nations. Among the young old (ages 65-69), death rates for men and women plummeted between 1950 and 1996; the female level in 1996 was less than one-fourth that in 1950. Major declines can be seen at older ages as well. As a consequence of these steep drops, life expectancy at age 65 rose 5.6 years for men and 8.2 years for women during the period 1950-1996. Under the mortality conditions of 1996, the average Japanese woman aged 65 could expect to live an additional 21.5 years and the average Japanese man of the same age nearly 17 years.

Myers (1996) used a decompositional technique to assess the age-specific impact of mortality decline on overall changes in life expectancy during the period 1950-1990 in six industrialized nations. The major conclusions of the study were as follows. First, the influence of old-age mortality changes was substantial. In Australia, for example, 40 and 28 percent of the overall female and male gains in life expectancy at birth, respectively, during the 40-year period was due to mortality improvements at ages 65 and over. Second, gains in life expectancy at ages 65 and over have generally accelerated over time, that is, were more rapid during the period 1970-1990 than during the preceding 20-year period. Third, increases in life expectancy due to changes at older ages have been more rapid for women than for men, which suggests that the gender differential in life expectancy may not be narrowing.

TABLE 2-3 Mortality Rates for Selected Older Age Groups in Japan: 1950, 1970, and 1996 (per 1,000 population)

	65-69		75-79		80-84	
Year	Male	Female	Male	Female	Male	Female
1950	51.6	35.7	114.4	87.1	177.9	142.9
1970	37.4	20.9	98.1	67.2	151.2	115.5
1996	19.5	8.2	51.2	26.2	86.7	49.6

SOURCE: Japan Statistics and Information Department (1990, 1999).

The importance of changes in mortality rates at older ages in relatively low-mortality nations has been examined from another perspective. Olshansky et al. (1991) calculated that from 1900 to 1985, most mortality declines in the United States occurred among infants, children, and women of childbearing age. The conditional probability of death under the age of 50 declined more than 70 percent for both men and women, with smaller declines after age 50. Because mortality rates are now so low at younger and middle ages, any significant additional gains in life expectancy must come from reductions in death rates among older population groups. If all U.S. deaths prior to the age of 50 were eliminated, the total gain in life expectancy at birth would be only 3.5 years.

Some countries are approaching the time when subsequent improvements in overall life expectancy will derive from changes not merely among the elderly, but primarily among the oldest old. Wilmoth et al. (2000), using detailed data for Sweden, have shown that mortality decline above age 70 was the major cause of the increase in maximum achieved life span in that country between 1861 and 1999. In a comprehensive study of death rates at ages 80 and over in the post-1950 period for 28 low-mortality countries, Kannisto (1994) demonstrated that old-age mortality had reached much lower levels than ever previously recorded, and that the decline had tended to accelerate in recent years. Perhaps surprisingly, there had been no perceptible convergence of national old-age mortality levels. The only commonality among the 28 countries was a speedier decline for women than for men, thus widening the female advantage in life expectancy at birth. Kannisto attributed the rapid decline in old-age mortality to period rather than cohort effects, citing in particular the effects of recent medical advances and the adoption of healthier lifestyles by better-educated, wealthier, and urban population subgroups. If this interpretation is correct, there is likely to have been a widening of socioeconomic differentials in old-age mortality, as has been suggested for adult populations in general in the United Kingdom, the United States, and other Western nations (Preston and Taubman, 1994; Marmot and Wilkinson, 1999). At the same time, there would appear to be great potential for further overall (national) improvements in old-age mortality to the extent that other social groups can benefit from technology and lifestyle changes. In any case, the great reductions in old-age mortality have caught many demographers and policy planners by surprise.

Old-Age Mortality in Developing Countries

The greater relative improvement in life expectancy at older versus younger ages is not yet widespread in developing regions of the world. However, the proportional increase in life expectancy at older ages is approaching or has surpassed the relative increase in life expectancy at birth in some developing countries, notably in Latin America and the Caribbean. As the epidemiological profile in the developing world changes, a greater share of all deaths is seen at older ages. Data compiled by the World Health Organization indicate that half or more of all female deaths occur after age 65 in numerous developing nations; the corresponding percentage for males typically is less, but exceeds half in several countries.

Given the problems with data and mortality measurement discussed earlier, one cannot confidently assess changes in mortality rates at old ages across developing regions. In general, countries in Latin America and the Caribbean are thought to have the most accurate mortality information and longest time series, with many nations having reasonable life table estimates dating back to 1950 or before. One analysis[10] of 19 countries (14 of which are in the western hemisphere) indicates that, with the exception of Belize around 1970, there was an unmistakable decline in Latin American/Caribbean death rates at age 65 during the second half of the 20th century and a corresponding increase in the number of years of life remaining for those persons who reach age 65. Gains for women typically were greater than for men; in Costa Rica, Panama, Puerto Rico, and Peru, more than 5 years was added to female life expectancy at age 65 between 1950 and 1990. In Singapore and Taiwan, improvements in older-age mortality were even more rapid. Mortality rates for those aged 65-69 dropped by more than 50 percent during the last half of the century, and the corresponding gains in life expectancy at age 65 for both men and women were greater than those seen in Latin America.

Short-term projections of life expectancy at age 65 in both developed and developing countries show that the female advantage in life expectancy at birth persists at older ages. In all 20 nations shown in Table 2-4, women who reach age 65 have higher remaining life expectancies than do elderly men. The gender gap is usually about 4 years in developed countries and 2-3 years in developing countries.

Major Cause-Specific Changes in Old-Age Mortality

The change in national mortality and disease profiles associated with population aging in developed countries has been well documented (Lopez, 1990; Lopez et al., 1995). At ages 65 and over, a majority of

---

[10]Using life tables compiled and evaluated by the U.S. Bureau of the Census, based on country-specific vital registration and survey data, estimates of death underregistration, and secondary sources/analyses.

TABLE 2-4 Life Expectancy at Age 65 in Selected
Countries, 2000

	Men	Women
Developed Countries		
Australia	17.5	21.6
Bulgaria	13.4	16.2
Canada	17.1	21.7
France	16.7	21.3
Germany	15.4	19.2
Italy	16.2	20.2
Japan	17.0	21.3
Russia	11.5	15.4
Sweden	16.4	20.3
United Kingdom	15.2	19.1
Developing Countries		
Brazil	14.1	17.9
China	13.1	15.6
Egypt	10.6	12.9
India	13.3	13.9
Kenya	13.3	15.1
Mexico	14.2	17.0
Peru	15.1	17.3
Thailand	14.2	17.7
Turkey	15.5	18.4
Zimbabwe	10.1	13.8

NOTE: Figures refer to the average number of years of remaining life for an individual who reaches age 65 in the year 2000.

SOURCE: Projected by the U.S. Bureau of the Census (2000)
based on the most recent data for each country.

developed countries have seen reductions in the proportions of deaths
from heart disease and stroke since 1950, often accompanied by a reduction in the death rate from these two diseases. Conversely, cancer rates
and proportional mortality from neoplasms have generally risen with
time, although the trend has varied by disease site. Multiple-decrement
life table analyses for selected developed countries have shown that the
sharp rise in cancer rates with age implies a doubling of deaths from
cancer in some countries during the period 1950-1990 (Myers, 1996).
Among older men, deaths have risen for most disease sites, with the
notable exception of stomach cancer. For older women, there is concern
about skyrocketing rates of lung cancer (Levi et al., 1992; Lopez, 1995) that
have resulted from the upsurge in tobacco consumption among women
in the 1960s and 1970s. In France, standardized death rates at ages 65-74

for cancers are now higher than for cardiovascular diseases for both men and women (Mesle and Vallin, 1999).

Median ages at death for most chronic conditions have increased over time (Myers and Manton, 1987). For example, from 1950 to 1990, the average age at death from heart disease for women in Canada increased by an estimated 7.5 years, of which 5.3 years is attributed to reductions in mortality at age 65 and over. In other words, the increase in life expectancy at older ages during recent decades is the result of reductions in age-specific rates for most major causes of death. Such reductions may result from the delayed onset of disease (due, perhaps, to better health promotion efforts), as well as from prolonged survival with a disease (perhaps reflecting better treatment of existing conditions).

The potential for additional years of life with chronic disease raises important issues about the quality of those additional years. Are we living healthier as well as longer lives, or are we spending an increasing portion of our older years with disabilities, mental disorders, and ill health? In aging societies, the answer to this question will have a profound impact on policies regarding national health and long-term care systems, and on the sufficiency of individual and collective retirement savings. As discussed in Chapter 6, the need to better understand trends in and causes of disability, both within and across countries, is a major challenge for gerontological research.

While cause-of-death data at older ages are problematic in every country in terms of precision and cross-national comparability, the problems are exacerbated in developing countries by underreporting of deaths, lack of causal information, inaccurate diagnoses, and ethnologic differences. On a broad scale, it appears clear that the general epidemiological transition already experienced in the developed world has occurred or is occurring in many developing nations as well.[11] Data from Taiwan shown in Table 2-5 exemplify the typical epidemiological shift in causes of death. The infectious and parasitic diseases that dominated Taiwanese mortality in the mid-1950s have given way to chronic and degenerative diseases. By 1976, cerebrovascular disease (primarily stroke) and cancers[12] had become the top killers, and the broader cardiovascular disease category—including cerebrovascular, heart, and hypertensive disease)—accounted for nearly 30 percent of all deaths. The role of cardiovascular diseases as

---

[11]This is not to say that there is a single, linear trajectory to the epidemiological transition. As Frenk et al. (1991) have shown for several Latin American countries, the "typical" stages of epidemiological transition may not follow a sequential order, but may in fact overlap or even reverse direction.

[12]It should be noted that cancers themselves may be infectious diseases, particularly in developing countries. Pisani et al. (1999) estimate that 16 percent of all cancer deaths worldwide in the early 1990s were due to infectious agents.

TABLE 2-5 Rank Order of the Ten Leading Causes of Death in Taiwan, 1956, 1976, and 1996

	1956	1976	1996
1	GDEC[a]	Cerebrovascular disease	Malignant neoplasms
2	Pneumonia	Malignant neoplasms	Cerebrovascular disease
3	Tuberculosis	Accidents	Accidents
4	Perinatal conditions	Heart disease	Heart disease
5	Vascular lesions of CNS[b]	Pneumonia	Diabetes mellitus
6	Heart disease	Tuberculosis	Cirrhosis/ chronic liver disease
7	Malignant neoplasms	Cirrhosis of the liver	Nephritis/nephrosis
8	Nephritis/nephrosis	Bronchitis[c]	Pneumonia
9	Bronchitis	Hypertensive disease	Hypertensive disease
10	Stomach/duodenum ulcer	Nephritis/nephrosis	Bronchitis[c]

[a]Includes gastritis, duodenitis, enteritis, and colitis (except diarrhea of newborns).
[b]CNS refers to the central nervous system.
[c]Includes emphysema and asthma.

SOURCE: Taiwan Department of Health (1997).

the principal cause of death also has been well documented in other parts of Asia (Ruzicka and Kane, 1991) and in a large majority of Latin American and Caribbean countries (Pan American Health Organization, 1998). With regard to causes of death at ages 65 and over, World Health Organization (1998) data for developing countries with reasonably reliable cause-of-death information suggest that more than half of all deaths in the 1990s in numerous nations (e.g., Argentina, Kazakstan, Tajikistan, Uzbekistan) were attributable to cardiovascular disease. The share of cancer deaths among the elderly is between 12 and 25 percent in most cases.

RELIABILITY OF DEMOGRAPHIC PROJECTIONS OF THE ELDERLY

Tomorrow's elderly, as noted earlier, already have been born, at least until the time horizon reaches the year 2065. Therefore, future fertility rates may affect the proportion of older persons in a given society, but not their number. Current and future mortality trends are of increasing concern to social scientists and policy planners because assumptions about these trends vary considerably and may have surprisingly divergent implications for future programs. Past population projections often have underestimated improvements in mortality rates, particularly among the oldest old. Consequently, global and national projections of the size of older populations generally have missed the mark and regularly have been revised upwards. For example, in its 1980 assessment of world population, the United Nations projected a global total of 760 million elderly (65+) by the year 2025. The latest United Nations (1999) assessment projects 817 million elderly, 57 million and roughly 8 percent more than forecast in 1980. On a national level, consistently low projections of the elderly population poorly serve planning in such areas as health care costs and delivery systems, pension scheme payouts, and housing design.

In industrial nations, mortality is now so low among children and young adults that improvements at these ages (except for mortality from violence and HIV/AIDS among young males), even if it occurs, can contribute very little to overall improvements in life expectancy (National Research Council, 2000). Hence, projection "errors" tend to be greatest at older ages. A series of studies by Keilman (cited in Lee and Miller, 2000) has identified systematic underestimation of the elderly population in projections for industrialized countries on the order of .5 percent per year for the elderly and about 1 percent per year for persons aged 85 and over. Over a 75-year period, these errors would compound so that the actual number of elderly could be 60 percent higher than expected, while the 85-and-over population could exceed current projections by 300 percent.

Such calculations lead some to argue that the actual numbers of tomorrow's elderly and especially the oldest old could be much higher than presently anticipated (see Box 2-2). Until recently, it was generally assumed that the human death rate increases with age in an exponential manner. Research has now documented that at very old ages, the rate of increase in the mortality rate tends to slow down,[13] and several hypotheses have been advanced as explanations for this phenomenon (see Horiuchi and Wilmoth, 1998, for one discussion of competing explanations). There is no empirical or theoretical basis for assuming that life expectancy will peak at some numerical limit in the future. This is especially so in light of recent medical advances, potential developments in gene therapy, and the realization that the rate of mortality increase in humans slows down at very advanced ages.

Methodological issues also are important in this context. Caselli (1996) has explored the usefulness of projecting mortality by cause of death, noting that the results provide a strong basis for implementing health promotion measures. Lee and Tuljapurkar (1998) argue that the usual method for dealing with uncertainty in population projections—i.e., the use of high/medium/low variants—is flawed. They and others (Lutz et al., 1998; National Research Council, 2000) posit that stochastic forecasts based on time series of vital rates offer important advantages,

---

[13]This has been demonstrated in nonhuman species as well; see, for example, Carey, 1997; Vaupel et al., 1998.

BOX 2-2
The Proliferation of Centenarians

As the average length of life increases, the concept of "oldest old" will change. We now have, for the first time in history, the opportunity to consider significant numeric growth of the population aged 100 and over. While people of extreme old age constitute a very small portion of the total population in most of the world, their numbers are of growing significance, especially in more developed nations. Hence it is increasingly important to have greater age detail about the very old. In the past, comparable population projections for the world's countries often grouped those aged 80 and over into a single open-ended category. Recently, agencies such as the United Nations Population Division and the U.S. Bureau of the Census's International Programs Center have produced or made plans to produce sets of international population projections that expand the range of older age groups to include an open-ended category of age 100 and over.

According to researchers in Europe, the number of centenarians has doubled each decade since 1950 in industrialized countries. Using reliable statistics from 10 western European countries and Japan, Vaupel and Jeune (1995) estimated that some 8,800 centenarians lived in these countries as of 1990, and that the number of centenarians grew at an average annual rate of approximately 7 percent between the early 1950s and the late 1980s. They also estimated that over the course of human history, the odds of living from birth to age 100 may have risen from 1 in 20 million to 1 in 50 for females in low-mortality nations such as Japan and Sweden.

There are several problems with obtaining accurate age data on very old people (Kestenbaum, 1992; Elo et al., 1996), and estimates of centenarians from censuses and other data sources should be scrutinized carefully. For example, the 1990 U.S. census recorded some 37,000 centenarians. Although the actual figure is thought to be closer to 28,000 because of age misreporting (Krach and Velkoff, 1999), the census figure represents a doubling of the population aged 100 and over from 1980 to 1990, similar to estimates for European nations. The potentially spectacular increase in numbers of centenarians is illustrated by data and projections for France. Dinh (1995) estimated that there were about 200 centenarians in France in 1950, and that by the year 2000 the number would be 8,500. His 50-year projections suggest there will be 41,000 people aged 100 and over by 2025, increasing to 150,000 in 2050. If these projections are realized, the number of centenarians in France will have multiplied by a factor of 750 in one century.

SOURCE: Excerpted from U.S. Bureau of the Census (in press).

---

particularly for mortality estimation,[14] and suggest exploring the value of cohort projections of life expectancy.

The upshot is that such views, coupled with expectations of future advances in a variety of medical and nonmedical technologies, may lead

---

[14]Lee and Tuljapurkar's favored model suggests that future increases in life expectancy in the United States will proceed approximately twice as fast as implied by projections of the U.S. Bureau of the Census and the U.S. Social Security Administration.

researchers to very different assumptions about the trajectory of human mortality and the numbers of tomorrow's elderly populations. For example, Figure 2-10 shows forecasts of the size of the U.S. population aged 85 and over through the year 2040, produced by the U.S. Bureau of the Census using two different mortality assumptions. These official projections are contrasted with those made by Guralnik et al. (1988), which show the effect of assuming a continuation of the 2 percent annual decline in death rates experienced during the 1980s. Much more optimistic forecasts of lowered death rates have resulted from mathematical simulations of reductions in known risk factors for chronic diseases, other morbidity, and mortality. One such simulation (Manton et al., 1993) generated an extreme upper bound projection of 54 million people aged 85 and over in the United States in 2040. While this and other projections are perhaps not the most likely, they underscore the potential impact of changes in adult mortality on the future size of the very old population and demonstrate the uncertainty inherent in projections of numbers and age composition. Indeed, this report and its recommendations are motivated in large part by the necessity to know more about health and mortality dynamics in aging populations and to increase our ability to factor uncertainty into program and policy planning.

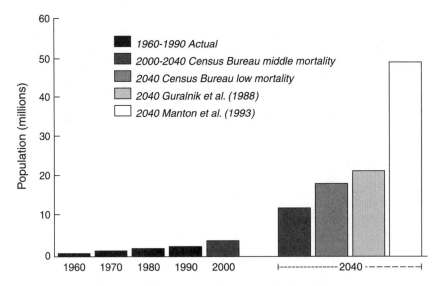

FIGURE 2-10 Forecasts of the U.S. population aged 85 and over.

REFERENCES

Binstock, R.
    1993   Health care costs around the world: Is aging a fiscal 'black hole?' *Generations* (Winter):37-42.
Bongaarts, J.
    2000   What's Next? Population Explosion or Decline? Available: http:// www.popcouncil.org/news_views/pop_momentum.html [February 28, 2001].
Carey, J.R.
    1997   What demographers can learn from fruit fly actuarial models and biology. *Demography* 34(1):17-30.
Caselli, G.
    1996   Future longevity among the elderly. In *Health and Mortality Among Elderly Populations*, G. Caselli and A.D. Lopez, eds. Oxford: Clarendon Press.
Caselli, G., and J. Vallin
    1990   Mortality and aging. *European Journal of Population* 6(1):1-25.
Chu, C.Y.C.
    1997   Age-distribution dynamics and aging indexes. *Demography* 34(4):551-563.
Coale, A.J., and S.C. Watkins, eds.
    1986   *The Decline of Fertility in Europe*. Princeton: Princeton University Press.
Condran, G.A., C.L. Himes, and S.H. Preston
    1991   Old-age mortality patterns in low-mortality countries: An evaluation of population and death data at advanced ages, 1950 to the present. *Population Bulletin of the United Nations* 30:23-60.
Day, J.C.
    1996   *Population Projections of the United States, by Age, Sex, Race and Hispanic Origin: 1995 to 2050*. U.S. Bureau of the Census, Current Population Reports, Series P25-1130. Washington, DC: U.S. Government Printing Office.
Dechter, A.R., and S.H. Preston
    1991   Age misreporting and its effects on adult mortality estimates in Latin America. *Population Bulletin of the United Nations* 31/32:1-16.
Dinh, Q.C.
    1995   Projection de la population yotale pour la France metropolitaine: Base RP90, horizons 1990-2050, *Demographie-Societe* 44. Paris: INSEE.
Eberstadt, N.
    2000   World depopulation. Last one turn off the lights. *The Milken Institute Review* First Quarter:37-48.
Elo, I.T., S.H. Preston, I. Rosenwaike, M. Hill, and T.P. Cheney
    1996   Consistency of age reporting on death certificates and social security records among elderly African Americans. *Social Science Research* 25:292-307.
Espenshade, T.
    1994   Can immigration slow U.S. population aging? *Journal of Policy Analysis and Management* 13(4):759-768.
Frenk, J., J.L. Bobadilla, C. Stern, T. Frejka, and R. Lozano
    1991   Elements for a theory of the health transition. *Health Transition Review* 1:21-38.
Gjonka, A., H. Brockmann, and H. Maier
    1999   Old-age Mortality in Germany Prior to and after Reunification. Paper presented during the Third European-American Research Colloquium on Social and Biological Determinants of Longevity, Max Planck Institute for Demographic Research, August, Rostok, Germany.

Grundy, E., M. Murphy, and N. Shelton
  1999   Looking beyond the household: Intergenerational perspectives on living kin and
         contacts with kin in Great Britain. *Population Trends* 97:19-27.
Guralnik, J.M., M. Yanagishita, and E.L. Schneider
  1988   Projecting the older population of the United States: Lessons from the past and
         prospects for the future. *Milbank Quarterly* 66:283-308.
Hill, M.E., S.H. Preston, and I. Rosenwaike
  2000   Age reporting among white Americans aged 85+: Results of a record linkage
         study. *Demography* 37(2):175-186.
Horiuchi, S., and J.R. Wilmoth
  1998   Deceleration in the age pattern of mortality at older ages. *Demography* 35(4):391-
         412.
Japan Statistics and Information Department
  1990   *Statistical Yearbook of Japan 1990*. Tokyo: Ministry of Health and Welfare.
  1999   *Statistical Yearbook of Japan 1999*. Tokyo: Ministry of Health and Welfare.
Jones, G.W., R.M. Douglas, J.C. Caldwell, and R.M. D'Souza, eds.
  1997   *The Continuing Demographic Transition*. Oxford: Clarendon Press.
Kannisto, V.
  1994   *Development of Oldest-Old Mortality, 1950-1990: Evidence from 28 Developed Coun-
         tries*. Monograph on Population Aging 1. Odense, Denmark: Odense University
         Press.
Kestenbaum, B.
  1992   A description of the extreme aged population based on improved Medicare en-
         rollment data. *Demography* 29(4):565-580.
Kim, Y.J., and R. Schoen
  1997   Population momentum expresses population aging. *Demography* 34(4):421-427.
Kinsella, K., and Y.J. Gist
  1995   *Older Workers, Retirement, and Pensions. A Comparative International Chartbook*. U.S.
         Census Bureau Report IPC/95-2RP. Washington, DC: U.S. Government Printing
         Office.
Kojima, H.
  1996   *Aging in Japan: Population Policy Implications*. Institute of Population Problems
         Reprint Series 25. Tokyo: Ministry of Health and Welfare.
Krach, C.A., and V.A. Velkoff
  1999   *Centenarians in the United States*. U.S. Census Bureau Current Population Reports
         P23-199. Washington, DC: U.S. Government Printing Office.
LeBras, H.
  1991   Demographic impact of post-war migration in selected OECD countries. In *Mi-
         gration: The Demographic Aspects*, pp. 15-26. Paris: Organization for Economic Co-
         operation and Development.
Lee, R.D.
  1994   The formal demography of population aging, transfers, and the economic life
         cycle. In *Demography of Aging*. Committee on Population. L.G. Martin and S.H.
         Preston, eds. Commission on Behavioral and Social Sciences and Education.
         Washington, DC: National Academy Press.
Lee, R.D., and T. Miller
  2000   Evaluating the Performance of the Lee-Carter Mortality Forecasts. Available:
         http://www.demog.berkeley.edu [February 28, 2001].
Lee, R.D., and S. Tuljapurkar
  1998   Population Forecasting for Fiscal Planning: Issues and Innovations. Available:
         http://www.demog.berkeley.edu [February 28, 2001].

Lesthaeghe, R.
2000   Europe's demographic issues: Fertility, household formation and replacement migration. In *United Nations Expert Group Meeting on Policy Responses to Population Ageing and Population Decline*, pp. 20/1-20/40. ESA/P/WP.163. New York: United Nations Department of Economic and Social Affairs.

Lesthaeghe, R., H. Page, and J. Surkyn
1988   *Are Immigrants Substitutes for Births?* IPD Working Paper 1988-3. Brussels: Inter-university Program in Demography.

Levi, F., C. La Vecchia, F. Lucchini, and E. Negri
1992   Trends in cancer mortality sex ratios in Europe, 1950-1989. *World Health Statistics Quarterly* 45(1):117-164.

Lopez, A.D.
1990   *Mortality Trends in the ECE Region: Prospects and Implications.* United Nations Economic Commission for Europe Seminar on Demographic and Economic Consequences and Implications of Changing Population Age Structures, Ottawa, 24-28 September. Report CES/SEM.28/R.36. Geneva: United Nations.

Lopez, A.D.
1995   The lung cancer epidemic in developed countries. In *Adult Mortality in Developed Countries: From Description to Explanation*, A.D. Lopez, G. Caselli, and T. Valkonen, eds. Oxford: Clarendon Press.

Lopez, A.D, G. Caselli, and T. Valkonen, eds.
1995   *Adult Mortality in Developed Countries: From Description to Explanation.* Oxford: Clarendon Press.

Lutz, W., W.C. Sanderson, and S. Scherbov
1998   Expert-based probabilistic population projections. *Population and Development Review* 24(Supplement):139-155.

Manton, K.G., B.H. Singer, and R.M. Suzman
1993   The scientific and policy needs for improved health forecasting models for elderly populations. In *Forecasting the Health of Elderly Populations*, K.G. Manton, B.H. Singer, and R.M. Suzman, eds. New York: Springer-Verlag.

Marmot, M., and R.G. Wilkinson
1999   *Social Determinants of Health.* Oxford: Oxford University Press.

McKeown, T.
1979   *The Role of Medicine: Dream, Mirage, or Nemesis?* Princeton: Princeton University Press.

Mesle, F., and J. Vallin
1999   Mortality Trends at Older and Oldest Ages in France Since 1950. Paper presented at the Third European-American Colloquium on Social and Biological Determinants of Longevity, 1-7 August, Rostock, Germany.

Moore, T.J.
1993   *Lifespan.* New York: Simon & Schuster.

Murray, C.J.L., and A.D. Lopez, eds.
1996   *The Global Burden of Disease.* Geneva: World Health Organization.

Myers, G.C.
1996   Comparative mortality trends among older persons in developed countries. In *Health and Mortality Among Elderly Populations*, G. Caselli and A.D. Lopez, eds. Oxford: Clarendon Press.

Myers, G.C., and K.G. Manton
1987   The rate of population aging: New views of epidemiologic transitions. In *Aging: The Universal Human Experience*, G.L. Maddox and E.W. Busse, eds. New York: Springer.

National Research Council
   2000   *Beyond Six Billion: Forecasting the World's Population.* Committee on Population. J.
           Bongaarts and R.A. Bulatao, eds. Commission on Behavioral and Social Sciences
           and Education. Washington, DC: National Academy Press.
Olshansky, S.J., M.A. Rudberg, B.A. Carnes, C.K. Cassel, and J.A. Brody
   1991   Trading off longer life for worsening health. *Journal of Aging and Health* 3(2):194-
           216.
Pan American Health Organization
   1998   *Health in the Americas.* Scientific Publication No. 569, Volume I. Washington, DC:
           Pan American Health Organization.
Peterson, P.G.
   1999   Gray dawn: The global aging crisis. *Foreign Affairs* 78(1):42-55.
Phillips, D., and H.P. Bartlett
   1995   Aging trends-Singapore. *Journal of Cross-Cultural Gerontology* 10(4):349-356.
Pisani, P., D.M. Parkin, F. Bray, and J. Ferlay
   1999   Estimates of the worldwide mortality from 25 cancers in 1990. *International Jour-
           nal of Cancer* 83(1):18-29.
Preston, S.H.
   1986   The relation between actual and intrinsic growth rates. *Population Studies* 40:343-
           351.
Preston, S.H., and M.R. Haines
   1991   *Fatal Years: Child Mortality in Late Nineteenth-Century America.* Princeton: Princeton
           University Press.
Preston, S.H., and P. Taubman
   1994   Socioeconomic differences in adult mortality and health status. In *Demography of
           Aging.* Committee on Population. L.G. Martin and S.H. Preston, eds. Commis-
           sion on Behavioral and Social Sciences and Education. Washington, DC: Na-
           tional Academy Press.
Ruzicka, L., and P. Kane
   1991   Mortality Transition and Cause of Death Structure in Asia. Paper prepared for
           the International Union for the Scientific Study of Population Seminar on Causes
           and Prevention of Adult Mortality in Developing Countries, October, Santiago,
           Chile.
Siampos, G.
   1990   Trends and future prospects of the female overlife by regions in Europe. *Statisti-
           cal Journal of the United Nations Economic Commission for Europe* 7:13-25.
Soldo, B.
   1996   Cross pressures on middle-aged adults: A broader view. *Journal of Gerontology:
           Social Sciences* 51B(6):S271-273.
Stanecki, K.A., and P.O. Way
   1999   Focus on HIV/AIDS in the developing world. In *World Population Profile: 1998,*
           T.M. McDevitt. U.S. Census Bureau Report WP/98. Washington, DC: U.S. Gov-
           ernment Printing Office.
Stolnitz, G.J.
   1992   Echo effects on aging of past vital-rate fluctuations in the ECE region. In *Demo-
           graphic Causes and Consequences of Population Aging,* G.J. Stolnitz, ed. Economic
           Studies No. 3. New York: United Nations.
Suzman, R.M., D.P. Willis, and K.G. Manton, eds.
   1992   *The Oldest Old.* New York: Oxford University Press.
Taiwan Department of Health
   1997   *Health and Vital Statistics. General Health Statistics 1996.* Taipei: Executive Yuan.

Thomlinson, R.
   1976   *Population Dynamics. Causes and Consequences of World Demographic Change.* New York: Random House.
Timaeus, I.M.
   1993   *Measurement of Adult Mortality in Less Developed Countries: A Comparative Review.* Technical Papers (53). Bethesda, MD: International Institute for Vital Registration and Statistics.
United Nations
   1988   Sex differentials in survivorship in the developing world: Levels, regional patterns and demographic determinants. *Population Bulletin of the United Nations* 25:51-64.
   1999   *World Population Prospects.* The 1998 Revision, ST/ESA/SER.A/177. New York: United Nations Department of Economic and Social Affairs.
   2000a   *Replacement Migration.* ESA/P/WP.160. New York: United Nations Department of Social and Economic Affairs.
   2000b   *United Nations Expert Group Meeting on Policy Responses to Population Ageing and Population Decline.* ESA/P/WP.163. New York: United Nations Department of Economic and Social Affairs.
U.S. Bureau of the Census
   2000   International Data Base. Available: http://www.census.gov/ipc/www/idbnew.html [February 28, 2001].
   in   *An Aging World 2001.* Washington, DC: U.S. Government Printing Office.
   press
Vaupel, J.W., J.R. Carey, K. Christensen, T.E. Johnson, A.I. Yashin, N.V. Holm, I.A. Iachine, V. Kannisto, A.A. Khazaeli, P. Liedo, V.D. Longo, Y. Zeng, K.G. Manton, and J.W. Curtsinger
   1998   Biodemographic trajectories of longevity. *Science* 280(May 8):855-860.
Vaupel, J.W., and B. Jeune
   1995   The emergence and proliferation of centenarians. In *Exceptional Longevity: From Prehistory to the Present*, B. Jeune and J.W. Vaupel, eds. Monograph on Population Aging 2. Odense, Denmark: Odense University Press.
Wilmoth, J.R., L.J. Deegan, H. Lundstrom, and S. Horiuchi
   2000   Increase of maximum life-span in Sweden, 1861-1999. *Science* 289:2366-2368.
World Health Organization
   1998   *World Health Statistics Annual 1996.* Geneva: World Health Organization.

3

Work, Retirement, and Pensions

Labor market participation and patterns of work among older men and women have changed dramatically over the past 20 years, as have pension systems and sources of retirement income. There are many key economic, health, and social factors behind these changes. Yet, as emphasized in Chapter 1, not all countries or all individuals within a country have experienced the same trends, and understanding these differences is central for identifying the key determinants of the changes that have occurred. Achieving such understanding, in turn, requires the collection of detailed scientific data for comparative study. The objective of this chapter is to set forth some basic facts about these changes, drawn from a wide range of experience across countries, and to suggest minimal data requirements for the successful understanding of these phenomena. A central theme is that much can be learned from careful comparative analyses of policy reforms and changes in work and retirement behavior across countries.

With regard to work patterns, there is evidence that retirement increasingly occurs in different forms (Lazear, 1986; Organization for Economic Co-operation and Development, 1995a; National Research Council, 1996). In fact, many countries that have experienced a decrease in labor market attachment among older workers have done so without any change in the normal retirement age. Although social norms and the demand for the labor supplied by older workers play a role, changes in retirement patterns also depend heavily on the precise form of early retirement provisions in pension and social security plans, as well as on the structure of income support and welfare programs for older individuals

(Burtless and Moffitt, 1984; Börsch-Supan and Schnabel, 1998, 1999). As a result, data with which to study retirement will need to include a wide range of information on potential income sources and earning opportunities (National Research Council, 1997; Hurd, 1998). Moreover, the collection of these data must begin much earlier than at normal retirement age, possibly as early as age 45. Health status also plays a role in retirement decisions (Bound et al., 1999), and it will therefore be necessary as well to stress the importance of accurate health and disability information. It may well be that changes in workplace environment or even the act of retirement itself may affect health and disability outcomes. Longitudinal data that record the timing of these work, retirement, and health events are therefore essential.

A further complication arises from the need to compute accurate summary measures of retirement incentives. As discussed below, different countries and different individuals within a country vary considerably with regard to the mix of private and public pension entitlements. Moreover, contribution periods and contribution rules can pose significant challenges for lifetime data collection. However, relatively simple summary measures can be collected through a sensible mix of longitudinal survey data and access to administrative sources. Indeed, the need to supplement standard sample survey data with administrative data is a major requirement for accurate analysis and inference, a theme to which we return in Chapter 8.

Measuring the work opportunities for older individuals requires careful consideration of the changing demand for older workers (Straka, 1992; Organization for Economic Cooperation and Development, 1995b). For example, the earnings profiles of those who remain in work may provide a misleading guide to the earnings opportunities of those who leave the labor force early. This will be especially true if those who withdraw early are predominantly from a single skill group or industry. For measuring changes in work opportunities there is no real alternative to having accurate earnings histories with skill and occupational information.

Comparative analysis is particularly effective in enhancing understanding of the issues surrounding work and retirement, and there already exist many successful comparative studies in this area (see, e.g., Quinn and Burkhauser, 1994; Gruber and Wise, 1998, 1999; Johnson, 1999; Hermalin and Chan, 2000; Borsch-Supan, 2000b; Disney and Johnson, in press). These studies have documented the differing experiences of various countries and have significantly enhanced understanding of the retirement process. Comparisons are particularly instructive among countries that have experienced differing trends in retirement but, on the basis of standard economic and demographic statistics, might otherwise appear rather similar.

A sophisticated comparative analysis can exploit changes in policy rules across countries to isolate the impact of policy from that of other macroeconomic and social changes. Gruber and Wise (1999) managed to uncover three important features in their analysis of 11 developed countries that could not easily be discerned from single-country studies. First was a strong correspondence between early and normal retirement ages and departure from the labor force. Second, public pension provisions in most countries were found to place a heavy tax burden on work past the age of early retirement eligibility and thus to provide a strong incentive to withdraw early from the labor force. Third, the implicit tax—and thus the incentive to leave the labor force was found to vary substantially among countries, as did retirement behavior. Through such cross-national comparisons, then, some general conclusions about the relationship between retirement incentives and retirement behavior can begin to be drawn.

The remainder of this chapter provides more detail on these issues. First, we consider the evidence on patterns of work and retirement across countries and highlight common trends, as well as note interesting differences in behavior. The following section addresses the measurement of retirement incentives and how they differ across countries. It also considers important policy reforms from around the world and their likely impact on retirement behavior. Finally, we take stock of the implications of these changes for data collection that is adequate to enable the accurate description of work patterns and retirement incentives at the approach of retirement age and thereafter. We realize that there are other, related issues that are not emphasized here. Some, such as the importance of health status and wealth, are discussed more thoroughly elsewhere in this volume; others are mentioned briefly at the end of this chapter.

PATTERNS OF WORK AND RETIREMENT
AROUND THE WORLD

This section reviews labor force participation rates for men and women across a wide array of countries. These contrasts are of interest in themselves, but they take on special relevance in any examination of the determinants of retirement behavior. They highlight the importance of comparative analysis by showing that countries that for most part are rather similar economically and demographically can display considerable variation in retirement patterns. Along with more detailed individual-level data, such comparisons offer some hope for teasing out the main explanations for the observed variations in retirement behavior.

While assessing the evidence on labor force participation, it is important to anticipate the discussion in the next section of the incentives to retire faced by individuals at older ages and consequently the mechanisms by which people support themselves when out of the labor market. This often means examining the role of early retirement. For example, Table 3-1 reveals that male labor force participation rates fall well before normal ages of retirement, indeed often well before eligibility for public pensions.

To study these aspects of retirement and retirement income requires an understanding of the full range of potential sources of income for older individuals, including disability schemes and private pensions in addition to public pension or social security arrangements. Recent reforms in pension systems and the growth of private schemes in many countries increase the range of data needed to adequately describe retirement incentives, a point to which we return in detail in the concluding section of the chapter.

The declining labor force participation of older persons and the general increase in female participation are the most significant feature of labor force change in the developed world over the past several decades. However, these changes have not been experienced in many developing countries, and there are vastly different trends even among developed countries in this regard. Japan and Belgium provide two of the most dramatic extremes. Figure 3-1 presents this contrast, with Germany included for comparison. The figure shows a surprisingly large decline in male participation with age in Belgium. By age 69, virtually no men in

TABLE 3-1 Normal Pension Ages, Early Retirement Ages, and Employment Rates for Men in Nine Countries, circa 1995

Country	Pension Age		Employment Rates (%)	
	Normal	Early	At Age 59	At Ages 60-64
Sweden	65	60	74	49
United Kingdom	65	60	62	50
United States	65	62	74	53
Germany	65	60	81[a]	35
Italy	60	55	47	30
Netherlands	65	60	57[a]	19
Australia	65	60	73	47
Japan	65	60	87	76
New Zealand[b]	65	63	80[a]	50

[a]Refers to ages 55-59.
[b]Pension age in New Zealand is currently being raised from 60 to 65; see Table 3-2.

SOURCES: Gruber and Wise (1999); Johnson (1999).

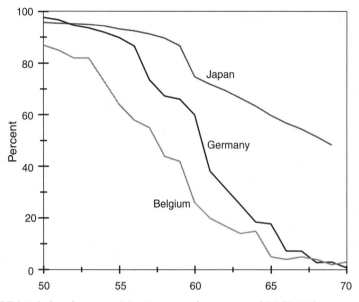

FIGURE 3-1 Labor force participation rates for men aged 50-70 in three countries:
Early-to-mid 1990s.
SOURCE: Gruber and Wise (1999). Reprinted with permission.

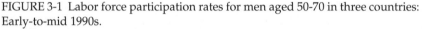

Belgium are working, whereas in Japan, almost half are still in the labor
force. Indeed, most men in Belgium are no longer in the labor force at age
65, and only about a quarter are working at age 60. In Japan, on the other
hand, nearly two-thirds are working at age 65 and three-quarters at age
60.

Figure 3-2, for Europe and North America and for Australasia and
Latin America, respectively, shows the labor force participation rates of
men aged 55 to 59 since 1970. Even at these early ages, before early
retirement ages in most public pension systems, wide differences in participation are apparent. As we have seen, Belgium has extremely low
levels of participation; the situation there contrasts with that in Sweden,
Denmark, and the United States, where participation rates have remained
at about 80 percent. Figure 3-2 shows the strong decline in Australia,
which contrasts with the relatively stable rates in Japan.

It is above age 60 that differences across countries are most apparent
(see Figures 3-3 and 3-4). Figure 3-3 shows the sharp declines in France,
Belgium, and Germany, which contrast with the much higher participation rates in the United States and Sweden. Among Australasian and
Latin American countries, there are equally sharp declines in Australia

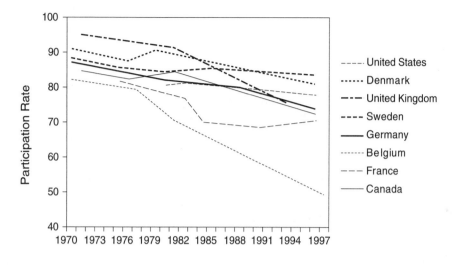

Years

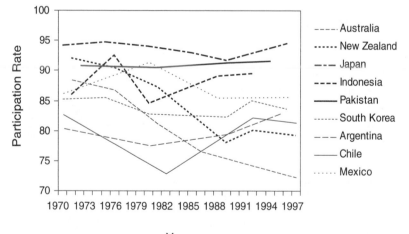

Years

FIGURE 3-2 Labor force participation rates for men aged 55-59 in two regions: Circa 1970 to circa 1998.
NOTE: Top panel—Europe and North America, bottom panel—Australasia and Latin America.
SOURCE: International Labour Office, various years.

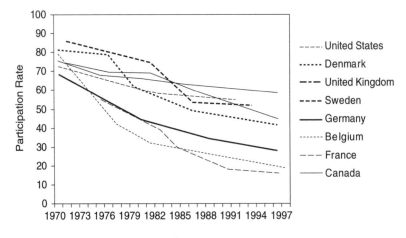

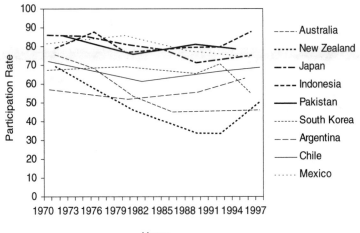

FIGURE 3-3 Labor force participation rates for men aged 60-64 in two regions: Circa 1970 to circa 1998.
NOTE: Top panel—Europe and North America, bottom panel—Australasia and Latin America.
SOURCE: International Labour Office, various years.

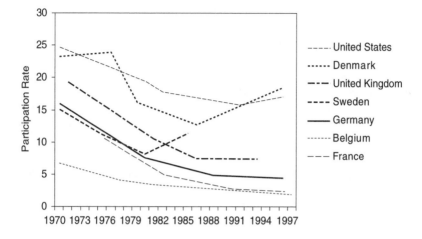

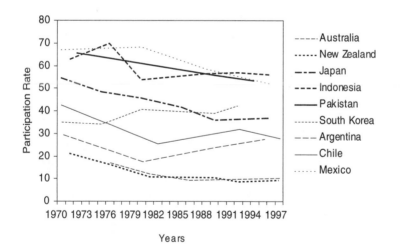

FIGURE 3-4 Labor force participation rates for men aged 65 and over in two regions: Circa 1970 to circa 1998.
NOTE: Top panel—Europe and North America, bottom panel—Australasia and Latin America.
SOURCE: International Labour Office, various years.

and New Zealand, whereas participation rates remain high in Indonesia and Japan.

An intriguing feature of Figure 3-3 is the rise in participation rates experienced by New Zealand in the mid- to late 1990s. This increase closely follows the raising of the retirement age to 65 and the change in indexation of retirement benefits, which is discussed further in the next section. Note from Figure 3-4 that there is little impact on those men aged 65-plus. Indeed, the retirement behavior of men of this age in New Zealand and Australia looks quite similar. The contrast for women is even more illuminating, as discussed below.

In general, the participation rates among men over age 65 show the most interesting variation in the Australasian and Latin American countries. Outside of New Zealand and Australia, men in this age group in these countries have relatively high participation rates. Men in Indonesia, Mexico, and Pakistan, for example, maintain rates above 50 percent into their late 60s. Of course, this high level of participation reflects in part less wealth than that of comparable men represented in the top panel of Figure 3-4. Similar experience has been documented in other developing countries. For example, Hermalin and Chan (2000) show high rates of male participation in Thailand and the Philippines. However, as that study also points out, such high rates are not common to all developing countries and depend on pension rules and coverage (the latter often being limited and highly selective), health factors, and family arrangements (see also Raymo and Cornman, 1999; Yashiro, 1997).

Underlying these changes in participation rates over time are secular changes experienced by all age cohorts, as well as aging effects experienced by each cohort through its lifetime. This is particularly the case for women. Figure 3-5, for example, shows the participation rates of Swedish women aged 55-59 increasing year by year. However, if we look at the behavior of the 1976 cohort in 1981, when they are in the 60-64 age group presented in Figure 3-6, we see the participation rate has fallen from around 58 percent to about 42 percent. Younger cohorts of women in many countries are exhibiting a high rate of labor market participation at all stages in their life cycle. But it is still true that their participation rate declines, often quite dramatically, with age. Thus for each cohort group, patterns of retirement for women can match quite closely the declines experienced by their male counterparts, even though their overall participation rates at older ages are often observed to rise steadily.

One useful contrast for older women is displayed in Figure 3-6, which shows falling rates of participation in France and extremely low rates in Belgium, mirroring the low attachment at older ages for men in both of these countries. These figures can be compared with the rising rates for older women in Sweden and the United States.

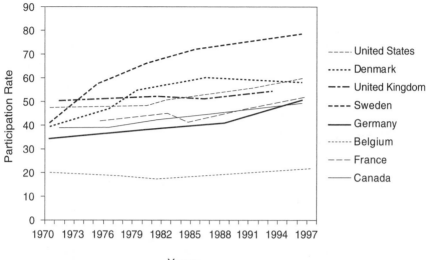

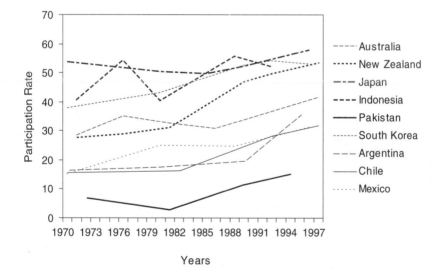

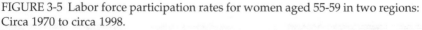

FIGURE 3-5 Labor force participation rates for women aged 55-59 in two regions:
Circa 1970 to circa 1998.
NOTE: Top panel—Europe and North America, bottom panel—Australasia and
Latin America.
SOURCE: International Labour Office, various years.

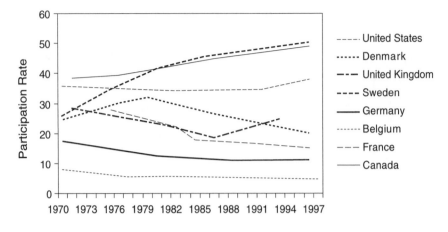

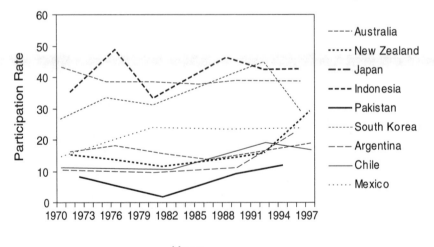

FIGURE 3-6 Labor force participation rates for women aged 60-64 in two regions: Circa 1970 to circa 1998.
NOTE: Top panel—Europe and North America, bottom panel—Australasia and Latin America.
SOURCE: International Labour Office, various years.

Low rates of female participation among women over age 60 have been a common feature in New Zealand and Australia. This situation reflects in part the state pension system and the retirement age for women, which, as in the United Kingdom, was set historically at 60. The impact of a rise in this age in New Zealand is again clearly displayed in the increasing participation rate for that country in Figure 3-6. This increase is much more dramatic than that in neighboring Australia, where a similar reform to the normal retirement age is being introduced at a much slower rate (see the discussion of Table 3-2 below).

In summary, not only do participation rates vary widely across countries, but they also show dramatic changes across time within countries. It is this difference in the participation rates across and within countries that presents an opportunity to use comparative analysis to identify the factors underlying such changes. Moreover, the size and systematic nature of these variations offer some hope that the major determinants of the differences can be revealed through careful statistical analysis.

RETIREMENT INCENTIVES AND PENSION ARRANGEMENTS

Researchers have long been interested in the dynamics of work and retirement (see, e.g., Sheshinski, 1978; Rust, 1989; Lumsdaine et al., 1992; Blau, 1994; Johnson et al., 1998; Tanner, 1998). Perhaps the most important argument in favor of more systematic collection of data on work and retirement is the opportunity to understand how features of retirement and other programs affect these decisions. To achieve such understanding requires evaluating the incentive effects of the provisions of retirement programs, which in turn depend both on the provisions and on individual work histories, marital status, and other individual and family circumstances. Thus it is important to be able to match detailed plan provisions with individual data.

Individual employment and earnings histories differ widely, as do individual retirement plans. For some countries, self-employment and part-time work among older workers are a growing feature of staged early retirement. In many nations worldwide, the growth of dual-career families almost certainly will have an influence on retirement patterns. Also in some countries, private retirement plans are becoming increasingly important and can involve difficult data requirements concerning the history of employer and employee contributions. Disability benefits and other welfare programs are also likely to be important in understanding patterns of retirement (see, e.g., Piachaud, 1986; Disney and Webb, 1991; Manton et al., 1997). Alongside the obvious need for detailed health and asset information, these considerations shape the data demands we consider briefly below.

Public Pension Reforms and Features

Table 3-2 illustrates the general types of reform that have occurred across a selection of Organization for Economic Cooperation and Development (OECD) countries. Shown are changes in normal retirement ages, in indexation procedures, and in pension calculations that have been introduced in recent years in each country. A majority of countries have seen some planned increase in retirement age or in the minimum years of contribution required to earn a full pension, at least for women. Recall the discussion in the last section of participation rates for women and men in New Zealand.

In many countries, benefits are indexed to some measure of inflation. As of the end of the 1990s, few countries indexed their pensions to gross wages (Australia being an important exception), although a majority had employed gross wage indexation in the previous two decades. A wage index is generally thought to reflect price increases plus growth in worker productivity, and thus leads to larger increases than indexation to a price index. Indexing benefits to a consumer price index is now common. The changes reduce the level of benefits or, equivalently, delay the age at which benefits can be received. Most countries employing an earnings-related scheme have made adjustments that will have the effect of reducing the eventual replacement rate; popular changes include expanding the earnings base on which the eventual pension is calculated.

For purposes of summarizing public pension reforms, Disney and Johnson (in press), from which much of this discussion is drawn, group OECD countries into a small number of broad categories. For example, France, Germany, and Italy have generous earnings-related public systems that provide high levels of benefits to most pensioners on the basis of a comprehensive system of social insurance. The United States, the United Kingdom, Japan, and Canada also employ earnings-related schemes. In the case of the two North American countries, however, these schemes are explicitly redistributive[1] and provide much lower replacement rates to high than to low earners. In the United Kingdom, there is an earnings-related pension, but it was introduced recently and is relatively small by comparison with the main flat-rate basic pension. Japan also has a mixed system, combining a flat and an earnings-related pension. New Zealand and the Netherlands both have flat-rate public pension schemes, and in both cases the pension is paid purely on the basis of past residence in the country, not a contributory record. Finally, Aus-

---

[1]Although the redistributive impact of Social Security in the United States all but disappears when a life-time view of incomes and differential mortality is accounted for (see Coronado et al., 2000).

TABLE 3-2 Changes to Public Pension Benefits in Nine OECD Countries

Country	Changes to Pension Age	Changes to Indexation	Changes to Benefit Calculation
Australia	Phased rise in pension age for women from 60 to 65 by 2013.	Indexation to wages formalized in 1997.	Ongoing tinkering with details of means test.
New Zealand	Rising from 60 to 65 in 2001.	Indexation to prices since 1993 but not to fall below 65% of average earnings.	Surcharge introduced but now being withdrawn.
Canada	None planned.	Already price indexed.	Introduction of a clawback on basic pension; series of minor changes to financing and benefits of second tier.
France	Minimum contribution duration rising from 37.5 to 40 years, reducing chance of retiring at 60.	Price indexation since 1987.	Wage base for pension calculation rising from best 10 years to best 25 years; earnings revalued to retirement by prices.
Germany	Women's pension age rising from 60 to 65 by 2004. Actuarial reductions being introduced for retirement before 65.	Indexation to net wages rather than gross wages from 1992.	1999 reform to cut replacement rate after 40-year earnings history from 72 to 64 percent; to be phased in through link to life expectancy.
Italy	Complex reforms raising pension ages and minimum years of contribution.	Move from wage to price indexation in 1992.	Move from traditional defined-benefit public scheme to "virtual" defined contribution, effectively based on each year's salary.
Japan	Age for receipt of basic pension rising from 60 to 65 between 2001 and 2013.	Move from gross wage to net wage indexation.	1985 act put a ceiling on pensions of 68 percent of average lifetime earnings.
United Kingdom	Women's pension age to rise from 60 to 65 between 2010 and 2020.	Basic pension indexed only to prices since 1980, greater of prices and earnings before that.	State earnings-related pensions based on average earnings, not best 20 years, to replace 20 percent of earnings, not 25 percent. Generosity to widows cut.
United States	Rising from 65 to 66 in 2009 and to 67 by 2027.	Price indexation.	No information.

SOURCE: Disney and Johnson (in press).

tralia is the only major country in which the public pension system consists entirely of a means-tested benefit for pensioners.

Tables 3-3 and 3-4, drawn from Disney and Johnson (in press) illustrate for a set of OECD countries the pension a single person would re-

TABLE 3-3 Alternative Measures of Replacement Rates by Relative Income Level for Single Men in Seven Countries, circa 1995

Country	Net Replacement (%)	Gross Replacement (%)	Net over National Average (%)	Gross over National Average (%)
Canada				
Half	76	59	50	35
Average	44	31	51	37
Twice	25	15	51	37
France				
Half	84	68	48	39
Average	84	70	95	79
Twice	73	56	165	136
Germany[a]				
Half	67 (79)	48	34 (40)	24
Average	72	45	72	45
Twice	75	40	150	80
Italy				
Quarter	103	103	32	24
Average	90	78	82	72
Three times	85	70	192	193
Netherlands				
Half	73	63	41	32
Average	43	32	41	32
Twice	25	16	41	32
United Kingdom				
Half	72	63	25	19
Average	50	44	34	26
Twice	35	33	48	39
United States[a]				
Half	65	47	32	23
Average	55	38	55	38
Twice	32	21	64	42

[a]In each case other than Germany and the United States, the replacement rate is calculated on the basis of the earnings distribution among workers approaching retirement age. In Germany and the United States, the replacement rate is based on overall average earnings, so the data on replacement rates for those two countries are not fully comparable with other national figures. The figures for Germany in parentheses include social assistance. See source for further details.

SOURCE: Disney and Johnson (in press).

TABLE 3-4 Alternative Measures of Replacement Rates by Relative
Income Level for Single Men in Australia, New Zealand, and Japan,
circa 1995

Country	Net Replacement (%)	Gross Replacement (%)	Net over National Average (%)	Gross over National Average (%)
Australia[a]				
Half	N/A	N/A	33	25
Average	N/A	N/A	33	25
Twice	N/A	N/A	33	25
New Zealand				
Half	75	66	38	33
Average	38	33	38	33
Twice	19	15	38	33
Japan				
Half	77	68	N/A	36
Average	56	49	N/A	49
Twice	43	36	N/A	72

[a]The figures for Australia are for the maximum benefit. Replacement rates are not really
relevant in this means-tested system.

NOTES: The replacement rate is calculated on the basis of the earnings distribution among
workers approaching retirement age. N/A = not available.

SOURCE: Disney and Johnson (in press).

ceive. This is expressed as four different proportions: (1) net pension as
a proportion of previous net earnings, (2) gross pension relative to previous gross earnings, (3) net pension as a proportion of national average net
earnings, and (4) gross pension as a proportion of national average gross
earnings. These figures are calculated on three bases: (1) for someone
with half average earnings during his/her life, (2) for someone with average earnings, and (3) for someone with twice average earnings. Naturally
this is a great simplification in that there is a broad range (the bases for
Italy are different, as shown in Table 3-3) of possible earnings histories
that can result in a large variety of eventual pension payments, but the
figures provide a good illustration of the nature and generosity of the
various systems.

The results are as expected. Italy, France, and Germany all have very
high replacement rates at all levels of income considered. Note also that
in these countries, pensioners with histories of high earnings receive pensions from the state that provide them with an income that is higher than
the average earnings of current workers.

Despite having important earnings-related elements, the systems of

the United Kingdom, the United States, and Canada provide lower replacement rates for higher than for lower earners. This is also true for
Japan (see Table 3-4). Indeed, Canada has almost a flat-rate system. Naturally the flat-rate Dutch and Australian systems offer the same cash level
of benefits whatever the previous earnings history and thus, relative to
earnings, provide higher retirement incomes to low than to high earners.

Two further issues are worthy of special attention in examining work
incentives in public pension schemes: the treatment of spouses and indexation.

Treatment of Spouses

There are two notable features of the treatment of spouses. The first is
that in fully earnings-related social insurance systems, only those who
have been in the labor market earn pensions in their own right, and married couples may receive no additional benefits at all. Married women
pensioners in such countries are likely to enjoy less financial independence than those in countries such as New Zealand and the Netherlands
where the benefit system is not work related. In a sense, the state systems
in Germany, France, and Italy almost mimic private provision in a number of other countries. They involve neither redistribution from rich to
poor nor, to a major extent, redistribution from men to women. Second,
in those countries that do provide extra pensions for couples, the relative
size of the pensions of single persons and married couples is quite similar
across countries, with the former tending to be in the range of 60-70
percent of the latter.

Indexation

One of the most important features of any pension system is the way
in which benefits are indexed. On the whole, the changes that have occurred have been toward less generous indexation procedures. Indexation of benefits in accordance with some form of earnings index ensures
that the incomes of pensioners will keep pace with the general living
standards of the rest of the population. Indexation of benefits in line with
prices will maintain the same real standard of living for the pensioner, but
a declining standard relative to other groups in the population. Indexation at a lower rate than this results in declining living standards.

In countries with an earnings-related system of benefits, there is another important aspect of indexation, which concerns how earnings are
revalued to retirement to calculate the initial pension level. Most OECD
countries effectively revalue in line with a measure of earnings growth.
But this does not mean that once in payment, pensions must rise in line

with earnings growth. State earnings-related pensions in the United Kingdom are a good example (see, e.g., Creedy et al., 1993; Dilnot et al., 1993). The initial payment is calculated by reference to previous earnings uprated to the year of retirement using an earnings index. But once in payment, the pension is raised each year only in line with prices. One interesting development has been that in recent years, both the Germans and Japanese have moved toward indexing their earnings-related pensions to a measure of after-tax earnings growth rather than of gross wages.

Retirement Incentives and Public Pensions

Two central features of public pension plans have an important effect on labor force participation incentives. The first is the age at which benefits are first available, called the early retirement age (see Table 3-1). The "normal" retirement age is also important, but typically much less so than the early retirement age. The extent to which people continue to work after the early retirement age is closely related to the second important feature of plan provisions, the pattern of benefit accrual. Suppose that at a given age a person has acquired entitlement to future benefits upon retirement. The present discounted value of these benefits is the person's public pension wealth (PPW) at that age (PPW_a). The key consideration for retirement decisions is how this wealth will evolve with continued work. If a man is aged 59, for example, what is the change in PPW if he retires at age 60 instead of age 59? The difference between PPW if retirement is at age a and PPW if retirement is at age a + 1, $PPW_{a+1} - PPW_a$, is called *PPW accrual*.

PPW accrual can be compared with net wage earnings over the year. If the accrual is positive, it adds to total compensation from working the additional year; if the accrual is negative, it reduces total compensation. The ratio of the accrual to net wage earnings is an implicit tax on earnings if the accrual is negative and an implicit subsidy to earnings if the accrual is positive. Thus a negative accrual discourages continuation in the labor force, and a positive accrual encourages continued participation. This accrual rate, along with the associated tax rate, is a key calculation in explaining individual retirement decisions. Table 3-5 presents accrual rate computations for public pensions across a number of countries. The pension accrual is negative at older ages in many countries. Consequently, continuation in the labor force means a loss of pension benefits, which imposes an implicit tax on work and provides an incentive to leave the labor force.

The magnitude of PPW accrual is determined by several provisions. The most important of these is the adjustment to benefits if a person works for another year. An additional year of work means a delay in receiving benefits, which will be received for one fewer year. In some countries, an "actuarial" adjustment is made such that benefits are increased to offset the fact that they are received for fewer years. In other countries, however, there is no such adjustment. The greater the adjustment, the greater is the inducement to continue working. If the adjustment is not large enough to offset the fewer years of benefit receipt, however, there is an incentive to leave the labor force. Second, a person who continues to work generally must pay taxes on earnings, lowering net public pension accrual. These tax payments make retirement more attractive. Third, the additional year of earnings is often used in the recomputation of public pension benefits, which are typically based on some measure of lifetime average earnings. Since earnings are often higher later in life than earlier, net accrual may rise, making retirement less attractive. This effect may be especially important for the younger old who are not fully vested in their public pension systems until they have paid in for some minimal number of years. Finally, a delay in receiving benefits raises the odds that the worker might die without being able to collect any benefits. This may be an important consideration for the oldest workers.

There is no completely satisfactory way to summarize the country-specific incentives for early retirement.[2] One crude measure is based on continued labor earnings once a person is eligible for public pension benefits. Gruber and Wise (1999) sum the implied tax rates on continued work beginning with the early retirement age—when a person is first eligible for public pension benefits—and continuing through age 69. They call this the "tax force" to retire (see the second-to-last column of Table 3-5).

Table 3-5 indicates a strong relationship between unused labor capacity and the tax rate on continued work. To understand the relationship more clearly, it is useful to divide the countries into three groups: (1) those with high unused capacity (Belgium, France, Italy, the Netherlands, and the United Kingdom); (2) a group with medium unused capacity (Germany, Spain, and Canada); and (3) a group with low unused capacity (the United States, Sweden, and, in particular, Japan). The average replacement rate at early retirement in the first group is 76.6 percent of median earnings, and the average tax on continued labor earnings in that year is 91.8 percent. In the third group, with the least unused labor capacity, the average replacement rate at the early retirement age is 50 percent, and the tax rate on continued earnings is 24.7 percent. These com-

---

[2]For a look at incentive effects in different nations and various problems related to their measurement, see Disney et al., 1994; Baker and Benjamin, 1996; Meghir and Whitehouse, 1997; Disney and Whitehouse, 1999; Peracchi and Viviano, 1999; and Börsch-Supan, 2000a.

TABLE 3-5 Retirement Incentives and Labor Market Behavior

Country	Unused Labor Capacity, Age 55 to 65 (%)[a]	Replacement Rate at ER Age (%)[b]	Accrual in Next Year (%)	Implicit Tax on Earnings in Next Year (%)	Tax Force, ER Age to 69[c]	Hazard Rate at Early Retirement Age (%)[d]
Belgium	67	77	−5.6	82	8.87	33
France	60	91	−7.0	80	7.25	65
Italy	59	75	−5.8	81	9.20	10
Netherlands	58	91	−12.8	141	8.32	70
United Kingdom	55	48	−10.0	75	3.77	22
Germany	48	62	−4.1	35	3.45	55
Spain	47	63	4.2	−23	2.49	20
Canada	45	20	−1.0	8	2.37	32
United States	37	41	0.2	−1	1.57	25
Sweden	35	54	−4.1	28	2.18	5
Japan	22	54	−3.9	47	1.65	12

[a]Unused labor capacity is defined as the proportion of persons aged 55 to 65 not in the labor force.

[b]ER = early retirement.

[c]Tax force is the summation of the implied tax rates on continued work beginning with the early retirement age—when a person is first eligible for public pension benefits—and running through age 69.

[d]Hazard rate at early retirement measures the percentage of working individuals who leave the labor market at the early retirement age.

NOTES:

Belgium: The public pension early retirement age is 60, but employees who are laid off are eligible for large benefits at younger ages. Thus the accrual, implicit tax, and tax force measures treat unemployment benefits as early retirement benefits available at age 55.

France: Counting public pension benefits, available at age 60, but not accounting for guaranteed income benefits for those losing their jobs at age 57 or older.

Italy: Public pension benefits for private-sector employees, not counting disability availability.

Netherlands: In addition to public pension benefits, the calculations account for virtually universal employer private pension benefits. The employer plan is assumed to provide for early retirement at age 60. There is no public pension early retirement in the Netherlands, but employer early retirement benefits are commonly available at age 60.

United Kingdom: Based on public pension benefits only, but counting "incapacity" benefits at 60 as early retirement benefits.

Germany: Counting public pension benefits and assuming a person is eligible for "early" disability benefits.

Spain: Based on RGSS (the main public pension program).

Canada: Counting public pension benefits only.

United States: Counting public pension benefits only.

Sweden: Counting public pension benefits only. The hazard rate at the early retirement age is the average of the rates between ages 59 and 61.

Japan: Assuming a "diminishing earnings" profile. The employment option is to work in the primary firm until age 60 and then in a secondary firm, where the worker would be eligible for the 25% wage subsidy if his/her earnings were low enough.

SOURCE: Gruber and Wise (1999).

parisons point to a rather strong correlation between public pension incentives and unused capacity.

Impact of Disability and Welfare Programs

Other government-provided programs may have an important effect on retirement. In many European countries, unemployment insurance and disability benefit programs essentially provide early retirement benefits before the official public pension early retirement age. In the mid-1990s in Belgium, for example, 22 percent of men were receiving unemployment or disability benefits at age 59. In France, 21 percent were receiving these benefits at that age, in the Netherlands 27 percent, in the United Kingdom 33 percent, and in Germany 37 percent. Even in Sweden, where departure rates are relatively low before age 60, 24 percent were receiving unemployment or disability benefits at age 59.

In the United States and Japan, on the other hand, only about 12 percent were receiving unemployment or disability benefits at age 59. In France, almost all those who are unemployed at age 60 begin to receive public pension benefits at that age and thereafter are officially classified as retired. In the Netherlands, the United Kingdom, Germany, and Sweden, the majority of persons receiving disability benefits before age 65 start to receive public pension benefits at that age and are classified as retired. Thus in many countries, one must be able to calculate accrual under various programs, in addition to accrual under the public pension program.

Employer-Provided Pensions

In addition to public pension plans, other pension programs may affect observed retirement patterns. One such program is employer-provided pension plans. For example, half of employees in the United States are covered by employer-provided plans, and about half of these are defined-benefit plans that have substantial retirement incentive effects. Employer-provided plans are also common in Canada, Japan, the United Kingdom, and the Netherlands, for example. In other countries, such as France, Germany, and Italy, employer plans are of negligible significance. Where such plans are salient, it is important to try to obtain the information that would allow calculation of accrual as is done for public pension plans. This task is often complicated because there is typically great variation in the provisions of employer plans. The Health and Retirement Survey in the United States (Juster and Suzman, 1995) has attempted to collect information on the provisions of respondent plans, with difficulty but with some success.

In a number of Latin American countries, most notably Chile, as well as in Switzerland, Singapore, and Australia, private pension savings have been made compulsory. In the United Kingdom and the United States, a series of legislative changes since the early 1980s has extended the range of options for tax-privileged pension saving to individual pension savings accounts. Even in countries such as Italy, new legislative frameworks have been set in place to facilitate the growth of private provision, though to little effect as yet.

Table 3-6 provides some idea of the extent of occupational pension coverage for a number of OECD countries studied by Disney and Johnson (in press). The first column shows the proportion of pensioners in receipt of private pension income, while the second displays the proportion of workers covered. The table confirms the obvious patterns. Coverage among workers ranges from around 90 percent in Japan and the Netherlands; almost 90 percent in Australia; about half in the United Kingdom, the United States, and Canada; around 40 percent in Germany; to under 20 percent in New Zealand, and less than 10 percent elsewhere. In general, occupational pensions are less prevalent among pensioners than among active workers. In part this is because not all pensioners are ex-workers. In addition, in some countries occupational pension schemes are not mature, so that more members of later generations participate. In Australia, the vast difference reflects two factors. First is the relatively recent introduction of compulsory membership for all employees. Sec-

TABLE 3-6 Occupational Pension Coverage, circa 1995

Country	% of Pensioners Receiving	% of Working Population Covered
Australia	c. 20% men, 7% women[a]	87%
Canada	54% men, 31% women	45%
France	Negligible	Negligible
Germany	21% men, 9% women	42%
Italy	Negligible	Negligible
Japan[b]	10%[a]	c. 90%
Netherlands	76% men, 23% women	c. 90%
New Zealand	21% men, 10% women	17%
United Kingdom	66% men, 32% women	48%
United States	48% men, 26% women	44%

[a]Figures on recipients for Japan and Australia are difficult to interpret since most occupational plans in these countries provide lump-sum benefits. Takayama (1996) estimates that 55% of retirees in Japan receive some lump-sum benefit.

[b]Japanese figures are for 1991.

SOURCES: Davis (1995); Takayama (1996); Bateman and Piggott (1997); Disney and Johnson (in press).

ond is the fact that most people take their accrued pension rights as a lump sum rather than as a pension, so that while they may have benefited from a private pension, they are not recorded as receiving any pension income. The same is true in Japan, where a large proportion of occupational schemes provide lump-sum benefits. To a large extent these features reflect the history and development of occupational schemes, which tended to emerge first in the public sector, especially among civil servants and the armed forces, and then to be negotiated between unions and larger companies, often taking the civil service scheme as a benchmark.

Table 3-7 compares the probability of receipt of occupational pensions among the recently retired according to sex and marital status. In all cases, married women are much less likely to receive such pensions than any other group. Interestingly, however, single never-married women are more likely to receive such pensions than are single men. Married men have the highest likelihood of receipt. The commonality of these patterns is striking and is of course a reflection of the work-related basis for receipt and lower levels of labor market attachment among women. On the other hand, it is among women that coverage continues to grow as work patterns change.

TABLE 3-7 Proportion of Recently Retired Persons Receiving Occupational Pensions, by Sex And Marital Status, circa 1995

Marital Status	Male	Female	Total
Canada			
Single (never married)	34.2	48.9	42.1
Single (other)	54.1	34.8	38.1
Married/cohabiting	56.3	25.3	42.1
All	54.1	30.8	40.8
Netherlands			
Single (never married)	61.7	67.7	63.6
Single (other)	83.8	60.6	66.8
Married/cohabiting	75.5	12.6	46.7
All	76.4	23.0	50.2
United Kingdom			
Single (never married)	54.6	56.2	55.2
Single (other)	56.4	44.8	49.1
Married/cohabiting	69.5	25.8	48.0
All	66.3	32.0	48.7
United States			
Single (never married)	33.5	39.7	36.9
Single (other)	41.9	31.0	34.0
Married/cohabiting	49.5	20.4	36.2
All	47.5	25.5	35.5

SOURCE: Johnson (1999).

It is interesting to examine how common receipt of private pensions is among the retired. Performing such an assessment in the same way as was done for public systems, by reference to what example people would receive, is difficult because the occupational systems are diverse and depend critically on work histories. Table 3-8 presents figures for four countries showing the proportions of pensioners' incomes that derive from private pensions. What is perhaps most striking is that in none of these countries do occupational pensions provide half of total income for pensioners. Indeed, only in the Netherlands does the proportion reach a third. In all four countries, the share of total income from private pensions is largest for couples and smallest for single (including never-married, divorced, and widowed) women. On the whole, receipt of private pensions is more important for younger than for older pensioners.

There are three important types of private pensions. In the United States, employer-provided pensions are of two types. The most common type used to be termed a defined-benefit plan, with benefits based on earnings, often those just before retirement. Such plans typically have provisions similar to those discussed above for public pension systems and generally provide large early retirement incentives, much like the public pension incentives in many countries. A second type of employer-provided pension is the defined-contribution plan. Under such a plan, contributions—typically a percentage of earnings—are made to an employee's account. The account grows according to the investment allocation of the account funds. At retirement, benefits depend on the accumulated assets in the employee's account. This type of plan has none of the incentive effects associated with defined-benefit plans. In the United States, a third form of private pension, the personal retirement plan, is the most rapidly growing form of retirement saving. Individual retirement accounts (IRAs) and 401(k) plans are the most common of these. IRAs are not provided through employers, whereas 401(k) plans are. Both have

TABLE 3-8 Share of Occupational Pensions in Total Family Income, circa 1995

Country	Couples	Single Men	Single Women
Canada[a]	26.9	23.7	20.4
Netherlands	37.3	35.7	22.9
United Kingdom	26.5	20.1	14.1
United States	21.4	21.9	16.7

[a]Includes income from individual accounts (RRSPs).

SOURCE: Johnson (1999).

key features of conventional employer-provided defined-contribution plans, but it is useful to distinguish them from the latter plans. Contributions to 401(k) plans have grown rapidly since their introduction in 1982, and contributions to these plans are now much larger than contributions to all other plans combined. The decline in defined-benefit plans in the United States has been particularly dramatic. Between 1980 and 1995, the proportion of full-time employees in medium and large private companies participating in a such a plan dropped from 84 to 52 percent. Again, IRAs and 401(k) plans have virtually none of the incentive effects of defined-benefit plans, and their rapid rise is therefore likely to change the incentive for early retirement faced by the typical worker.[3]

The use of public-sector disability benefit schemes to finance early retirement has already been mentioned. Occupational pensions can also be used as a vehicle for early retirement. In the Netherlands, such schemes often pay for early retirement, guaranteeing employees a benefit of 70-80 percent of previous earnings up to age 65. In the past, the costs of early retirement were often covered on a pay-as-you-go rather than a funded basis. Firms are now dealing with the extra costs imposed by the funding approach by reducing benefits or increasing minimum eligibility ages.

The role that privately provided pensions can play in promoting early retirement is often neglected, and this can make it difficult to understand retirement behavior in countries with a large private sector. It is often unclear how one should regard this type of early retirement. To the extent that individuals have accumulated adequate funds to retire at 55 rather than 65, they are simply enjoying the fruits of their own labor and savings, and such early retirement can be seen as an indicator of the success of the system. Pensions, however, are rarely that simple. In final occupational salary schemes, the costs of early retirement are often borne by scheme participants other than those who benefit. In addition, the structure of such schemes, which tend to be most generous to long-staying and older individuals, can make companies less willing than they might otherwise be to take on older workers; some have even argued that the structure encourages the sacking of incumbents. On the other hand, the fact that such schemes can be used effectively to ease the pain of workforce redundancies indicates that they may perform a more important role in the welfare state than simply the provision of retirement pen-

---

[3]An important point with regard to private pension provisions is the ability of people to allocate their resources across time in a sensible manner. The desirability of privatizing some or all of public pension programs depends in large part on this ability, and the monitoring/measurement of its impact will become increasingly important to the extent that countries reformulate their pension schemes to incorporate greater emphasis on a private pillar.

sions. Finally, where occupational pensions are unfunded, as in much of the public sector in the United Kingdom, early retirement can be used as in state pay-as-you-go systems to relieve current pressures, but in a way that leads to growing cost pressures for the future.

The important role of occupational pensions in the tendency to early retirement in the United Kingdom is illustrated in the top panel of Figure 3-7, which shows employment survival curves for men with and without an occupational pension (Blundell and Johnson, 1998; Blundell and Tanner, 1999). Those without an occupational pension, who tend to be much lower paid and less skilled, leave the labor force more rapidly in their 40s and early 50s. But the interesting point is that after about age 55, those with an occupational pension start leaving employment very rapidly indeed. The bottom panel of Figure 3-7 shows the same survival probabilities for women, and the retirement age of 60 is clearly visible.

More detailed analysis of the effects on retirement behavior of incentives built into occupational schemes has been carried out in the United States by Lumsdaine et al. (1990, 1994) and Stock and Wise (1990a, 1990b). These studies have revealed very substantial effects of the specific incentives for workers to retire at particular ages that are offered by many U.S. occupational pension plans. Thus people react to the design of private pension plans in much the same way as they make use of generous government-sponsored early retirement programs.

KEY DATA REQUIREMENTS

To understand trends in work and retirement and to assess the impact of ongoing pension reforms and changes in retirement incentives, one must gather information on work histories and longitudinal data on earnings, marital status, health status, and disability. While long earnings histories are not typically needed under defined-benefit regimes (which are often based on the last few years of wages), such data are required to measure opportunities in work, as argued above. Moreover, many of the more recent pension reforms move in the direction of defining pension amounts on the basis of an individual's working history or payroll tax payments over the life cycle. Private pension funds are also shifting from final-salary benefits to average-salary benefits or even to defined-contribution schemes (see, e.g., Disney and Whitehouse, 1992, 1999). In addition, reforms tend to allow for more freedom in choice of retirement age. Such reforms thus provide interesting evidence about the influence of scheme-specific details on retirement behavior.

This is not to diminish the importance of social factors (changes in marital status, partner's employment status, social participation, social networks) and health issues (functional ability and cognitive function) in

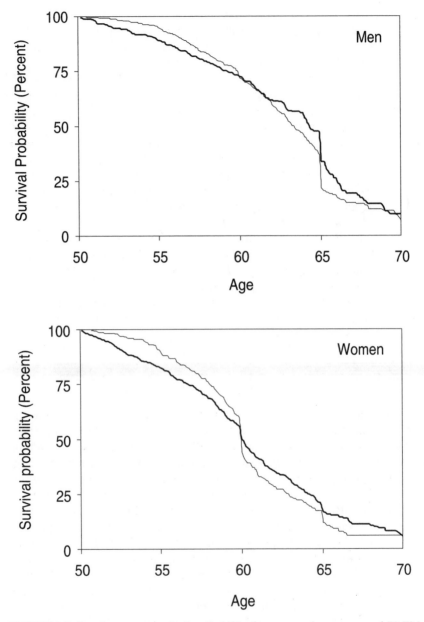

FIGURE 3-7 Employment survival probability for men and women aged 50-70 in the United Kingdom: Circa 1989.
NOTE: Bold—Occupational pensions, Light—State Social Security pensions.
SOURCE: Blundell and Tanner (1999).

the decision to retire. Retirement changes roles within a household, and a related issue is synchronization in the retirement decisions of couples. Changing roles related to retirement are also likely to affect social participation. But the form these changes take and the resulting impact on social participation depend on economic resources, preexisting social networks, and functional ability and cognitive functioning. It is also possible that individuals' perceptions and expectations regarding retirement and aging may influence changes in their social participation. In particular, expectations regarding future dependency and illness may become self-fulfilling, but such expectations may themselves be dependent on social position prior to retirement and local context (such as access to public transport).

Public Pension Plan Provisions and Personal Attributes

Understanding individual retirement decisions and how they relate to retirement programs requires evaluating the incentive effects of the programs' various provisions. Those effects in turn depend both on the plan provisions and on individual work histories, marital status, and other individual and family circumstances. As noted earlier, continuation in the labor force can mean a loss in public pension benefits. In many countries, this loss of benefits can offset a large fraction of the wage earnings a person would receive from continued work. Thus there is an implicit tax on work, and total compensation can be much less than net wage earnings.

Given the variation in the magnitude of the public pension tax on work from country to country, the details of plan provisions must be known precisely. In addition, to conduct microanalysis of the effect of those provisions on individual retirement decisions, employment histories, family status, and other circumstances that determine individual accrual rates must also be known. Thus it is important to be able to match detailed plan provisions with individual survey data.

Plan provisions are typically recorded in administrative documents and can usually be obtained rather easily. Data on individual attributes can be gathered from many different sources. For instance, in many countries administrative data collected as part of public pension programs include the individual data used to determine benefits, and in this sense are ideal. These data files are also typically very large and may allow analysis by birth cohort, for example. Administrative data, however, do not typically include information on other individual attributes, such as health status, that may have an important effect on retirement decisions. Surveys such as the Health and Retirement Survey in the United States include such data. They may also include administrative data that can be used in conjunction with the survey data (for example, the Health and Retirement Survey obtains Social Security earnings histories). Thus one must take a flexible approach to data collection.

Disability, Unemployment, and Private Pension Plan Provisions

In many countries, disability and unemployment insurance programs effectively provide for early retirement before the explicit public pension early retirement age. In Germany, for example, the path to retirement for most employees is not the public pension system narrowly defined, but rather unemployment and disability insurance programs. Such programs are also important in France, Belgium, the Netherlands, and other countries. Thus in addressing public pension reform, these programs must be considered as well. Ideally, one should also know which paths to retirement are available to each person. One who is eligible for disability benefits, for example, typically faces much greater early retirement incentives than one not eligible for these benefits. Eligibility usually depends on program provisions and individual circumstances that are often difficult to determine from administrative or survey data. For this reason, a new way to obtain these data may be desirable. Perhaps surveys could collect the necessary individual information, which, together with plan provisions, would allow determination of eligibility.

The public pension system is the principal source of retirement benefits in many countries, whereas in others it is only one of multiple sources of retirement support. In the United States, the United Kingdom, the Netherlands, Canada, and Japan, for example, employer-provided pension plans are a key source of benefits. Indeed in some countries, such as the United States, employer-provided benefits are often integrated with public pension benefits. The incentive effects of these private defined-benefit plans are quite similar to those of public pension programs. Thus in some countries it may be necessary to consider public and private plans jointly. Where the latter plans are prevalent, it is important to try to obtain the information needed to calculate accrual for these plans, just as for public plans. This task is often complicated by great variation in the provisions of employer plans.

As noted above, the most dramatic change in retirement saving in the United States is the growth in individual retirement saving plans. Individuals must decide how much to contribute to these accounts, how to invest their contributions, and how to withdraw funds after retirement. In 1980, almost 92 percent of pension plan contributions were to traditional employer-provided plans, and about 64 percent of these contributions were to conventional defined-benefit plans. Today, almost 60 percent of contributions are to personal retirement accounts, including 401(k),

IRA, and other plans. Including employer-provided (non-401[k]) defined-contribution plans, more than 76 percent of contributions are to plans controlled in large measure by individuals. For persons retiring three decades from now, personal assets in 401(k) plans alone are likely to be substantially greater than public pension wealth (see Poterba and Samwick, 1999; Poterba and Wise, 1999; Poterba et al., 1999). As noted earlier, a critical feature of these plans is that they have none of the retirement incentive effects of public pension and other defined-benefit programs. Thus they must be considered by those attempting to understand future retirement incentives.

Other Related Data

In addition to financial incentives to retire, a comprehensive analysis of retirement should account for individual attributes, in particular health status, but also job attributes that may affect the benefit gained from working. Such effects could be additional costs of early retirement beyond the implicit financial tax on work discussed earlier. This observation also raises the question of "productive activity" and how it might be measured; it would surely include more than paid employment.

The goals of data collection should also be conditioned by looking forward. What issues are likely to arise? Gradual withdrawal from the labor force, which is uncommon now but may become more prevalent in the future, is one such issue. The increased entry of women into the labor force has promoted more flexible work arrangements, and computers have facilitated work at home. What would facilitate gradual rather than precipitous departure from the labor force? How would firm institutional arrangements have to be changed? What information would help answer these questions?

There are also close connections between retirement and the domains discussed in other chapters of this report. Saving for retirement and health status are obviously related to retirement. Perhaps less obvious is the relationship between demographic projections and retirement incentives. For example, projected dependency ratios may depend importantly on pension plan provisions and their effect on the proportion of older persons out of the labor force.

Because the provisions of public pension plans often constitute strong incentives for early retirement, it may be valuable to understand the reasons for such provisions. There are two distinct issues here. First, while it appears clear that public pension provisions affect labor force participation, it is also apparent that in at least some instances the provisions were adopted to encourage older workers to leave the labor force. For example, anecdotal evidence suggests that in some countries, it was thought that the withdrawal of older employees from the workforce would provide more job opportunities for young workers. This possibility does not call into question a causal interpretation of the relationship between plan provisions and retirement. To the extent that it is true, it simply means that in some instances the provisions were adopted for a particular reason—and the data show that they worked.

The second issue, however, does complicate data analysis. It can be argued that to some extent at least, public pension provisions were adopted to accommodate existing labor force participation patterns, rather than the patterns being determined by the provisions. For example, early retirement benefits could be provided to support persons who are unable to find work and thus already out of the labor force. Early retirement programs related to disability and unemployment could also have been adopted to accommodate preexisting labor force departure rates, and this possibility must temper a causal interpretation of the relationship between program provisions and retirement.

To address either or both of these issues requires historical data on unemployment rates, which are typically available from existing country data sources. But complete analysis may also require study of legislative records and other less quantitative data sources. If a goal is to understand how a given system might be improved, it is often useful to understand as well how it came about in the first place.

Throughout this chapter, we have focused on individual attributes and the incentives faced by individuals, and on corresponding data collection. We have given little attention to macro labor market analysis (e.g., labor demand for older workers) and macro determinants of retirement (e.g., the role of pensions in the labor market; see Gustman et al., 1994), age-related changes in productivity, or the potential importance of firm goals and changing firm characteristics. In many respects, this latter arena is almost a separate direction of study requiring a separate data collection effort, and we have not explicitly addressed what is likely to become an important area of inquiry (see, e.g., National Research Council, 1997; Haltiwanger et al., 1999a; 2000). Some countries have administrative data that link individual attributes to the firms in which people work and thus to characteristics of the firms (Lane et al., 1998; Abowd and Karmarz, 1999; Haltiwanger et al., 1999b). In principle, this sort of connection could be drawn as an add-on to individual-based data collection efforts. It might also be important to study firm internal labor markets and institutional arrangements that might, for example, affect the possibility for older workers to withdraw gradually from the labor force. In some countries, such as the United States, age discrimination laws may have an important effect on these arrangements. In many instances, it would be difficult for an older worker to obtain a lower wage while assuming less responsibility in order to stay in the labor force longer. These issues have not been forgotten, but merely are not emphasized in this chapter.

Finally, it is surely the case that cultural values and social preferences affect the generosity of retirement plans, and changing preferences may have affected recent changes in retirement plans. We have chosen in this chapter to avoid focusing on social preferences and cultural values, instead emphasizing systematic quantitative data collection, consistent with the focus of the volume as a whole. Indeed the key illustrative analysis presented in the chapter shows that the incentive effects of plan provisions appear to be highly comparable over countries with widely varying social histories.

RECOMMENDATIONS

3-1. National and cross-national studies should focus on the retirement incentive effects of the provisions of public pension plans. The magnitude of social security taxes on work differs greatly from country to country, and must be understood through careful monitoring of the details of plan provisions and conversion of those provisions into economically meaningful measures—such as benefit accrual rates—that can be related to individual retirement decisions. These measures can then be compared across nations to examine differential policy effects.

3-2. The nature and effects of disability and unemployment insurance programs should be considered when analyzing retirement schemes and individual retirement choices. Disability and unemployment insurance programs in many countries effectively provide for early retirement before the explicit early retirement age and must be considered in conjunction with the public pension program itself. One must be able to calculate accrual under both types of programs. Data also are needed on the paths to retirement that are available to individuals, in particular on the interaction between eligibility criteria and individual circumstances.

3-3. Research into patterns of work and retirement should include consideration of the interaction of private retirement plans and public programs. A growing number of countries, including many in the developing world, now have compulsory private pension schemes. Such schemes are likely to proliferate as nations attempt to reform and/or extend pension coverage. A critical feature of these plans is that they have none of the retirement incentive effects of public and other defined-benefit programs. Where these plans are prevalent, it is necessary to collect information that will allow calculation of accrual as a means of understanding likely associated retirement incentives.

3-4. To understand individual retirement choices, information on individual work histories, earnings histories, health status, saving, and other individual attributes should be collected in addition to data on public and private plan provisions. The most effective way to collect the broad array of individual data on the determinants of retirement choices is through longitudinal surveys that address a range of behavioral domains. Data from such surveys can often be supplemented with administrative data files that provide earnings histories, and are in fact used currently to analyze retirement behavior in many countries.

REFERENCES

Abowd, J.M., and F. Kramarz
    1999   Econometric analysis of linked employer-employee data. *Labour Economics* 6:53-
            74.
Baker, M., and D. Benjamin
    1996   Early Retirement Provisions and the Labour Force Behavior of Older Men: Evi-
            dence from Canada. Unpublished paper. University of Toronto.
Bateman, H., and J. Piggott
    1997   *Private Pensions in OECD Countries – Australia.* Labour Market and Social Policy
            Occasional Papers 23. Paris: Organization for Economic Co-operation and Devel-
            opment.
Blau, D.
    1994   Labour force dynamics of older men. *Econometrica* 62:117-156.
Blundell, R., and P. Johnson
    1998   Pensions and labor force participation in the UK. *American Economic Review*
            88(2):173-178.
Blundell, R.W., and S. Tanner
    1999   Labour Force Participation and Retirement in the UK. Paper prepared for the
            Panel on a Research Agenda and New Data for an Aging World, Committee on
            Population, National Research Council.
Börsch-Supan, A.
    2000a   Data and Research on Retirement in Germany. Paper prepared for the Panel on a
            Research Agenda and New Data for an Aging World, Committee on Population,
            National Research Council.
    2000b   Incentive effects of social security on labour force participation: Evidence in Ger-
            many and across Europe. *Journal of Public Economics* 78(1-2):25-49.
Börsch-Supan, A., and R. Schnabel
    1998   Social security and declining labour force participation in Germany. *American
            Economic Review* 88(2):173-178.
    1999   Social security and retirement in Germany. In *International Comparison of Social
            Security Systems*, J. Gruber and D. Wise, eds. Chicago: The University of Chicago
            Press.
Bound, J., M. Schoenbaum, T.R. Stinebrickner, and T. Waidmann
    1999   The dynamic effect of health on the labor force transitions of older workers.
            Labour Economics 6(2):179-202.

Burtless, G., and R. Moffitt
    1984   The effect of Social Security benefits on the labor supply of the aged. In *Retirement and Economic Behavior*, H. Aaron and G. Burtless, eds., pp. 135-175. Washington, DC: Brookings Institution.
Coronado, J.L., D. Fullerton, and T. Glass
    2000   *The Progressivity of Social Security*. NBER Working Paper 7520. Cambridge, MA: National Bureau of Economic Research.
Creedy, J., R. Disney, and E. Whitehouse
    1993   The earnings-related state pension, indexation and lifetime redistribution in the UK. *Review of Income and Wealth* 39(3):257-278.
Davis, E.P.
    1995   *Pension Funds*. Oxford: Clarendon Press.
Dilnot, A., R. Disney, P. Johnson, and E. Whitehouse
    1993   *Pension Policy in the UK: An Economic Analysis*. London: Institute for Fiscal Studies.
Disney, R., and P. Johnson
    in   *Pension Systems and Retirement Incomes Across OECD Countries*. Cheltenham, UK:
    press   Edward Elgar.
Disney, R., and S. Webb
    1991   Why are there so many long-term sick in Britain. *Economic Journal* 1011:252-262.
Disney, R., S. Webb, C. Meghir, and E. Whitehouse
    1994   Retirement behaviour in Britain. *Fiscal Studies* 15(1):24-43.
Disney, R., and E. Whitehouse
    1992   *The Personal Pension Stampede*. London: Institute for Fiscal Studies.
    1999   *Pension Plans and Retirement Incentives*. Working Paper, May. Washington, DC: World Bank.
Gruber, J., and D.A. Wise
    1998   Social Security and retirement: An international comparison. *American Economic Review Papers and Proceedings* 88(2):158-163.
Gruber, J., and D.A. Wise, eds.
    1999   *Social Security and Retirement Around the World*. Chicago: University of Chicago Press.
Gustman, A.L., O.S. Mitchell, and T.L. Steinmeier
    1994   The role of pensions in the labor market: A survey of the literature. *Industrial and Labor Relations Review* 47(3):417-438.
Haltiwanger, J.C., J. Lane, and J. Spletzer
    1999a Productivity differences across employers: The role of employer size, age, and human capital. *American Economic Review* 89(2):94-98.
    2000   Wages, Productivity, and the Dynamic Interaction of Businesses and Workers. Unpublished paper. University of Maryland.
Haltiwanger, J.C., J. Lane, J. Spletzer, J. Theeuwes, and K. Troske
    1999b *The Creation and Analysis of Employer and Employee Matched Data*. Amsterdam: North-Holland.
Hermalin, A.I., and A. Chan
    2000   *Work and Retirement Among the Older Population in Four Asian Countries: A Comparative Analysis*. CAS Research Paper Series No. 22. Singapore: Centre for Advanced Studies, National University of Singapore.
Hurd, M.
    1998   Symposium on assets, incomes and retirement. *Fiscal Studies* 19(2):141-151.
International Labour Office
    var.   Year Book of Labour Statistics. Geneva: International Labour Office.
    years

Johnson, P.
    1999 *Pension Provision and Pensioners' Incomes in Ten OECD Countries.* Monograph.
          London: Institute for Fiscal Studies.
Johnson, P., G. Stears, and S. Webb
    1998 The dynamics of incomes and occupational pensions after retirement. *Fiscal Studies* 19(2):197-215
Juster, F.T., and R. Suzman
    1995 An overview of the health and retirement study. *Journal of Human Resources* 30(Supplement):S7-S56.
Lane, J., S. Burgess, and J. Theeuwes
    1998 The uses of longitudinal matched employer/employee data in labor market analysis. *Proceedings of the American Statistical Association.*
Lazear, E.
    1986 Retirement from the labour force. In *Handbook of Labour Economics,* O. Ashenfelter and R. Layard, eds. Amsterdam: North-Holland.
Lumsdaine, R., J. Stock, and D. Wise
    1990 Efficient windows and labor force reduction. *Journal of Public Economics* 43:131-159.
    1992 Three models of retirement: Computational complexity versus predictive validity. In *Topics in the Economics of Aging,* D. Wise, ed., pp. 21-57. Chicago: University of Chicago Press.
    1994 Pension plan provisions and retirement: Men and women, Medicare, and models. In *Studies in the Economics of Aging,* D. Wise, ed. Chicago: University of Chicago Press.
Manton, K.G., L. Corder, and E. Stallard
    1997 Chronic disability trends in elderly United States populations: 1982-1994. *Proceedings of the National Academy of Sciences, Medical Sciences* 94:2593-2598.
Meghir, C., and E. Whitehouse
    1997 Labour market transitions and retirement of men in the UK. *Journal of Econometrics* 79:327-354.
National Research Council
    1996 *Assessing Knowledge of Retirement Behavior.* Panel on Retirement Income Modeling. E.A. Hanushek and N.L. Maritato, eds. Commission on Behavioral and Social Sciences and Education. Washington, DC: National Academy Press.
    1997 *Assessing Policies for Retirement Income: Needs for Data, Research and Models.* Panel on Retirement Income Modeling. C.F. Citro and E.A. Hanushek, eds. Commission on Behavioral and Social Sciences and Education. Washington, DC: National Academy Press.
Organization for Economic Co-operation and Development
    1995a *The Transition from Work to Retirement.* Social Policy Studies Series #16. Paris: Organization for Economic Co-Operation and Development.
    1995b *The Labor Market and Older Workers.* Social Policy Studies Series #17. Paris: Organization for Economic Co-Operation and Development.
Peracchi, F., and E. Viviano
    1999 *Italian Micro-Data on Work and Retirement.* Paper prepared for the Panel on a Research Agenda and New Data for an Aging World, Committee on Population, National Research Council.
Piachaud, D.
    1986 Disability, retirement and unemployment of older men. *Journal of Social Policy* 15:145-162.

Poterba, J.M., and A. Samwick
   1999   *Taxation and Household Portfolio Composition: U.S. Evidence from the 1980s and 1990s.*
          NBER Working Paper W7392, October. Cambridge, MA: National Bureau of
          Economic Research.
Poterba, J.M., S.F. Venti, and D.A. Wise
   1999   *Implications of Rising Personal Retirement Saving.* NBER Working Paper W6295,
          March. Cambridge, MA: National Bureau of Economic Research.
Poterba, J.M., and D.A Wise
   1999   *Individual Financial Decisions in Retirement Saving Plans and the Provision of Re-*
          sources for Retirement. NBER Working Paper W5762, March. Cambridge, MA:
          National Bureau of Economic Research.
Quinn, J.F., and R.V. Burkhauser
   1994   Retirement and labor force behavior of the elderly. In *Demography of Aging.* Com-
          mittee on Population. L.G. Martin and S.H. Preston, eds., pp. 50-101. Commis-
          sion on Behavioral and Social Sciences and Education. Washington, DC: Na-
          tional Academy Press.
Raymo, J.M., and J.C. Cornman
   1999   Labor force status transitions at older ages in the Philippines, Singapore, Taiwan,
          and Thailand, 1970-1990. *Journal of Cross-Cultural Gerontology* 14:221-244.
Rust, J.
   1989   A dynamic programming model of retirement behaviour. In *The Economics of*
          Aging, D. Wise, ed. Chicago: Chicago University Press for the National Bureau of
          Economic Research.
Sheshinski, E.
   1978   A model of social security and retirement decisions. *Journal of Public Economics*
          10:337-360.
Stock, J.H., and D.A. Wise
   1990a Pensions, the option value of work, and retirement. *Econometrica* 58(5):1151-1180.
   1990b The pension inducement to retire: An option value analysis. In *Issues in the Eco-*
          nomics of Aging, D. Wise, ed. Chicago: University of Chicago Press.
Straka, J.W.
   1992   *The Demand for Older Workers: The Neglected Side of a Labor Market.* Studies in
          Income Distribution, 15. Washington, DC: Social Security Administration.
Takayama, N.
   1996   *Possible Effects of Ageing on the Equilibrium of the Public Pension System in Japan.*
          Reprint Series No. 170. Tokyo: Institute of Economic Research, Hitotsubashi Uni-
          versity.
Tanner, S.
   1998   The dynamics of male retirement behaviour. *Fiscal Studies* 19(2):175-196.
Yashiro, N.
   1997   The economic position of the elderly in Japan. In *The Economic Effects of Aging in*
          the United States and Japan, M. Hurd and N. Yashiro, eds. Chicago: University of
          Chicago Press.

4

Private Wealth and Income Security: International Comparisons

Income security during retirement is a primary social achievement of the 20th century. As individuals retired from work at younger ages and life spans increased, the period between the formal end of work and death became one of the most significant stages of life. This enormous accomplishment, however, was accompanied by fundamental public policy challenges associated with the risks posed by population aging. The two most basic challenges were (1) that individuals would have sufficient income security during their retirement years so that retirement did not necessarily imply a substantial decline in living standards and (2) that individuals would have protection against the increasing risks of falling into poor health.

During the last century, industrialized nations responded to the problem of having sufficient income to achieve a decent standard of living during retirement by developing the now-familiar three-tiered system: the primary role of the public tier is to guarantee through governmental transfers at least a minimum income standard during retirement; the second tier is based on employer-provided pensions; and the third tier consists of wealth accumulation through private household savings (see also Chapter 3). As discussed below, individual countries in North America, Europe, and Asia have placed differing emphasis on these three tiers in devising their own unique schemes. Yet despite this cross-country diversity in policy, it is generally recognized that collectively, people in all of these countries are much better able now than they were 50 or even 25 years ago to enjoy reasonable income security during their old age.

At the same time, it is also widely acknowledged that whatever their past successes, the systems currently in place must eventually be substantially revised if the goal of adequate income security is to continue to be met in this century. Some of the challenges to the current systems stem from the demographic forces discussed in Chapter 2. First, the large baby boom cohorts born after World War II in various countries will be entering their retirement years during the first few decades of the 21st century. Issues associated with the sheer size of these cohorts are compounded by large increases in older-age life expectancy throughout Asia, Europe, and North America, which now face the new demographic reality of a constantly declining ratio of workers to retirees. This new demography implies that the financial costs of maintaining the existing income benefits of the old pay-as-you-go public-tier systems are not sustainable.

The major domestic political challenge of the 21st century concerns how countries will adapt their old-age income security and health insurance systems to meet this challenge. In this chapter we do not advocate any particular system over others. However, one option that most countries are likely to consider involves relying on individual private savings and wealth accumulation to offset any reductions that may take place in the level of public-tier support. How realistic is it to assume that individuals will save sufficiently over their lifetime to contribute significantly to their own income needs during retirement? To answer this question, one must first understand the basic motivations for household wealth accumulation. Why do some households save so little while others— even those with similar incomes—appear to accumulate so much wealth? Do individuals save primarily to leave bequests to their heirs; to reconcile differences in the timing of income and consumption over the life cycle; or to insure against future uncertainty regarding income, unemployment, or health? What role do financial inheritances play in perpetuating wealth inequalities across generations? These are basic and important research questions that require good theoretical and empirical scholarship, as well as high-quality data on household savings and wealth.

A central question regarding income security for the aged is whether individuals and families will assume greater responsibility for their own retirement if current government programs are scaled back because of budgetary pressures. In particular, will households accumulate more private wealth during their working years to finance their retirement years? A promising research strategy for answering this question is based on international comparisons. As suggested above, there is a great deal of variation in the way different countries finance the retirement of their older populations, placing differing weights on publicly provided pensions, private or employer-provided pensions, and private savings. For example, as a general rule the countries of continental Europe place much more emphasis than the United States on income security through a public-tier system. Yet some European countries rely almost exclusively on an integrated public tier, while others, such as the United Kingdom, use a combination of private- and public-sector resources. These combinations may produce quite different rates of income replacement during retirement, and therefore have differing implications for the incentives for private savings. For example, a public-sector benefit that provided almost complete income replacement would reduce and possibly even eliminate incentives for private retirement savings.

To address these basic questions, the panel pursued the following strategy. Because there exists much less research in Europe than in the United States on these issues, we commissioned papers from four European countries, selected on the basis of the following criteria: (1) they currently had wealth data from household surveys that were of sufficient quality to allow something useful to be learned about patterns of household wealth accumulation in the country; (2) differences in household savings across these countries span most of the variation that exists within Europe; and (3) distinguished researchers with impressive backgrounds on these topics were available to write the papers. The four countries selected were the Netherlands (Alessie and Kapteyn, 1999), Italy (Jappelli and Pistaferri, 1999), Germany (Börsch-Supan, 1999), and the United Kingdom (Banks and Tanner, 1999). To extend the comparisons beyond Europe, we also commissioned a paper on Japan (Kitamura and Takayama, 2000), a country with relatively high rates of household wealth accumulation that is experiencing population aging at a very rapid rate.

The remainder of this chapter is organized as follows. The first section highlights the main theoretical issues that arise with household savings and wealth accumulation. As we demonstrate, these theoretical questions transcend national boundaries. The second section describes the most important wealth surveys now in place in the United States, the above four European countries, and Japan and reviews the relevant data quality and measurement issues. The third section documents the most salient patterns of household wealth accumulation in the United States, Europe, and Japan, based on the data from these surveys. The final section presents the panel's recommendations regarding the policy and research questions in the domain of wealth accumulation that should be of highest priority, as well as the steps necessary to establish the research infrastructure required to address them.

WEALTH ACCUMULATION:
RESEARCH FRAMEWORK AND KEY QUESTIONS

A number of questions must be addressed in examining aggregate rates of savings across countries. For example, are the reasons for savings unique to nations, or do some motivations transcend national boundaries? Are the citizens of some countries savers, while those of others are spenders? Do institutions and national policies matter for aggregate national savings?

An immense literature now exists on motives for wealth accumulation and savings (for an excellent survey, see Browning and Lusardi, 1996). The starting point for a wealth accumulation framework is typically the life-cycle model (or life-cycle hypothesis), which emphasizes savings (and dissavings) to deal with timing issues surrounding non-coincidence in income and consumption (see Box 4-1). According to this theory, individuals will tend to want to smooth consumption (to keep the marginal utility of consumption constant across periods), so that they will save when income is high and dissave when income is low. Browning

---

BOX 4-1
Difficulties with Data on Consumption

Given the importance attached to consumption in various models, the reader might expect this chapter to emphasize the value of collecting consumption data. However, while consumption is an important variable for measuring well-being and for understanding the dynamics of asset change, this report focuses on the measurement of income and assets, partly on grounds of practicality. The problem is that the collection of reliable consumption data typically takes several hours of survey time; is subject to substantial bias (the consumption level is usually underestimated); and effectively precludes adequate attention to such critical areas as health status, labor force participation, detailed measurement of income and assets, and measurement of family structure and transfers. Thus while we recognize that consumption is a useful indicator of well-being, we do not think it feasible to include a direct measure of consumption in a dataset designed to provide the most useful, policy-relevant data on aging.

There is a method of collecting consumption data that does not use up all the available survey space. This method has been used on an experimental basis, with results that can fairly be described as promising. The idea is to collect consumption data indirectly, by measuring income level, asset change from one period to the next, and capital gains over the same period. Consumption is measured as the difference between income and savings, and savings is measured as the change in net worth plus (or minus) capital losses (gains).

The problem with this indirect method of measuring consumption is that, while it appears to provide an unbiased measure of consumption, it is subject to extremely large measurement errors. The first difference in net worth is a highly noisy variable, net worth in each period has a substantial measurement error, and the difference in net worth has an even larger measurement error.

and Lusardi (1996) provide a concise summary of some of the major implications of the theory in its purest form (the certainty-equivalence model): the path of consumption should be independent of the path of income, the elderly should run down their assets, and anticipated changes in income should have no effect on consumption. All three of these fundamental implications have been disputed empirically: consumption appears to be too sensitive to income, the elderly may not dissave since wealth profiles appear not to turn down (perhaps), and much work has been done in an attempt to separate anticipated from unanticipated income changes.

These failures of the life-cycle model have led to a number of attempts to extend or enrich the theory so these facts can be explained. A good deal of this recent work has incorporated uncertainty into the model, adding risk aversion (or precautionary savings) as a primary savings motive. At least under some conditions, uncertainty causes individuals to discount future incomes more heavily and to place a high value on social insurance schemes (such as public pension annuities) that reduce risk. Uncertainty about future income will tend to increase current savings, and, at least in earlier portions of the life cycle, consumption will tend to follow income.

In one important variant of this model, impatience for the present duels with prudence as individuals attempt to maintain a "buffer stock" of a small amount of wealth to deal with future uncertainty. The buffer stock remains small because of impatience. Another avenue explored in recent work involves liquidity constraints, i.e., the idea that individuals cannot borrow and lend at the same interest rate. Given these constraints, individuals will not be able to borrow as much as they might want to finance their current consumption. Once again in this case, consumption will tend to follow income more closely.

Another motive for saving involves bequests. Tests of a bequest motive are of three types. The first is based on the main prediction of the life-cycle hypothesis: that in the absence of a bequest motive, bequeathable wealth should decline at sufficiently advanced ages. The second type of test is based on variation in the rate of wealth change as a function of covariates that are assumed to be related to the strength of a bequest motive. An example is provided by comparing the rates among those with and without children; a consistent finding is that there is little difference. One difficulty in testing for the importance of bequest motives relates to the distinct possibility that some considerable proportion of bequests are "accidents" (see Yaari, 1965). Since individuals cannot foresee with certainty the time of their deaths, they may run the risk of dying too late, having run out of resources to finance their consumption. To guard against this risk, they will accumulate wealth; thus those who die early will leave bequests even though they do not have a bequest motive per se. As a practical empirical matter, however, it has proven difficult to distinguish between altruistic and accidental bequests. A third type of test is based on direct questions about savings motives. For example, Alessie et al. (1995) found that people who say they have thought about leaving a bequest save more than others.

A related but somewhat different aspect of bequests involves the extent to which past inheritances can explain the diversity in current wealth holdings by households. It turns out that financial inheritances received represent but a fraction of total net worth, so that levels and distributions of wealth would be largely the same even if the maximum contribution of financial inheritances were taken into account. For example, in the U.S. Panel Study of Income Dynamics (PSID), it was found that only one in five households had received any financial inheritances as of 1984. Smith (1999b) estimates that inheritances would account for only 13 percent of PSID 1984 wealth values, as well as 13 percent of the increment in wealth between 1984 and 1994.

Another branch of the recent literature rejects rationality in its traditional form as applied to savings behavior. Some of this literature stems from a discouragement with our ability to explain the wide diversity in savings and wealth among individuals. The nonrational theories take a number of forms, including separate mental accounts (e.g., Thaler and Shefrin, 1981) and hyperbolic discounting (Laibson, 1997).

In the context of this summary of the theory, a number of key research questions arise that could be addressed by cross-national analysis. These questions include the following:

1. Do the elderly dissave (a key prediction of the life-cycle model)? The life-cycle model does not imply that in the presence of uncertainty, one should start running down assets immediately after retirement, as has been stressed, for instance, by Hurd (1998). If and when individuals start depleting their wealth holdings depends on family composition, mortality risks, utility parameters, and the possible presence of a bequest motive. Thus in a formal sense, simply looking at whether the elderly dissave after retirement is not sufficient to determine the validity of the life-cycle hypothesis. However, absent a bequest motive, the hypothesis does imply that wealth should start declining *sooner or later*. The evidence on this matter is mixed. Hurd (1987) and Alessie et al. (1999) present evidence that this is indeed the case. Others, however—most notably Börsch-Supan and Stahl (1991) and Börsch-Supan (1992)—find no evidence for dissaving at all. Börsch-Supan and Stahl offer as an explanation that at some point, the elderly are simply no longer able to consume as much as they had originally planned because of physical (and perhaps mental) restrictions. In terms of economic theory, this would represent an unanticipated change in tastes.[1] More generally, unanticipated shocks (e.g., a runup of the stock market) may throw consumers off their planned consumption paths. To shed further light on this research question, one would clearly need accurate knowledge of the actual assets and liabilities of households over time. In addition, however, one would need information about the state of physical and mental health of individuals within those households and the extent to which this state was anticipated. Similarly, one would need to know the extent to which households' capital gains or losses were anticipated. There is a clear role for cross-country comparisons here, since stock markets and housing markets are certainly not perfectly correlated across countries; thus differences in movement may be exploited to identify different types of (anticipated or unanticipated) shocks.

2. *Is there an important bequest motive for savings?* One would like to know more about the various potential beneficiaries of bequests—not just relatives, but also charities. A particularly important heir is likely to be the spouse, if present. Given differential mortality between men and women, it is important to know the extent to which household planning of consumption takes into account the needs of the longest-living spouse (usually the woman) (Hurd, 1998). Cross-country comparisons are important here as well in view of the vastly different tax treatments of bequests in different countries and the variations in living arrangements that exist across countries.

3. *Do social insurance programs for retirement income have the effect of reducing household savings and wealth? What is the effect on national savings?* This is a research subject with a lengthy history (see, e.g., Feldstein, 1974; Browning and Lusardi, 1996). The main problem in investigating this issue is how to deal with individual unobserved heterogeneity. In many countries, public pension benefits are related to an individual's earnings history. Thus people who have spent much of their lives in the labor force will generally receive higher benefits than those with a less consistent labor market history. The former individuals may also be the ones who, by personality or habit, save more. They may, for instance, be more risk averse than people whose labor force attachment is looser. The result is a spurious positive correlation between savings and public pension benefits, whereas the life-cycle hypothesis would suggest a negative relationship. The use of panel data (as by Alessie et al., 1997) may circumvent this problem to some extent, as one can allow for fixed individual effects. However, use of these data leads to inaccurate results, since the remain-

---

[1]Even if consumption constraints are fully anticipated, it is conceivable that wealth will increase in old age. This may occur if one cannot borrow against future annuity income and if annuity income is higher than the upper limit on consumption.

ing variation in public pension entitlements across individuals is too limited to allow for statistically significant conclusions. A more promising approach may be that taken by Kapteyn et al. (1999), who exploit the fact that different cohorts have lived (and are living) under different expectations about their retirement provisions. According to the life-cycle hypothesis, this variation in expectations should translate into different wealth accumulation patterns across generations. The results obtained by Kapteyn et al. suggest that this is indeed the case. Also here, one would like to exploit differences in institutional arrangements across countries to obtain more reliable estimates of the effect of public pension provisions on national savings rates. The effect of survivor provisions in public pension programs on savings rates of multiperson households warrants special attention.

4. *What is the interaction between private pensions on the one hand and private savings and wealth accumulation on the other?* The issues under this question are similar to those with public pensions, except that there is generally greater individual freedom in the choice of private versus public pension arrangements. Thus the possibility of spurious positive correlations between individual wealth accumulation and pension rights is even stronger: people who save a great deal also tend to have more generous pension arrangements. Comparisons across countries open up additional identification possibilities. For instance, in the Netherlands most private pensions are tied to one's occupation, thereby severely limiting individual freedom of choice, whereas in the United States individual choice is much greater. Comparison of savings rates across such institutional arrangements would provide insight into the interrelationships between institutions and savings. For both this and the previous research question, it is of paramount importance to collect adequate (possibly administrative) data on individual work histories, characteristics of pension plans, fiscal treatment of such plans, and the like.

5. *Is consumption smooth before and after retirement?* On the one hand, the answer to this question is a crucial test of the life-cycle hypothesis, since retirement is generally fully anticipated; hence according to the life-cycle hypothesis, consumption should not be affected by retirement except for the effects of the new way of life (more leisure and possibly fewer work-related expenses). Yet empirical evidence appears to suggest that consumption declines considerably after retirement (see, e.g., Hamermesh, 1984; Banks et al., 1998). The fact that, for example, Health and Retirement Survey (HRS) data indicate that about a quarter of U.S. households arrive at (or close to) retirement with only modest amounts of wealth (less than $30,000; see Lusardi, 1999) in itself suggests that many households do not plan adequately for retirement. Generally, tests of income smoothing around retirement are hampered by the fact that hardly any reliable

panel dataset exists that would allow one to follow consumption patterns before and after retirement closely. The collection of such data is of clear importance.

6. *What is the effect of capital gains on active savings?* If capital gains were fully anticipated, posing this research question would amount to asking what is the marginal propensity to consume out of wealth. Estimates of this marginal propensity are large enough to entail substantial risk of an economic recession if, for instance, the stock market were to suffer a major setback. Conceivably, the uncertainty involved in the value of stock holdings may reduce the tendency to consume out of capital gains. Nevertheless, Juster et al. (1999) find that $1.00 of capital gains in stocks reduces active saving by about 0.17 (see also Poterba, 2000). They also find that this effect is large enough to explain the dramatic decline in active saving in the United States since the 1980s. In view of the obvious importance of active saving to provide for old age in the future, more detailed analysis of the relationship between capital gains and active savings in different countries is required. Next to the availability of excellent wealth data, the first priority would be to have data on the extent to which capital gains are anticipated and how certain individuals feel about the value of their stock holdings. As indicated with respect to research question 1, movements in stock market prices and real estate values show enough variation across countries that these differences can be exploited to learn more about the effect of capital gains on savings.

7. *What are the effects of health shocks on wealth accumulation and vice versa?* The robust positive relationship between health and wealth is a much-studied phenomenon, but a single comprehensive explanation for this relationship appears to be lacking (see, e.g., Smith, 1999a). The effects of health shocks on wealth accumulation may be quite different across countries. In countries where individuals are generally fully insured against any major adverse health event, out-of-pocket health-related expenditures cannot be an important mechanism for the translation of adverse health shocks into lower wealth accumulation. Under those circumstances, health shocks would instead have an indirect effect, for instance through a less successful labor market history. Here as before, one runs into the problem of disentangling unobservable individual traits and observable factors. For example, people with potentially poor health may generally have less energy; hence even before a major illness occurred, they would already have earned less (and accumulated less) than other observationally equivalent individuals. Thus to shed light on the exact mechanisms involved, accurate earnings and illness histories are necessary. Cross-country comparisons can then help in identifying the exact role played by institutions. Regarding the effect of wealth, or more generally socioeconomic status, Hurd et al. (1998) find only weak evi-

dence for a causal link between socioeconomic status and changes in health over a 2-year period, controlling for various health status measures at the beginning of the period. On the other hand, they do establish a statistically quite significant effect of health status on wealth changes over the same period. Their findings suggest that at least at older ages, differential access to health care is not a major factor in explaining the correlation between health and wealth. As Hurd et al. suggest, the fact that one does see a strong relationship between socioeconomic status and morbidity and mortality in a cross section of the elderly population may point to unobserved genetic and behavioral factors that influence both socioeconomic status and health at later ages. Clearly, one would like to be able to identify these factors, for which one would again need accurate earnings and illness histories. Further, the effect of health and wealth is likely to interact with living arrangements and family situations, which again points to the need for a multidisciplinary approach to data collection.

8. *What is the effect of tax-preferred savings vehicles on household savings?* This is a research question with a long history, especially in the United States (see, e.g., Venti and Wise, 1989, 1990, 1991; Gale and Scholz, 1994). The importance of the issue hardly requires amplification. Tax subsidies on savings may easily involve very substantial amounts; hence the effectiveness of these instruments must be evaluated carefully. To this end, one would need household panel data (among other things, to be able to correct for unobserved individual heterogeneity). A related issue has to do with the composition of household portfolios (see Poterba, 1999). In many cases, income (positive or negative) from different assets (or liabilities) is taxed differently. Examples include whether capital gains are taxed and whether mortgage and other interest payments are deductible. The differential tax treatment of income relative to different assets and liabilities has significant effects on the composition of household portfolios (see, e.g., Hochguertel et al., 1997; King and Leape, 1998; Poterba and Samwick, 1999). It may be difficult to disentangle the effects of household income and taxes through empirical work, given the systematic relationship between marginal tax rates and income. Since understanding the role of institutions is even more crucial here than is the case for some of the other research questions, it would be desirable for the data to span time periods covering (several) policy changes and/or countries with different policies regarding the fiscal treatment of saving.

9. *Do the elderly consume their housing wealth?* Despite considerable research into this issue (e.g., Venti and Wise, 1989, 1990, 1991; Sheiner and Weil, 1992), the evidence appears to be mixed. Although there are some indications that the elderly may consume their housing wealth, a great majority may not do so. Reverse mortgage schemes have met with mixed success, and the factors that determine the success of such schemes are as

yet incompletely understood. Beyond the collection of data on actual behavior, an obvious approach is to ask elderly individuals directly why (or why not) they would consider consuming their housing wealth.

10. *How does household wealth interact with labor market (retirement) decisions?* Such interaction occurs in at least two ways. Those who have accumulated significant amounts of wealth may be expected to retire earlier than others, simply because they can afford to. In economic terms, they are consuming part of their wealth in the form of leisure. Conversely, those arriving at retirement age without significant wealth holdings may decide to return to the labor market at least part time to supplement the annuity income they are drawing from public and/or other pensions. Modeling of the interplay between wealth accumulation and labor force participation is technically complex (see, e.g., Blundell et al., 1997). The technical complications of estimating a theory-consistent model usually force researchers to estimate models that are rather loosely related to theory. Here there appears to be considerable scope for the use of subjective information, obtained, for example, by asking individuals directly about preferences and constraints (e.g., whether a job would be available if they wanted one).

11. *Are there demographic effects in the stock market?* One of the explanations sometimes given for the sharply increasing stock market prices over recent years is that demographic demand is high. Put simply, the baby boomers have reached a stage in their life cycle at which they have both the resources and the need to save for old age. They invest their money in part in the stock market, thus driving prices up (e.g., Bergantino, 1997). If this explanation is quantitatively important, one may expect the opposite stock movement in prices once the baby boom generation starts retiring. As a result, the value of an individual's stock may be much lower in retirement than is currently anticipated. Apart from studying long-term movements in stock market prices (as does Bergantino, 1997), an obvious way of learning more about the potential importance of this phenomenon is by studying household portfolios on the basis of microdata and interviewing households about their investment motives and expectations for the future. Cross-national variation in stock market performance should be useful in identifying the salience of demographic effects.

DATA SOURCES

There has been renewed interest in the United States, Europe, and Asia in the measurement of and motives for household wealth accumulation and savings behavior. Recently, wealth data have proliferated in these three regions as some prominent surveys have incorporated wealth modules. Moreover, many of these surveys have panel designs so that changes in wealth and savings can be investigated. Encouraged by these newly available data, researchers have formulated theoretical models focused on fundamental hypotheses about why people save (Deaton, 1992). While the issues examined are extremely diverse, these models are linked by a common need: reasonably reliable wealth and savings data to test the models' basic implications. Indeed, data quality is an issue of long-standing concern among researchers interested in wealth accumulation (Curtin et al., 1989).

This section describes in detail some important new data sources for studying the process of household wealth accumulation that have emerged in the last two decades in the United States, the four European countries selected for study by the panel, and Japan. These surveys are listed in Box 4-2. The approaches used to measure household wealth

---

BOX 4-2
Surveys of Household Wealth:
United States, Four European Countries, and Japan

United States
- Panel Study of Income Dynamics
- Health and Retirement Survey
- Asset and Health Dynamics Among the Oldest Old Survey
- Survey of Consumer Finances
- Survey of Income and Program Participation

Netherlands
- Socio-Economic Panel
- CentER Savings Survey

Italy
- Survey of Household Income and Wealth

Germany
- Income and Expenditure Survey
- German Socio-Economic Panel
- Soll und Haben Survey

United Kingdom
- Financial Research Survey
- British Household Panel Study

Japan
- Family Saving Survey
- National Survey of Family Income and Expenditure
- Basic Survey of Japanese Living Conditions

differ significantly among these surveys, and a number of innovative measurement strategies have been introduced.

In all countries, assets are widely believed to be poorly reported in household surveys. Indeed, the rewards for collecting household wealth data have been considered so meager that in the past, many countries simply have not made the attempt. This pessimism stems from a number of sources. First, there has been a fear that asking sensitive questions about individuals' wealth would lead otherwise willing respondents to refuse to participate in household surveys. Second, item nonresponse has been pervasive, and reported values have apparently been subject to large errors. While a number of prominent surveys throughout the world have included wealth modules, their quality has been viewed with justified skepticism, partly because of numerous missing values. Third, it is widely known that in almost all countries, the distribution of wealth is highly skewed, with relatively small numbers of households possessing a relatively large fraction of the national wealth. Unless this extreme concentration of wealth is addressed in the survey design, large portions of national wealth will be missing in the household survey.

United States

In the United States, there has been tremendous growth and improvement during the last decade in household surveys that contain significant wealth modules. These surveys include the PSID, HRS, the Asset and Health Dynamics Among the Oldest Old (AHEAD) Survey, the Survey of Consumer Finances (SCF), and the Survey of Income and Program Participation (SIPP).

PSID has gathered almost 30 years of extensive economic and demographic data on a nationally representative sample of approximately 5,000 (original) families and 35,000 individuals in those families. PSID spans all age groups, making it possible to examine wealth data across the complete life cycle. Wealth modules were included in the 1984, 1989, and 1994 waves of the survey. Another wealth module was included in 1999 and will be used every 2 years thereafter. These wealth modules incorporate transaction questions about purchases and sales so that in principle, active and passive savings can be distinguished.

Two new surveys with wealth modules for selected age populations are HRS and AHEAD. HRS is a national longitudinal sample of about 7,600 households (12,654 individuals) in which at least one person is a member of the birth cohorts of 1931-1941 (51-61 years old at baseline). HRS's principal objective is to monitor economic transitions in work, income, and wealth, as well as changes in health status. The first wave of data was collected in 1992, with a baseline response rate of 82 percent.

The first three HRS waves are now available,[2] and follow-ups are planned every 2 years.

The companion survey to HRS—AHEAD—includes 6,052 households (8,211 individuals) with at least one member from the birth cohort of 1923 or before, thus with at least one person aged 70 or over in 1993. The baseline AHEAD interview was conducted in 1993 using computer-assisted telephone techniques for respondents aged 70-79 and computer-assisted in-person interviews for those aged 80 and over. In both surveys, blacks, Hispanics, and residents of the state of Florida were oversampled at a rate of two to one. The baseline response rate was 81 percent, and as with HRS, a follow-up is planned every 2 years.

An important advantage of PSID, HRS, and AHEAD is that they include questions that measure many components of household wealth. In addition to housing equity (with separate detail for first and second homes), the following 11 categories are used in HRS: other real estate; vehicles; business equity; individual retirement account or Keogh; stocks or mutual funds; checking, savings, or money market funds; certificates of deposit, government savings bonds, or treasury bills; other bonds; trusts and estates; other assets; and other debt. The definition of personal net worth in PSID closely parallels that used in HRS and AHEAD, but fewer and somewhat broader categories are used.

A fourth microsurvey is SCF, whose primary purpose is to obtain detailed measures of all components of household wealth. Like PSID, SCF represents the full age distribution. Since it was designed primarily as a wealth survey, SCF no doubt provides the most detailed measurement of household wealth available from a household survey, with literally hundreds of questions on wealth holdings. Many of the balances that are combined in the other surveys (such as checking and savings accounts) are probed separately in SCF. For example, checking accounts alone are separately divided into as many as seven different accounts.

Because wealth holdings are known to be extremely positively skewed, SCF combines a representative area-probability sample with a special oversample of very high-income households. The oversample is obtained by a match with Internal Revenue Service (IRS) records. One problem with the oversample is that the initial response rate was low. Some minor revisions were incorporated in the oversampling used in the SCFs conducted in 1983, 1989, 1992, 1995, and 1998.

A final set of surveys is SIPP, which has included short wealth modules since its inception. The asset coverage of SIPP is similar to that of the

---

[2]The household survey has been linked to major administrative records—Social Security and, as the respondents age, their Medicare files. In addition, summaries of pension plans are being linked to HRS.

other surveys (except SCF), and offers the advantage that one can track time-series changes in wealth holdings since the mid-1980s. In contrast to the other microsurveys, SIPP has not made use of follow-up brackets in its wealth module.

To evaluate the quality of household surveys, one must have a standard against which the survey data can be compared. One approach to monitoring household savings and wealth accumulation over time relies on yearly data provided by the Federal Reserve on household balance sheets (Flow of Funds [FOF]). FOF data not only track trends in aggregate household net worth, but also provide details on the components that make up these aggregates.

All of these microdatasets have unique features that need to be examined carefully to ensure comparability. HRS and AHEAD are large random samples of the aging population, while PSID, SCF, and SIPP include all age groups in their sampling frames. All studies but SIPP use innovative techniques to ensure high-quality financial data (Juster and Smith, 1997). For example, PSID was the first study to use the unfolding bracket technique to mitigate the missing data problem in the measurement of household assets, and HRS and AHEAD followed suit. SCF is designed to represent the full range of the wealth distribution through the use of special sampling frames that are known to represent all high-wealth households. None of the other microdatasets (PSID, HRS, AHEAD, or SIPP) has adequate representation at the upper end of the wealth distribution. Finally, SCF obtains great detail with over 100 questions, while all the other surveys rely on fewer than 15 questions.

Despite the recent growth and improvement in household surveys containing significant wealth modules, use of these instruments to measure household wealth is beset by a number of problems. Some of the most salient of these problems, along with some of the innovations used to resolve them, are listed in Table 4-1 and discussed below. What do we now know about the effectiveness of these innovations? The quality of household wealth data appears to have risen significantly over time. Better measures of wealth are related to the use of unfolding brackets that reduce item nonresponse, oversampling of very wealthy households, and the number of questions asked. On the other hand, some of the innovations bring new problems as well.

High Rates of Item Nonresponse

The problem of widespread nonresponse to wealth questions has always plagued surveys with wealth modules. Standard techniques for imputing missing values may not help if the nonresponses differ from the responses in unobservable ways. The impact of using unfolding brackets

TABLE 4-1 Measurement Issues in Wealth Surveys

Problem	Solution
High rates of item nonresponse	Unfolding brackets
Extreme heterogeneity of wealth	Oversampling of extremely wealthy
Insufficiently comprehensive wealth concept	Use of three definitions:
	• Household wealth = housing equity + tangible assets + all financial assets
	• Household wealth = housing wealth + employer-provided pension wealth
	• Household wealth = housing wealth + employer-provided pension wealth + social security wealth
Psychometric measurement issues, such as anchoring	Random entry brackets
Repeated measurement issues in panel surveys	Across-wave links

to convert missing data on wealth components into a set of categorical brackets is dramatic. On average, 90 percent of households that report not knowing the value of their asset component are willing to provide answers to these categorical bracket questions, while almost 50 percent of households that refuse to provide an estimate are willing to answer the bracket questions. The value of unfolding brackets is not simply in reducing item nonresponse, but also in obtaining more accurate measures of asset values. Juster and Smith (1997) conclude that use of this simple device increases estimates of total nonhousing net worth in the population by amounts on the order of 20 percent for the HRS sample. As is almost always the case, increases in net worth estimates bring them more in line with external control totals, and this is a quality gain.

The only survey that has not used this technique is SIPP, whose asset values are considerably below estimates from all the other surveys. For this reason, some view SIPP's wealth module with suspicion.

Extreme Heterogeneity of Wealth

Given the extraordinary skew to the wealth distribution, estimates of mean wealth are quite sensitive to whether super-rich households are included in the sampling frame. For example, the top 1 percent of SCF households possess 34 percent of total household wealth, while the upper .1 percent possess 13 percent. Not surprisingly, then, since SCF makes a special effort to include very high-income households in its sample, mean wealth in that survey is quite a bit higher than that in the other household surveys.

Juster et al. (1999) have evaluated the impact of this oversampling of the rich in SCF. The wealthiest PSID household would fall in the 99.935th percentile of SCF; thus PSID represents none of the wealthiest 6 in 10,000 American households. Yet this is not an unambiguous gain. The extremely wealthy remain a very difficult population to sample, and SCF response rates in this subsample are often extremely low. The result is time-series estimates of mean household wealth that are much more variable in SCF than in any of the other household surveys (and more variable relative to the FOF benchmark). PSID and HRS should never be used to describe the savings and wealth behaviors of the always intriguing but somewhat elusive extreme elite, but they may be able to describe behavior well into the 99th percentile of the population.

Comprehensiveness of Wealth Concept

Variability in the comprehensiveness of the wealth concept reduces comparability across surveys. Given the widely different ownership rates of various assets and the differing distribution of values for each asset, estimates of total household wealth will be sensitive to how inclusive the measure of wealth is. For example, stock market wealth tends to be far more unevenly distributed than wealth held in checking and savings accounts. Thus measures of household wealth that exclude stock market equity will exhibit less inequality than measures that include it. It is therefore important that the measures of net worth used in household surveys be as comprehensive as possible.[3] The main issue that arises here concerns the number of questions that must be asked to obtain a comprehensive measure. The new U.S. surveys reviewed above vary a great deal in this regard, with SCF at one extreme (more than 100) and PSID at the other (7 nonhousing questions). Nonetheless, it appears that one can characterize total household wealth holdings for the overwhelming majority of households with a relatively moderate number of questions (see Juster et al., 1999). It may be noted that some components of household wealth are measured more easily than others. At least with relatively short wealth modules, it is especially difficult to distinguish between busi-

---

[3]The role (and thus measurement) of capital gains in this regard is important, but difficult to measure accurately and comprehensively. Obviously, realized rates of return are an important source for differences in wealth levels both within and across countries. Other than some data from PSID and HRS in the United States and data expected from the British Household Panel Study, we know very little about the capital gains component of portfolio composition.

ness and property assets and to itemize the subcomponents of the financial wealth portfolio.

In addition to the need to obtain a comprehensive measure of household wealth, wealth distributions are extremely sensitive to whether employer-provided pensions and public pensions are included in the wealth measure (see also Chapter 3). This is particularly true of countries where households save little, but can expect to have generous pension and other social security benefits. Alessie et al. (1995), for example, report that median private wealth (net worth) in the age bracket 55-59 in the Netherlands is only approximately 11 percent of median total wealth (private wealth + social security wealth + pension wealth). In the age bracket 60-64, the share of private wealth in total wealth for the median household is even less—about 8 percent.

Psychometric Issues

A number of psychometric issues arise in the measurement of wealth. For example, there is a substantial methodological literature on what are termed anchoring effects. The idea is that respondents to a survey question will make inferences about the true state of the world from the specific phrasing of the question. In effect, for respondents who lack any idea of the size of their checking and savings accounts, a sequence that starts with $100 will convey the impression that small numbers are more likely to be correct than large ones, while a sequence starting with $100,000 will convey the opposite impression—that large numbers are more plausibly correct than small ones. Results based on HRS and AHEAD suggest that these anchoring effects are quite strong: the median asset value for subsamples given a low entry point is only half as large as the median for subsamples given a much higher entry point (Hurd, 1999).

The precise phrasing of wealth questions also matters. For example, when respondents in the HRS, AHEAD, and PSID are asked about the value of their asset holdings, the initial question is phrased, "Is it more than x?," where the value of x depends on the asset. But there are alternative ways to phrase what is essentially the same question, with the obvious possibilities being, "Is it x or more?" or "Is it more than x, less than x, or what?" The distinction among these three questions lies in whether the rounded number specified by x is associated with a yes or a no response, and whether respondents have an opportunity to indicate that their asset holdings are just about the same amount as the rounded number, neither more nor less. With respect to a yes or no response, there is the risk of acquiescence bias, whereby respondents would rather agree than disagree with a statement. Thus an answer labeled "yes" will tend to be chosen more often than one labeled "no" (Hurd, 1999). On the basis of analyses of data from HRS and AHEAD, it appears that there is little difference between the "x or more" and "more than x" versions. But the balanced question (Is it more than x, less than x, or what?) appears to provide a somewhat different distribution of responses, with some respondents reporting that "just about x" is the correct answer. Thus, although the use of brackets has reduced item nonresponse dramatically (as discussed earlier), the ensuing psychometric problems of anchoring and acquiescence bias still need to be addressed.

Another recent innovation in HRS and AHEAD is combining the economic modules that deal with net worth and with income. The idea is that for some income sources, data quality is enhanced if questions about assets and income are combined into a single question sequence. The gain is in the reporting of income from assets; the usual practice of having an asset module followed some time later or preceded by an income module means that questions about asset holdings are asked at a different point in the questionnaire than questions about the income from those assets. In HRS-3 and AHEAD-2, a question sequence was tried that starts with assets, moves directly to questions about income from assets, and then proceeds to questions about income amounts and periodicity. Juster et al. (2000) report that rates of missing data on income from assets are cut roughly in half by this procedure, and that mean income representing the return on assets is almost doubled. This doubling of income appears to be a quality gain since it aligns reported income from assets with the national accounts.

Repeated Measurement in Panel Surveys

A final data quality issue concerns panel use of these wealth modules to evaluate household savings behavior. Panel estimates in the United States must rely basically on HRS, AHEAD, and PSID. When successive waves of wealth modules are used to compute the wealth accumulation and savings of households, the verdict on quality must be more cautious. This need for caution stems in part from the larger role often played by measurement error in a first-difference formulation. In addition, however, few systematic attempts have been made to improve wealth measurement in panel surveys by exploiting the fact that respondents may help resolve some of the large discrepancies that arise in asset values. This is indeed an area in which much work needs to be done.

Four European Countries and Japan

The situation in Europe and Japan with respect to the quality and availability of microdata on wealth is quite diverse. In the last decade, a number of attempts have been made in several countries to improve wealth measurement. Each of the five countries selected for inclusion in this study has followed a somewhat different approach to wealth measurement. The diversity of outcomes among the five countries may be informative about the value of alternative approaches.

The Netherlands

The research on the Netherlands commissioned for this study was based on the Socio-Economic Panel (SEP), a representative panel survey conducted by Statistics Netherlands (see Alessie and Kapteyn, 1999, for details). SEP covers about 5,000 households and is representative of the Dutch population, with the exception of those living in institutions such as nursing homes. It contains detailed information about a number of household demographic characteristics and collects data on household income and wealth. SEP has some desirable attributes: it has been conducted annually since 1984 so that time-series changes can readily be analyzed, and it is a panel so that individual changes over time can be isolated. As is common for most wealth surveys, wealthy households are not oversampled in SEP. Because of problems in collecting the data, no asset and debt information has been gathered on the self-employed since 1990.

In SEP, each respondent in the household is asked to complete a short questionnaire on his/her assets and liabilities. The form of the questions and the timing (May of each year) have been chosen to parallel the filing of tax returns. This in principle should help in obtaining data that are somewhat similar to tax data. Nevertheless, there is a fair amount of item nonresponse, which hampers the calculation of total wealth. An analysis by Alessie et al. (1993) shows that item nonresponse leads to an underestimation of total net worth of households in SEP. The underlying reason is simply that richer households must answer more questions and thus have a higher probability of missing an item. If one then deletes all households with at least one missing item, the rich households will be underrepresented and hence also their population characteristics, such as mean net worth. Alessie et al. find that this case-wise deletion depresses an estimate of mean net worth by approximately 10 percent.

The assets distinguished in SEP include (1) checking accounts; (2) savings and deposit accounts; (3) savings certificates (certificates of deposit); (4) bonds and mortgage bonds; (5) shares, mutual funds, options, and other securities; (6) value of the primary residence; (7) other real estate (not used for own residence); (8) value of car(s); (9) net worth of own company (for the self-employed); (10) life insurance mortgage; (11) other life insurance with a saving element (starting date of the insurance,

insurance premium); and (12) other assets. These assets are reported at the current market value. The liabilities include (1) personal loans; (2) revolving credit; (3) debt with mail orders, retail debt; (4) other purchases on credit; (5) hire-purchase; (6) remaining mortgage debt; (7) collateral-based loans; (8) debt with relatives and friends; (9) other outstanding debt, unpaid bills; and (10) debt not already mentioned. These categories have varied somewhat across the duration of the panel. The definitions of net worth, housing equity, and financial assets are quite close to those used in the major U.S. surveys. No information is available on cash holdings or occupational pensions.

A second, smaller panel with wealth information is the so-called CentER Savings Survey (CSS). The panel covers roughly 2,000 households and has collected extensive information on assets and liabilities since 1993. CSS is actually part of the so-called CentER-panel, a panel of about 2,000 households that answer questions every week on their computers (either their own or ones provided by CentERdata, the survey research agency running the panel). The computers of the panel members are linked to the central computer at CentERdata (today via Internet, in the past directly via a modem). The setup of a computer panel allows for computer-assisted interviewing; panel members can answer questions when it is convenient for them, and it is easy to go back to households to collect more information if needed. For the purpose of collecting data on wealth, the flexibility of the instrument is of particular importance. There are no constraints on the length of the questionnaire (one simply spreads questionnaires over several weeks, if needed), which makes it possible to collect a vast amount of information on the same households. Also, it is easy to enrich datasets with new information by fielding new questions when needed.[4] Despite these potential advantages, it has taken a number of years to exploit the technology in a way that does lead to better data. Alessie et al. (1999) report satisfactory outcomes of the comparison of CSS data with external sources.

Italy

The main wealth data for Italy come from the Bank of Italy Survey of Household Income and Wealth (SHIW), whose main purpose is to collect detailed data on demographics, household consumption, income, and

---

[4]An important example of this is the addition of psychological modules. In addition to such objective information as wealth, income, and labor market status, CSS contains extensive information on expectations, savings motives, risk aversion, time preferences, and the like. Several questions in the psychological module were added after they proved valuable in other surveys (e.g., HRS).

balance sheets. This survey is representative of the Italian population and has been fielded biannually since 1984, although financial wealth data have been publicly available only since 1989 (see Jappelli and Pistaferri, 1999). Beginning in 1989, some but not all of the households were reinterviewed in subsequent panels. For example, the panel component has increased over time: in 1989, 29 percent of the households were reinterviewed, and by 1995, 45 percent were reinterviewed. Net worth is the sum of household financial assets and net real assets. Financial assets include transaction and savings accounts, certificates of deposit, government bonds, corporate bonds, stocks, mutual funds, life insurance, cash value of defined-contribution pension funds, and foreign assets. Net real assets include real estate, business, valuables, and the stock of durables net of liabilities. Liabilities are the sum of mortgage and other real estate debt, consumer credit, personal loans, and credit card debt. Exact values are requested for real assets, but financial assets are only coded into categories.

Germany

The most useful source of household wealth data for Germany is the German Income and Expenditure Survey (EVS), which has a design roughly comparable to the U.S. Consumer Expenditure Survey. EVS has been conducted since 1963 every fifth year by the German Federal Statistical Office (see Börsch-Supan, 1999). It is representative of 98 percent of the German population, the remaining 2 percent comprising those living in institutions and the super-rich. Börsch-Supan (1999) reports that only those with a monthly net income of 35,000 DM (or roughly $17,000 per month) or less are included in the survey. The main purpose of EVS is to provide a comprehensive picture of the economic situation of private households. The data include information on basic household characteristics, income by source, flows of consumption and saving expenditures by detailed categories, home ownership, and stocks of wealth by asset categories and debt. Sample sizes are around 50,000 households in each wave so that quite large cell sizes exist in all age categories, even old ages. In the past, these data have been accessible only by special permission from the German Federal Statistics Office. However, the 1993 survey was provided to all researchers as a scientific file.

EVS is primarily a consumption survey. As with many such surveys, each household keeps a monthly and at times daily household book recording all income sources and important expenditures, including all savings flows. Unrealized capital gains remain unreported. The survey concludes with a final interview at the end of the survey year, during which the household is asked to report its financial circumstances (in particular, the stock of wealth) and public transfer payments. This interview also serves as a control on the information given during the survey period. For example, one can check stock figures against flow data, and it is possible to deduce interest income. The data allow for the construction of two savings measures: income minus consumption and the balance between purchases and sales of assets. When information is aggregated within age classes, both measures appear to match quite closely.

Another survey conducted in Germany, the German Socio-Economic Panel (GSOEP), is an annual panel study of some 6,000 households with a design that corresponds to the U.S. PSID. The panel started in 1984, and 14 waves through 1997 are currently available. In 1990, the West German panel was augmented by an East German sample, permitting analysis of the transition in East Germany. The data are used extensively in Germany and are available to all interested researchers at a nominal cost.[5]

While the GSOEP data have proven to be extremely useful for examining income and employment dynamics, they have shortcomings for use in research on savings behavior and wealth accumulation. Savings behavior has not been a major focus of the GSOEP questionnaire, and the only information on wealth that has been requested systematically in a panel is the presence of a set of assets (stocks, bonds, savings certificates, mutual funds, life insurance contracts, building society savings contracts, other financial assets, and real estate). This set of dummy variables permits a simple analysis of households' asset choices over time. In addition, the 1988 wave included a set of questions on the amount of money held in the above assets. However, item nonresponse was unusually high, and the experiment has not been repeated.

A third dataset containing information on asset holdings of households in Germany is the Soll und Haben Survey commissioned by Spiegel-Verlag. The survey covers about 5,000 West German individuals in 1980, 1984, 1989, and 1995. In 1995, about 1,000 East Germans were also included.

United Kingdom

Despite its rich tradition of high-quality surveys on consumption and income and its position as one of the financial capitals of the world, the United Kingdom has only limited household surveys that collect good wealth data (see Banks and Tanner, 1999). The most useful is the Financial Research Survey, an ongoing survey that gathers information on

---

[5]Increasing interest in the GSOEP data in the United States prompted the construction of an English-language user file. Wagner et al. (1993) report on the usefulness of the German panel data and provide English-language code books.

around 4,800 individuals per month. Information is obtained on all financial assets and liabilities held, with banded data on balances for most. The survey also has demographic variables relating to the household to which the individual belongs; some data on income; and summary information on other financial products, such as pensions, mortgages, and insurance. There is no oversampling of high-wealth households. Detailed information is collected on categories such as savings accounts and deposit accounts at the bank or building society, National Savings products, tax-favored vehicles (such as tax-exempt special savings accounts and personal equity plans), stocks and bonds, unit trusts, and investment trusts. Summary information relating to the ownership of housing wealth and mortgages, life insurance policies, private pensions, and loan and checking account balances is collected, but neither self-assessed wealth values nor the information required to impute estimates of these values is collected for these categories. Finally, no information is gathered on the value of fixed assets or business assets (for the self-employed); information on asset values is collected within categorical limits, rather than in exact amounts. Another distinguishing characteristic is that household data are collected at the individual, not the household level.

The British Household Panel Study does not collect information on stocks of wealth or savings as part of the regular annual questionnaire. However, wave 5 (1995) included a battery of questions on wealth and assets (Banks and Tanner, 1999).

Japan

Japan has three major microdata surveys that collect information on financial assets and liabilities: the Family Saving Survey, the National Survey of Family Income and Expenditure (NSFIE), and the Basic Survey of Japanese Living Conditions. None are panel surveys. Kitamura and Takayama (2000) conclude that for purposes of describing financial household behavior, NSFIE, conducted every 5 years since 1959, is the most reliable source of information. For their analysis, they were able to use four different cross sections of NSFIE: 1979 (53,000 observations), 1984 (54,000 observations), 1989 (59,100 observations), and 1994 (56,000 observations). The response rate in 1989 was 85 percent, which is quite a bit higher than that for other household surveys in Japan (for instance, the Family Income and Expenditure Survey had a response rate of about 55 percent in 1990).

Comparisons between aggregates obtained from NSFIE and FOF and National Accounts data suggest a 40 percent underreporting of financial assets in NSFIE. Kitamura and Takayama offer three explanations for the discrepancy: (1) selective nonresponse, since wealthy households are less willing to participate in the survey; (2) underreporting by self-employed households; and (3) statistical errors in the FOF and National Accounts data.

Since NSFIE measures assets, income, and expenditures, one can construct both a savings measure (income minus consumption) and a wealth measure from the data. Net worth is calculated as the sum of net financial assets, net housing assets, and consumer durables.

The Japanese wealth data have some unique characteristics relative to wealth data for other countries, and these characteristics help explain certain features of the Japanese data. Two factors should be borne in mind when comparing Japanese data with those from other countries. First, it is common practice in Japan for workers to receive several years' worth of earnings as a "going-away present" when they reach the age of 55 and are expected to leave the firm in which they have worked for many years. These payments, which can be thought of as similar to the value of a defined-contribution pension plan in the United States, are counted as part of household wealth since they represent financial assets owned by the household. In countries with defined-contribution pension plans, the value of such plans typically is *not* included in estimates of household wealth. However, since such payments usually go only to those 55 or older, they cannot explain any of the pre-age-55 patterns that also distinguish Japanese households from those of other countries. Second, a large proportion of Japanese wealth is held in the form of home equity; for example, about two-thirds of total net worth in Japan consists of housing equity. This is presumably due to the country's high housing prices.

Assessing the Content and Quality of
United States Versus European and Japanese Surveys

Not surprisingly, many of the problems described earlier for U.S. wealth surveys also plague the surveys of Europe and Japan. If anything, there appears to be more concern in Europe that including questions on wealth in household surveys will make individuals more reluctant to participate in a survey at all and will also lead to high rates of attrition in panel surveys. For example, in the 1989 SHIW, 9,427 households refused to participate, compared with 8,274 that agreed to participate. However, this problem appears to be diminishing with time. In 1995, 3,653 households refused, compared with 8,135 that participated (Brandolini, 1999). This is still a high rate of refusal by the standards of most of the more prominent American surveys, but it is not at all clear what unique role the wealth module plays in this refusal to participate. It is remarkable, as noted above, that response rates on the financial survey in Japan appear to be better than those on other comparable household surveys.

Another generic problem is overall high rates of individual item nonresponse to wealth questions. Most European and Japanese wealth surveys have not adopted the unfolding bracket techniques that have proven so successful in reducing item nonresponse in the United States. There are some exceptions, however: the British Household Panel Survey uses unfolding brackets after a "don't know" response, while the Financial Research Survey collects wealth values in bands (Banks and Tanner, 1999). It is not clear, however, whether this was done for the purpose of improving response rates. The Italian SHIW collected data on financial assets in 14 brackets in 1991, 1993, and 1995. For real assets, the exact value was elicited.

Table 4-2 provides a checklist for the surveys of the United States, Europe, and Japan in terms of their sample design and survey content. The surveys are quite comparable across many dimensions. First, with the exception of SCF, none of the other household surveys in Japan, Europe, or the United States have high-income or high-wealth oversamples. Second, with the exception of the British Financial Research Survey (which measures only financial wealth), the definition of household wealth is remarkably similar in all countries. Third, sample sizes in the European surveys are at a minimum at least as large as those of the best American surveys.[6]

There are some differences as well. Many of the European countries, as well as Japan, have no panel wealth data, so individual-level decisions on wealth accumulation cannot be modeled. Moreover, most European and Japanese household surveys have not yet attempted to integrate measures of employer-provided pensions into their household data. Finally, the European surveys and the Japanese NSFIE have tended to be regarded as economic surveys only. As a consequence, they do not include other domains of life that may either affect or be strongly influenced by income and wealth. One notable domain largely absent from both the best European surveys and the Japanese NSFIE is health, which has been shown to interact strongly with economic status (Smith, 1999a). The Dutch

---

[6]The American HRS has evolved into a number of interrelated surveys, each representing a different set of birth cohorts. For example, the original HRS sample with a sample size of 12,654 individuals represented the birth cohorts of 1931-1941. The original AHEAD cohort with a sample size of 8,211 individuals represented the birth cohorts of 1923 and earlier. In 1998, these samples were supplemented by two new cohorts: the so-called War-Babies (those born between 1942 and 1947, with 2,511 individuals) and the Children of the Depression (representing those born between 1924 and 1930, with 2,355 individuals). In the year 2004, a new cohort, representing the Early Boomers (those born between 1948 and 1954), will be added. A common instrument is now used in all surveys. The net result is a continuing survey design that will replenished itself so that all cohorts can be studied in their pre- and postretirement years.

TABLE 4-2 Wealth Data: Survey Design and Content Checklist

	United States			Europe Netherlands		Italy	Germany	United Kingdom		Japan
	HRS	PSID	SCF	SEP	CSS	SHIW	EVS	FRS	BHPS	NSFIE
Sample Frame										
Sample sizes	7,600	5,000	2,000-3,000	5,000	2,000	8,000	50,000	58,400	5,500	50,000
Age groups	51-61	All	All	All	All	All	All	All	All	All
Wealthy oversample	No	No	Yes	No	No	No	No	No	No	No
Panel features	Yes	Yes	No	Yes	Yes	Yes	No	No	Not yet	No
Survey Content										
Income	Yes	Yes	Yes	Yes	Yes	Yes	Yes	Yes	Yes	Yes
Housing equity	Yes	Yes	Yes	Yes	Yes	Yes	Yes	No	Yes	Yes
Financial assets	Yes	Yes	Yes	Yes	Yes	Yes	Yes	Yes	Yes	Yes
Consumption	No	No	No	No	No	Yes	Yes	No	No	Yes
Unfolding brackets	Yes	Yes	Yes	No	No	No	No	No	Yes	No
Employer-provided pensions	Yes	No	No	No	Yes	Part	No	No	No	No
Health	Yes	Yes	No	No	Yes	No	No	No	No	No
Individual (I) or household (H) assets	H	H	H	H&I	H&I	H	H	I	H or I	H

NOTES: HRS = Health and Retirement Survey; PSID = Panel Study of Income Dynamics; SCF = Survey of Consumer Finances; SEP = Socio-Economic Panel; CSS = CentER Savings Survey; SHIW = Survey of Household Income and Wealth; EVS = Income and Expenditure Survey; FRS = Financial Research Survey; BHPS = British Household Panel Study; NSFIE = National Survey of Family Income and Expenditure

CentER Savings Survey is an exception, having a limited set of questions on health (including life expectancy, phrased in terms of the chances that the respondent will survive to some target age; self-assessed health; smoking; drinking; height; and weight).

Comparisons with External Controls

United States

One check on the validity of household wealth data is to compare them with other aggregate national accounts of household wealth. In the United States, the most common comparison is with the FOF accounts. Such comparisons have been conducted for a number of household surveys, in particular PSID and SCF. For example, Juster et al. (1999) report that similarly defined SCF totals were quite close to those available from FOF in most years. In contrast, the PSID totals were about three-fourths of the FOF totals. Most of the discrepancy between PSID and SCF resulted from the latter's oversample of the extremely wealthy. For example, excluding that part of the SCF oversample, aggregate PSID wealth was more than 90 percent of the comparable SCF figure.

Comparisons with external controls have also been conducted on individual-level asset categories. The most detailed study to date is that by Curtin et al. (1989). In comparing the most complete U.S. household survey (SCF) with the federal FOF accounts, they find considerable variability across different asset categories in how closely figures from SCF match those from FOF. For example, the SCF estimates of net equity in housing are substantially higher than the FOF estimates, apparently because FOF data do not make an appropriate correction for land values. In contrast, survey estimates of wealth in checking and savings accounts, bonds, and money market shares are much lower than FOF at least in art because FOF household data include liquid assets held by non-corporate business. Interestingly, FOF and survey estimates of stock holdings are almost identical.

The Netherlands

The Dutch flow-of-funds account data do not include the stock of wealth and its composition. However, Statistics Netherlands produces publications on the composition and distribution of wealth based largely on tax records—the so-called Income Panel Survey (IPS) data. The Dutch tax records are informative about wealth holdings only for households in the higher income and wealth brackets. Hence Statistics Netherlands supplements these administrative data with survey data from SEP.

Alessie and Kapteyn (1999) compare their own calculated wealth figures based on SEP with the figures published by Statistics Netherlands. Not surprisingly, the data match well for the lower wealth deciles (because Statistics Netherlands uses SEP for these figures as well). For the higher deciles, SEP indicates lower figures for total wealth holdings than those of IPS. For instance, at the 90th percentile, the SEP figures are 13 percent below those of IPS. At the 95th percentile, the discrepancy is 21 percent.

Alessie et al. (1999) compare CSS and IPS data. They find that the CSS data indicate a 12 percent higher average net worth than that suggested by the IPS data. This discrepancy is due in part to what appears to be an underestimation of home ownership in the IPS data. Moreover, the average house value in CSS may be somewhat of an overestimation. In comparison with IPS, CSS shows a balance in checking and savings accounts that is 20 percent lower. Ownership rates for stocks, bonds, and mutual funds are considerably higher (about twice as large) in CSS than in IPS, but the unconditional means of the total value of stocks, bonds, and mutual funds are about equal. Figures for consumer credit in the two sources match quite well.

Italy

Jappelli and Pistaferri (1999) compare aggregate savings rates and aggregate wealth-to-income ratios computed on the basis of SHIW with the same concepts derived from national accounts. Savings rates based on the SHIW microdata are typically some 60 percent higher than those based on the national accounts. For example, for 1989 the national accounts imply a savings rate of 16.3 percent, whereas SHIW implies a rate of 26.4 percent, although trends in these rates over time are quite similar. The discrepancy is attributable in part to the fact that savings in SHIW are measured as income minus consumption, but consumption is not well measured, leading to a systematic downward bias. The wealth-income ratio derived from SHIW corresponds much better with the national accounts data. If one assumes that income is reasonably measured, the implication is that wealth is also fairly well measured in SHIW, at least on average.

Germany

Börsch-Supan (1999) compares income and transfer data from EVS with aggregate data from the national income and product accounts (NIPA). For 1993 he finds that the EVS figures match the NIPA data quite well. For instance, gross labor income in EVS is on average about 98 percent of the corresponding figure in the NIPA. However, a comparison of 1983 EVS figures on the value of financial assets with financial assets held by private households as reported by the Bundesbank shows that the former are only 29 percent of the latter. There are several reasons for this discrepancy. First, the Bundesbank includes nonprofit organizations in its definition of private households. Correcting for this practice would probably raise the 29 percent figure to something on the order of 40-60 percent (Lang, 1997). Second, EVS does not cover cash, checking accounts, and the cash value of whole life insurance and private pension claims, which would represent about 33 percent of all financial assets held by private households. Third, stocks reported by EVS appear to include only 43.5 percent of all stocks held by private households. Undoubtedly, this is due largely to the fact that the top 2 percent of the income distribution is not represented in EVS. EVS appears to overestimate home ownership as well.

United Kingdom

Official United Kingdom data on wealth stem from two fiscal sources: wealth tax and inheritance tax. Estimation of the wealth distribution on the basis of this information is wrought with obvious problems. Since the microdata for the United Kingdom are relatively weak, a comparison of the two sources is likely to be unreliable.

Japan

As mentioned above, Kitamura and Takayama (2000) compare the NSFIE data with both flow-of-funds and national accounts data and find a difference of about 40 percent.

PATTERNS OF HOUSEHOLD WEALTH ACCUMULATION

As in the other four research domains addressed in this report, cross-national research on savings and wealth is an important tool for understanding why households save at such varying rates and why they have such different levels of household wealth. There are two reasons for the importance of such research on wealth. First, countries differ across many dimensions in their observed patterns of household savings and wealth. Even with similar national incomes, some countries have high levels of household wealth, while others exhibit little evidence of much private wealth accumulation. Second, there is also a great deal of variation across countries in the constraints, incentives, and institutions that affect the private savings decisions of households. For example, an important public policy question is how government programs that provide income security during retirement affect household savings and wealth accumulation. This is a difficult question to answer using data from a single country, since variation among the individual components of a country's public program are relatively rare, and within-country changes tend not to be dramatic. In addition, there is a legitimate question about the extent to which within-country changes in program parameters are exogenous. In contrast, variations across countries in the way income security during retirement is provided are much larger, and thus offer considerable statistical power in testing how the design of public income security programs affects household wealth accumulation.

This section first describes what the panel believes are the most salient patterns of household wealth accumulation in the United States. These are the basic facts that theories of household wealth accumulation and savings must be able to explain if they are to be taken seriously as keys to understanding household savings. We next present a parallel summary of the most salient patterns observed in Europe and Japan, based largely on research results summarized in the papers commissioned for this study. We then examine cross-country variations in wealth levels and wealth inequality and explore some of the explanations for these variations.

Patterns of Household Wealth Accumulation: United States

Figure 4-1 highlights some of the more salient attributes of wealth distribution in the United States. The figures shown are based on PSID data, which span the entire age distribution. It is clear, first, that wealth distribution is extremely unequal in the United States. Counting all assets (including net home equity), the net worth of the median household is about $50,000. In sharp contrast, the top 5 percent of households typically have more than 10 times that amount, while the bottom third have virtually no net worth at all. If anything, indeed, reliance on PSID leads to a substantial understatement of the extent of wealth inequality since it excludes the super-rich.

Inequality is even more dramatic in financial assets alone (see Figure 4-2). Most American households have very few financial assets, but a few have a great deal. Median financial wealth is only a few thousand dollars.

It is important to understand two basic patterns in household wealth holdings—the age profile and the relation of wealth to household income. Household wealth and household income have distinctive age gradients, but the gradient is much sharper for wealth than for income, so that wealth-income ratios increase over the life cycle. For example, wealth at age 50 is about twice as high as population wealth and about 10 times higher than the wealth of those household heads under age 35.

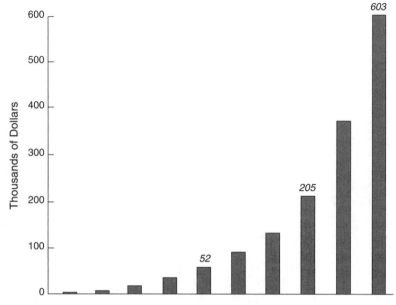

FIGURE 4-1 Distribution of net worth in the United States: 1994.
SOURCE: Smith (in press).

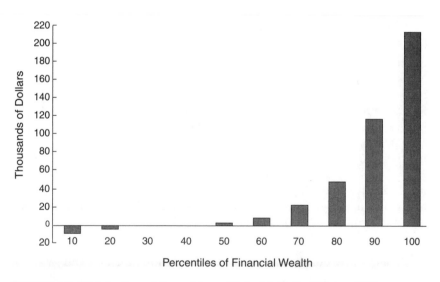

FIGURE 4-2 Distribution of financial wealth in the United States: 1994.
SOURCE: Smith (in press).

A critical question about the age-wealth gradient concerns whether wealth declines at older ages. A principal implication of the life-cycle model is that households will eventually dissave during the postretirement period as their consumption exceeds their income. Whether this is in fact the case is much in dispute, in part because of the small samples at this phase of the life cycle and the existence of other contaminating factors, including across-cohort increases in wealth and differential mortality by wealth. There is no dispute that just before and during retirement, the general pattern of extreme heterogeneity in wealth holdings continues to apply, with many households having almost no household wealth. This generalization is even more accurate with regard to financial assets.

To what extent can income disparities account for these large wealth disparities? Household income and wealth (as well as all key components of wealth) are strongly positively related, albeit in a highly nonlinear way. Financial assets and total net worth all increase at a more rapid rate than income as one moves from lower-income to higher-income households. To illustrate, in PSID, the median value of the total net worth of households in the median income decile is approximately $37,000. Net worth doubles between the 5th and 7th income deciles, doubles again between the 7th and 9th income deciles, and almost doubles once more between the 9th and 10th deciles. Households in the highest-income decile have six times the wealth of the median average-income household and almost 400 times as much wealth as those households in the lowest average-income decile. The increases in income across deciles are considerably smaller.

Yet it is easy to overemphasize the importance of income in determining household savings behavior and wealth. While not as frequently discussed, the diversity in wealth holdings even among households with similar incomes is enormous. Among median-income households, total net worth varies from $285,000 for those in the top 5 percent to only $8,400 for those in the bottom 20 percent. Similarly, financial assets for median-income households vary from $105,000 (the top 5 percent) to $0 or less among the lowest 40 percent. The within-income diversity of wealth holdings holds true even among households in the lowest-income decile. About 1 in 10 such households has more than $80,000 in wealth, while more than half have $1,000 or less. At the other end of the spectrum, 1 in every 5 households in the top decile of average household income has accumulated less than $15,000 in financial assets.

Patterns of Household Wealth Accumulation: Europe and Japan

For a number of reasons, much less is currently known about motives and patterns of wealth accumulation in western Europe than in the United

States. One reason is that European countries have lagged behind the United States in the collection of good household wealth data within their better household surveys. Fortunately, this situation is now changing rapidly in many (but not all) European countries. The panel took advantage of this positive development by encouraging new research on patterns of wealth accumulation and savings in several European countries. In addition, the Japanese NSFIE, conducted since 1959, provides invaluable information about savings and wealth patterns. We summarize the most important findings from these studies.

Cross-Country Variation in Wealth Levels and Wealth Inequality

Wealth Levels

Table 4-3 summarizes data from an OECD (1998) report on cross-country variation in household wealth accumulation. To standardize the comparison as much as possible, the data listed in the table are ratios of wealth to after-tax income for couples around age 55. The variation observed across the countries listed in this table can best be described as enormous. For example, the ratio of total household wealth to after-tax income (shown in Table 4-3 as total net worth) ranges from a high of 8 in Japan to a low of 2 in the Netherlands.[7] Even within Europe, the degree of variation is impressive. On the low end are Sweden and the Netherlands, with ratios around 2, while on the high end are France, Italy, and the United Kingdom, with average ratios of around 5. Considerable variation across these countries can also be observed in ratios of financial wealth to income. In Europe, Germany joins Sweden and the Netherlands in the lower tier, with mean levels of financial wealth representing a half-year or less of income.

Why do these countries at roughly similar levels of economic development differ so much in their private wealth holdings? Table 4-4 lists some basic summary statistics on household wealth in the five countries for which the panel commissioned papers. In light of the extreme skew that exists in most wealth distributions, both mean and median levels of household wealth are shown when available. Note that because financial wealth accumulation is of interest in its own right, this table, like Table 4-3, provides data for total net worth as well as financial wealth.

---

[7]It should be noted here that the Japanese NSFIE dataset excludes two significant categories of individuals: agricultural households and single-person households. This might be expected to produce an upward bias in the measure of total net worth shown in Table 4-3.

TABLE 4-3 Illustrative Wealth Income Ratios by
Country

Country	Total Net Worth	Financial Wealth
France	4.8	1.5
Germany	3.0	0.5
Italy	4.8	1.3
Japan	8.0	1.7
Netherlands	2.0	0.4
Sweden	2.1	–0.1
United Kingdom	6.0	0.7

NOTES: Data may not be strictly comparable because of different
sample selection procedures (for example, the inclusion or exclusion of
very-high-income households). Total net worth estimated by visual
inspection.

SOURCE: Organization for Economic Co-operation and Development
(1998).

Among the countries listed in Table 4-4, per capita income differences
are relatively small. By comparison, however, cross-national household
wealth differences are large. As suggested by Table 4-4, the lowest household wealth levels are observed in the Netherlands—well less than half of
the levels in Germany and a third of those in Italy. The disparities in
financial wealth among the European countries listed are considerably

TABLE 4-4 Level of Wealth Across Countries

Measure	Japan	Netherlands	Italy	Germany	U.K.	U.S.
Mean Net	4,291	100,995	154,385	245,265	N/A	158,500
Worth	(397,046)	(46,458)	(154,385)	(130,194)		
Median Net	2,733	42,847	92,909	117,394	N/A	50,600
Worth	(252,884)	(19,710)	(92,909)	(62,317)		
Mean Financial	1,279	24,917	20,377	61,557	7,136	53,300
Assets	(118,346)	(11,462)	(20,377)	(32,677)	(11,632)	
Median Financial	765	7,240	7,349	33,751	554	4,200
Assets	(70,785)	(3,330)	(7,349)	(17,916)	(903)	

NOTES: Amounts for Japan are in 10,000 1994 yen, for the Netherlands in 1987 guilders, for
Italy in 1995 Euros, for Germany in Deutschmarks, for the United Kingdom in 1997 pounds,
and for the United States in 1996 dollars. Figures in parentheses show the crude conversion
to 1996 U.S. dollars. N/A = not available.

SOURCES: Kitamura and Takayama (2000); Alessie and Kapteyn (1999); Japelli and
Pistaferri (1999); Börsch-Supan (1999); Banks and Tanner (1999); Smith and Smeeding (1998).

smaller. For all countries listed, mean financial wealth is relatively small, amounting to little more than a year's income. Most dramatic, Japan has by far the largest mean and median wealth levels. The United States has the second-highest mean wealth levels, but this appears to be largely the consequence of a relatively small number of households having significant amounts of financial wealth. Median household and financial wealth is actually less in the United States than in Italy or Germany.

Wealth Inequality

The second salient aspect of household wealth holdings is that they are distributed quite unequally across households. The large differences between median and mean wealth in Table 4-4 suggest that inequality is a common characteristic of wealth holdings in all the countries shown. There are many ways to measure inequality, but two of the most common are the wealth share of the top 1 percent and the Gini coefficient. Table 4-5 lists these two summary measures for a number of countries. Just as there are large cross-national differences in wealth levels, there are correspondingly large differences in dispersion. The United States appears to be in a class by itself on this metric, with wealth inequality far in excess of that of any of the other countries listed. For example, one-third of household wealth in the United States is held by only 1 percent of the population. The country nearest to the United States on this metric is France, with 26 percent. At the other extreme, the most egalitarian country listed is Sweden, where the top 1 percent of the population controls 16 percent of household wealth—half the U.S. statistic.

Tables 4-6 and 4-7 show in more detail the extent of inequality for the countries for which the panel commissioned papers that provided rel-

TABLE 4-5 Inequality Measures across Countries

Country	Wealth Share of Top 1%	Gini Coefficient
United States	35	79
Canada	17	69
France	26	71
Denmark	25	N/A
Germany	23	69
Sweden	16	59
Japan	N/A	52

NOTE: N/A = not available.

SOURCE: Davies and Shorrocks (1999).

TABLE 4-6 International Comparisons of Wealth Inequality for Total Net Worth (deciles relative to median)

Decile	Japan	Netherlands	Italy	Germany	United States
10	.13	.00	.07	.03	.00
20	.29	.07	.19	.10	.06
30	.50	.21	.42	.24	.24
40	.74	.47	.69	.51	N/A
50	1.00	1.00	1.00	1.00	1.00
60	1.30	1.81	1.33	1.46	N/A
70	1.70	2.83	1.77	1.92	2.41
80	2.25	3.99	2.40	2.42	N/A
90	3.37	6.10	3.66	3.46	7.12

NOTE: N/A = not available.

SOURCES: Kitamura and Takayama (2000); Alessie and Kapteyn (1999); Japelli and Pistaferri (1999); Börsch-Supan (1999); Smith (in press).

evant data. To eliminate the local currency problem, a straightforward way of measuring inequality is to index wealth holdings at selected deciles relative to the median. This procedure is followed for total household wealth in Table 4-6 and for total financial wealth in Table 4-7.

All countries in these tables are characterized by considerable household wealth inequality, but there also exists much variation across countries in the extent of this inequality. Inequality in financial wealth is clearly much higher in the United States than in any of the other countries

TABLE 4-7 International Comparisons of Wealth Inequality for Total Financial Net Worth (deciles relative to median)

Decile	Japan	Netherlands	Italy	Germany	U.K.	United States
10	.16	−.65	.06	.02	0	−1.48
20	.36	.01	.14	.18	0	−.26
30	.55	.23	.39	.39	0	0
40	.76	.57	.66	.66	.22	N/A
50	1.00	1.00	1.00	1.00	1.00	1.00
60	1.31	1.61	1.16	1.40	2.53	N/A
70	1.75	2.60	2.23	1.91	3.98	6.52
80	2.48	4.30	3.74	2.74	9.12	N/A
90	3.91	8.26	6.59	4.34	20.60	34.60

NOTE: N/A = not available.

SOURCES: Kitamura and Takayama (2000); Alessie and Kapteyn (1999); Japelli and Pistaferri (1999); Börsch-Supan (1999); Banks and Tanner (1999); Smith (in press).

shown and is lowest in Japan, with Germany a close second. In the United States, for example, households in the 90th financial wealth percentile have 35 times as much wealth as the median household. In this ranking, the United Kingdom is a distant second, with households in the 90th percentile having 20 times as much financial wealth as the median household. Thus while wealth inequality is thought to be high in the other European countries and Japan, it is considerably lower than in either the United States or the United Kingdom.

One reason wealth inequality is higher in the United States is that income inequality is also higher, yet this is not a sufficient explanation for the extent of the difference between the United States and Europe on this measure. Once again, the issue is not so much the behavior of the typical household in these countries, but why the top fifth of U.S. households accumulate so much wealth relative to the top fifth in Europe or Japan. Possible answers certainly include the effects of the tax and welfare systems in the various countries.

There is also considerable divergence among these countries with regard to trends in wealth inequality during the last few decades. The trend in the United States is clearly toward increasing wealth inequality (Smith, 1999a), at an even more rapid rate than the growth in income inequality. In contrast, Alessie and Kapteyn (1999) demonstrate that wealth inequality has been declining in the Netherlands during the same period. The differing patterns in the two countries appear to be due to price trends for two different assets in the wealth portfolio. In the United States, rising wealth inequality is largely the consequence of a very rapid increase in equity prices (Juster et al., 1999). Stock market equities are a minor part of the wealth portfolio of middle- and lower-income households in the United States, but a much larger part of the portfolio of higher-income households. Consequently, the major beneficiaries of the stock market boom in the United States have been the wealthy. In contrast, the major asset driving inequality in the Netherlands has been the home. Between 1987 and 1996, housing prices in the Netherlands doubled. Over the same period, home ownership increased from 42.7 to 50.5 percent. Since housing represents a larger portion of the portfolio of not-so-rich households than of the rich, the dispersion of the wealth distribution has been somewhat compressed. With regard to the other countries shown in Tables 4-6 and 4-7, Jappelli and Pistaferri (1999) report that in Italy, wealth inequality has risen slightly over the last decade or so. Kitamura and Takayama (2000) suspect that wealth inequality in Japan rose between 1984 and 1994, but they have not calculated a Gini coefficient for 1994.

Explanations for Wealth Differences Across Countries

Income differences among countries are unlikely to explain much of the cross-national disparity discussed above since income per capita is roughly similar in all the countries examined. The explanation is more likely to lie in differences among the countries in their institutions and their incentives to save. These institutional differences may reside in housing or insurance markets or in the way income insurance schemes have been structured.

Home Ownership

In most countries, the single most important asset people possess is their own home. In the United States, for example, housing equity represents one-third of total net worth, but even this statistic severely understates the role of home equity for most Americans. Home ownership is even more salient for the typical household, often being its only asset of much value. The extent to which individuals can own and subsequently build up equity in their home is probably the most crucial determinant of the level and distribution of wealth in any country.

Home equity is influenced by several personal, market, and institutional factors that vary considerably across countries. At the personal level, the three most critical attributes are age, marital status, and income. Home ownership rates vary considerably with age: people typically save for a down payment when they are young, often upgrade their homes during middle age as their families and income grow, and perhaps move once again during their retirement to a smaller home with more location-specific amenities. Income is clearly a critical determinant of the value of the home one can afford, and marital status is the best single indicator of family formation. But in addition to these personal-level attributes, countries differ in their housing markets and credit institutions—differences that strongly impact the ability of households to own and finance a home.[8] Finally, country-specific housing market price cycles can create substantial capital gains or losses on the existing stock of homes.

Table 4-8 lists rates of home ownership for single and married couples at ages 55 and 67 for selected OECD countries. In most countries, more than 80 percent of couples own a home by age 55. The two principal exceptions to this widespread prevalence of home ownership are the Netherlands and Germany. Rates of home ownership have traditionally

---

[8]It might also be argued that in some countries more than others, cities are places people want to live in, and renting is more common as a result. Further, housing subsidies for the middle class differ by country.

TABLE 4-8 Proportion of Families Reporting Housing Wealth

Country	Age 55		Age 67	
	All Singles	All Couples	All Singles	All Couples
Australia	56.5	85.7	67.2	91.6
France	65.0	80.0	65.0	84.0
Germany	32.4	58.8	36.2	57.6
Italy	69.5	83.2	63.4	82.4
Japan	55.6	83.7	73.8	91.7
Netherlands	32.8	59.7	18.6	40.8
Sweden	44.2	84.2	38.9	75.0
United Kingdom	45.7	75.1	42.3	66.2
United States	56.3	89.8	65.8	88.3

SOURCE: Organization for Economic Co-operation and Development (1998).

been much lower in the Netherlands than in the rest of Europe because of a heavily regulated housing market for a long period after World War II. Now that the market is deregulated, ownership rates have been increasing rapidly in the last decade. As mentioned above, Alessie and Kapteyn (1999) report that between 1987 and 1996, the rate of home ownership increased in the Netherlands from 43 to 51 percent.

Italy is an important special case that illustrates the role credit market imperfections can play in wealth accumulation (see Jappelli and Pistaferri, 1999). Imperfections in the Italian housing mortgage market have been pervasive in the last few decades as compared with the situation in the rest of Europe. These imperfections are manifested in the form of very high down payments (40 to 50 percent of purchase prices), a shorter mortgage maturity (20 years), and higher interest rates. Italians still strive to own their own homes, but given these credit imperfections must rely more on their own savings (as well as transfers from their relatives) to meet down payment requirements. The result is a very low rate of home ownership among younger Italians as they struggle to save for this purpose. The relatively high rates of wealth accumulation in Italy shown in Table 4-4 can best be understood as a consequence of the high rates of household savings required for home ownership. As Italy has developed economically over the last two decades, capital markets in housing have improved, and the savings required to finance a home have decreased. Indeed, Jappelli and Pistaferri (1999) conclude that improvements in the Italian mortgage lending market are the most likely explanation for the steep decline in Italian savings rates that has taken place in the last decade.

Cohort Trends

For the United States, the four European countries for which the panel commissioned papers, and Japan, one of the most salient patterns in household wealth accumulation is the very strong trends across cohorts. In all these countries, younger cohorts have considerably more household wealth than did older cohorts at the same age.

Figure 4-3 shows median net worth and financial wealth, respectively, by age and cohort for the Netherlands. Each line in the figure represents median net worth (top panel) or median financial wealth (bottom panel) of a 5-year birth cohort. For instance, the lines labeled 63 represent those born between 1961 and 1965. The figures illustrate a steep growth in net worth between 1987 and 1995 for all cohorts except the elderly. In part this reflects the rise in housing prices referred to earlier. Since home ownership is much less prevalent among the elderly than among the young, the median net worth of the elderly is less affected by a boom in the real estate market than is the net worth of other households. The figures also illustrate the misleading picture that a purely cross-sectional analysis would provide. For instance, the lower end of each line gives the median net worth of a birth cohort in 1987. If we connect the lower end of all lines, we obtain a cross-sectional age-wealth profile for 1987, which is nicely hump shaped as the life-cycle hypothesis would predict. Obviously, this is an artifact, as the cohort graphs clearly demonstrate. Financial wealth also exhibits substantial cohort effects, but they are less important in monetary terms.

Figure 4-4 illustrates cohort effects for Italy. Although these effects are clearly present here as well, a cross-sectional profile would be less misleading than in the Dutch case. Figure 4-5 illustrates the similarly strong cohort effects revealed by Japanese data between 1979 and 1994.

Income Replacement

There is considerable variation in the way different countries finance the retirement of their older populations. In particular, countries place differing weights on publicly provided pensions, private or employer-provided pensions, and private savings. Some European countries rely almost exclusively on an integrated public tier, while others, such as the United Kingdom, use a combination of private- and public-sector resources. These combinations may produce differing rates of income replacement during retirement, and therefore have different implications with regard to incentives for private savings. For example, a public-sector benefit that provided almost complete income replacement would reduce and possibly even eliminate incentives for private retirement savings.

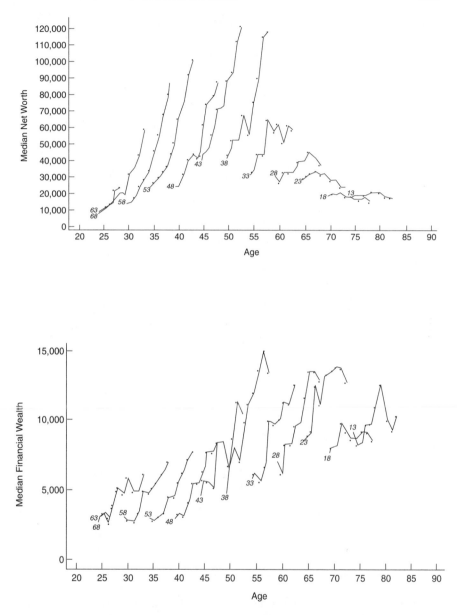

FIGURE 4-3 Median net worth and financial wealth by age of household head and cohort in the Netherlands: 1987 to 1996.
SOURCE: Alessie and Kapteyn (1999).

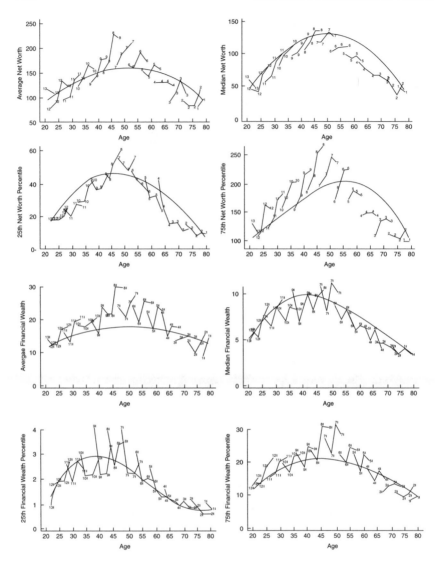

FIGURE 4-4 Measures of net worth by age of household head and cohort in Italy: 1989 to 1995.

NOTES: These figures plot wealth by age of 13 cohorts: cohort 1 includes all households whose head was born between 1905 and 1909, cohort 2 those born between 1910 and 1914, and so on up to cohort 13, those born between 1965 and 1969. Each cohort is observed at four different times, one for each cross section. The line in each graph is obtained by regressing wealth on a fourth-order polynomial, a full set of dummies, and a set of restricted time dummies. The data are drawn from the 1989-1995 SHIW. Values are converted in thousands of 1995 Euros.

SOURCE: Jappelli and Pistaferri (1999).

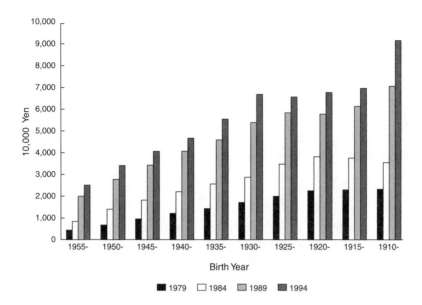

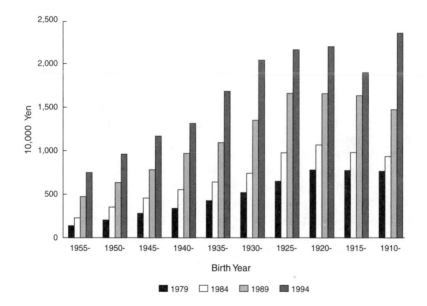

FIGURE 4-5 Net worth and net financial assets by birth year of household head in Japan: 1979 to 1994.
SOURCE: Kitamura and Takayama (2000).

TABLE 4-9 Replacement Rates for the Retired Population

Country	All Disposable Income	Public Transfers Only
France	80	61
Germany	85	63
Italy	80	25
Japan	76	42
Netherlands	78	50
Sweden	78	75
United Kingdom	68	35

SOURCE: Organization for Economic Co-operation and Development (1998).

Table 4-9, based on a recent OECD study, lists rates of income replacement during retirement for six European countries and Japan. In each country, these numbers were computed in a cross section as the ratio of the after-tax incomes of individuals at age 67 to the after-tax incomes of individuals at age 55. In addition to total income replacement rates, the table shows retirement income replacement based only on the public-tier program.

Throughout Europe, total income replacement rates are about .8 and are similar across countries. If anything, retirement income replacement is understated in these tables since income growth across cohorts implies that the incomes of those currently age 55 are higher than the incomes of those currently age 67 when they were age 55. Just 1 percent income growth per year would lead to essentially complete income replacement in virtually all European countries. Even without taking work-related costs into account, on average many European workers are better off when they retire than when they are working.

The similarity across European countries in total retirement income replacement rates disappears when we examine public transfers only—a reflection of differences in the way the various countries have designed their old-age pension systems. Since the portion of the system that lies formally outside the public tier is usually heavily controlled (or at least influenced) by the respective governments as well, it generally makes sense to examine the total retirement system, not just the public transfer portion.

Retirement Income Security

An important policy issue across all Western countries is the extent to which government social insurance programs during retirement substitute for or crowd out private savings (see Smith and Smeeding, 1998, and

TABLE 4-10 Retirement Income Security Systems

Country	Poverty Rate as % of GDP (circa 1992)		Guaranteed Minimum as % of Median National Income	Social Retirement Pensions as % of GDP		
	40%	50%		1995	2030	Diff
United States	13.4	22.7	34	4.1	6.6	2.5
Germany	4.5	8.1	52	11.1	16.5	5.4
United Kingdom	10.9	30.5	43	4.5	5.5	1.0
Canada	1.5	7.1	56	5.2	9.0	3.8
Australia	7.1	28.6	51	2.6	2.9	0.3
The Netherlands	3.0	4.4	66	6.0	11.2	5.2
Sweden	1.5	6.4	63	11.8	15.0	3.2

SOURCE: Smith and Smeeding (1998).

the discussion in Chapter 3 of this report). Most modern nations face challenges of an aging population that are similar to that in the United States. Nearly every country has a pay-as-you-go social retirement scheme that will be put to the financial and political test over the next 30 years. Each nation also has some mix of employer-provided pensions, own savings, earnings, and targeted benefits for the poor that helps them meet income security goals.

Income security policy goals include preventing poverty in old age, encouraging private savings, encouraging work at older ages, and ensuring desired rates of income replacement in retirement. What differs across countries is the extent to which each of these goals is pursued and the costs incurred. Table 4-10 summarizes several salient features of retirement income security systems for seven modern nations.

Poverty rates in old age vary substantially across nations. The first two columns of Table 4-10 show the percentage of persons aged 65 and over with disposable incomes (adjusted for differences in family size) of less than 40 or 50 percent of the overall national median disposable income. The table also shows the minimum guaranteed income for a single, older person as a percentage of the same adjusted national median income for each nation.[9] Nations with relatively low minimum benefits

---

[9]These minimum income systems usually involve two items: a flat old-age security benefit within the social retirement system, and some type of income or income and asset means-tested general revenue-financed "welfare" benefit for older persons. In the United States, the system involves the result of combining Old-Age and Survivor's Insurance (OASI), Supplemental Security Income (SSI), and food stamps. In many other nations, the flat old-age security benefit (minimum social security benefit) is higher, and the income-tested benefit is higher still. In Sweden, the policy goal is to have a guarantee at or above 60 percent of the median.

(United States, United Kingdom) have relatively higher poverty rates. Other nations with well-targeted, high-participation-rate welfare systems (e.g., Canada) or those with relatively high lower-tier social retirement benefit levels (the Netherlands, Sweden, Germany) have lower overall poverty rates. Australia is unique in that it has no social security system, only a means-tested income support system, financed by general revenues to prevent old-age poverty. While this system produces only a 7 percent poverty rate at 40 percent of the median income, it results in a 29 percent rate at half of the median.

These data also raise the question of what is meant by the generosity of a program. In the United States, for example, if social security is evaluated on the basis of replacement of income before retirement, it is a generous program indeed. Another definition of generosity is how much income is received relative to the median income of the society. On this basis, the U.S. system appears far less generous than those of other nations.[10]

Table 4-10 also summarizes the OECD forecast for the financial cost of the social retirement system alone (as a percentage of GDP) if it were to continue its current level of benefits and participation rates over the next 30 years. Most American analysts are concerned about the future of the U.S. social security system, which would consume 6.6 percent of GDP in the year 2030. The gap between this figure and that for 1995, which must be made up by either benefit reductions or tax increases, is 2.5 percent of GDP. In contrast, the nations with high social retirement benefits—Germany, the Netherlands, and Sweden—are confronting much larger gaps while also starting from much higher bases; Canada faces a larger gap while starting from a slightly higher base. Each of these nations relies heavily on its social retirement system to finance old-age income support. For the median elderly person, German, Dutch, and Swedish social retirement benefits make up 84, 73, and 90 percent of disposable income, respectively. These figures compare with about 60 to 63 percent in the United States and Canada (Smeeding, 1997). According to most analyses, including those of the OECD (1998) and the World Bank (1994), these benefit levels cannot be sustained.

Two nations—the United Kingdom and Australia—face a lesser problem. As mentioned earlier, Australia has no social security system, so it faces no explicit age-driven social security deficit problem. The United

---

[10]As discussed above, earnings and income inequality in the United States is much higher than in European countries at all ages. For the American system to achieve the same retirement-age poverty rates as other countries, it would have to have replacement rates that were well in excess of 1 for a large subgroup of the elderly. These levels of replacement would raise serious questions about such a system's effect on work effort and savings.

Kingdom has reduced its future outlays by designing a two-tier system: a low (roughly 40 percent of median income) flat-tier benefit supplemented by welfare benefits, and an upper tier that allows participants to invest their contributions in private assets, not government securities. Sweden also recently privatized a portion of its social retirement system, but it still faces high expected outlays resulting from the generosity of the current system and the cost of converting to a privately financed system.

Concepts of Wealth

One limitation of many household surveys is that they do not measure a large source of wealth—annuities paid during retirement—that is especially relevant just before and during retirement. This is an especially important issue for international comparisons given the differing extent to which countries rely on government annuities during retirement and on employer-provided pensions. For example, the two important annuities in the U.S. system are social security and private pensions. Social security is an almost universal public-sector retirement annuity wherein the benefit is tied to past earnings through a progressive formula. Employer-provided pensions typically also are related to salary, but they are far from universal and are much more common in larger private firms. For example, 53 percent of HRS respondents report that they are covered by a pension. Fortunately, HRS has made a determined effort to measure both social security and pension wealth.[11]

Table 4-11 lists wealth-income ratios for the subcomponents of wealth across schooling groups in the United States. This table documents some stark contrasts in the relative progressivity of these components. Financial assets are by far the most unequally distributed component; relative to household income, financial assets are 3.3 times larger among college graduates as compared with those who did not graduate from high school. Pensions are also regressive in their distribution, reflecting the greater prevalence of employer-provided pensions among high-wage workers. In contrast, social security is quite progressive, with social security wealth-income ratios being three times larger among high school dropouts than among college graduates. The final row in Table 4-11 combines all forms of household wealth. Compared with household wealth alone, total wealth is distributed relatively uniformly across schooling groups.

The other European countries for which wealth data are available (along with Japan) have not yet developed integrated datasets that can

---

[11]The numbers reported here were derived from respondents' reports of their future expected Social Security and pension annuities. See Smith (1995) for the details of this calculation.

TABLE 4-11 Wealth-Income Ratios by Components of Wealth in the
United States

		Education of Household Head			
Type of Assets	All	No High School Diploma	High School Diploma	Some College	College
Financial Assets	1.47	0.63	1.15	1.46	2.07
Household Assets	4.84	3.69	4.18	5.00	5.74
Social Security	2.12	3.28	2.65	1.96	1.33
Pensions	1.85	1.25	1.74	1.69	2.26
Total Wealth	8.81	8.22	8.57	8.65	9.33

NOTE: Data are from wave 1 of The Health and Retirement Survey, conducted in 1992.

SOURCE: Juster et al. (1999).

simultaneously inform us about levels of household wealth and wealth in the form of employer-provided and government-supported pensions. Such data are a high priority since they could go a long way toward reconciling cross-country differences in levels of private household wealth. For example, the fact that many of the continental European countries rely much more heavily on government-financed than employer-provided pensions may explain their relatively low levels of private wealth accumulation.

RECOMMENDATIONS

4-1. Countries should address the pressing need for longitudinal microdata comprising extensive measures of economic status that can illuminate the relationship between income and wealth on the one hand, and financial incentives to retire, various dimensions of health status, and intergenerational transfers on the other. In most countries, the requisite data on economic status pertinent to policy making simply do not exist. A number of recent surveys have demonstrated that relatively short wealth modules can capture most of the salient attributes of the household wealth distribution. Countries should build upon and extend existing survey models (such as the Health and Retirement Survey in the United States) that have been shown to provide high-quality data on wealth and savings in addition to information on interrelated realms of life.

4-2. Given the overarching need for longitudinal microdata on economic status, researchers and policy makers should pay close attention to novel and potentially revolutionary ways of collecting such data. Several recent innovations in collecting household wealth and income data have been found to greatly improve the quality of such information and should be further developed. These include the use of unfolding brackets to reduce item nonresponse and produce more accurate estimates of household wealth, the integration of income and asset questions, and the use of randomly varying anchor points. One particular high-priority research question is how to use the panel nature of repeated questions on household wealth to reduce across-wave measurement error.

The fact that a vast majority of households in developed countries will soon be connected to the Internet opens up promising new means of data collection, such as those used in the Dutch CentER Savings Survey. Rather than computer-assisted person-to-person interviewing or computer-assisted telephone interviewing, one can use computers or equivalent media (e.g., set-top boxes) not only to ask questions directly, but also to present questions in novel ways and perform cross-wave checking on line.

4-3. Similarly defined microdata should be collected in different countries to exploit institutional differences and advance our understanding of the effects of policies on individual-level wealth accumulation. One issue that could be illuminated by comparative cross-national research is the extent to which public income provisions discourage or drive out private savings. To assess institutional and policy effects, it is essential that data collection efforts in different countries be well coordinated, that similar information be collected, and that procedures (e.g., sampling and quality control) be synchronized to the extent possible. Such synchronization can be achieved largely through the exchange of information among various scientific groups involved in new data collection efforts. The goal is not necessarily to have standardized instruments and identical survey design protocols in all countries. Each country has unique institutional features and policy priorities that should help shape survey implementation.

REFERENCES

Alessie, R., S. Hochguertel, and A. Van Soest
  1999   Household Portfolios in The Netherlands. Paper prepared for the Conference on Household Portfolios, European University Institute, Florence.
Alessie, R., and A. Kapteyn
  1999   Wealth and Savings: Data and Trends in The Netherlands. Paper prepared for the Panel on a Research Agenda and New Data for an Aging World, Committee on Population, National Research Council.
Alessie, R., A. Kapteyn, and F. Klijn
  1997   Mandatory pensions and personal savings in The Netherlands. *De Economist* 145:291-324.
Alessie, R., A. Lusardi, and A. Kapteyn
  1995   Saving and wealth holdings of the elderly. *Ricerche Economiche* 49:293-315.

1999   Saving after retirement: Evidence from three different surveys. *Labour Economics* 6:277-310.

Alessie, R., M. Pradhan, and C. Zandvliet

1993   *An Exploratory Analysis of the Socio-Economic Panel with Regard to the Financial Position of Households.* VSB Progress Report 14. The Netherlands: Tilburg University.

Banks, J., R. Blundell, and S. Tanner

1998   Is there a retirement savings puzzle? *American Economic Review* 88:769-788.

Banks, J., and S. Tanner

1999   Household Wealth in the UK: Evidence from Survey Data. Paper prepared for the Panel on a Research Agenda and New Data for an Aging World, Committee on Population, National Research Council.

Bergantino, S.M.

1997   Booms, Busts and Babies: The Effect of Demographics on Housing and Stock Prices. Working Paper. Cambridge, MA: Massachusetts Institute of Technology.

Blundell, R., T. Magnac, and C. Meghir

1997   Savings and labor-market transitions. *Journal of Business & Economic Statistics* 15:153-164.

Börsch-Supan, A.

1992   Saving and consumption patterns of the elderly: The German case. *Journal of Population Economics* 5:289-303.

1999   Data and Research on Saving in Germany. Paper prepared for the Panel on a Research Agenda and New Data for an Aging World, Committee on Population, National Research Council. Available: Department of Economics, University of Mannheim, Germany.

Börsch-Supan, A., and K. Stahl

1991   Life cycle saving and consumption constraints: Theory, empirical evidence and fiscal implications. *Journal of Population Economics* 4:233-255.

Brandolini, A.

1999   The Personal Distribution of Income in Post-war Italy: Source Description, Data Quality, and the Time Pattern of Income Inequality. Temi di Discussione 350. Rome: Bank of Italy.

Browning, M., and A. Lusardi

1996   Household saving: Micro theories and micro facts. *Journal of Economic Literature* 34:1797-1855.

Curtin R., F.T. Juster, and J. Morgan

1989   Survey estimates of wealth: An assessment of quality. In *The Measurement of Saving, Investment, and Wealth*, R.E. Lipsey and H.S. Tice, eds. Chicago: University of Chicago Press.

Davies, J.B., and A.F. Shorrocks

1999   The distribution of wealth. In *Handbook of Income Distribution*, A.B. Atkinson and F. Bourguignon, eds. Amsterdam: North-Holland.

Deaton, A.

1992   *Understanding Consumption.* Oxford: Oxford University Press.

Feldstein, M.

1974   Social security, induced retirement, and aggregate capital accumulation. *Journal of Political Economy* 82:905-926.

Gale, W.G., and J.K. Scholz

1994   Intergenerational transfers and the accumulation of wealth. *Journal of Economic Perspectives* 8(4):145-160.

Hamermesh, D.
  1984 Consumption during retirement: The missing link in the life cycle. *The Review of Economics and Statistics* 66:1-7.
Hochguertel, S., R. Alessie, and A. Van Soest
  1997 Saving accounts versus stocks and bonds in household portfolio allocation. *Scandinavian Journal of Economics* 99:81-97.
Hurd, M.
  1987 Saving of the elderly and desired bequests. *American Economic Review* 77:289-312.
  1998 *Mortality Risk and Consumption by Couples.* Working Paper. Santa Monica, CA: RAND.
  1999 Anchoring and acquiescence bias in measuring assets in household surveys. *Journal of Risk and Uncertainty* 19:111-136.
Hurd, M., D. McFadden, and A. Merrill
  1998 *Healthy, Wealthy, and Wise? Socioeconomic Status, Morbidity, and Mortality among the Elderly.* Working Paper. Santa Monica, CA: RAND.
Jappelli, T., and L. Pistaferri
  1999 The Dynamics of Household Wealth Accumulation in Italy. Paper prepared for the Panel on a Research Agenda and New Data for an Aging World. Committee on Population, National Research Council.
Juster, F.T., M. Hurd, and J.P. Smith
  2000 Enhancing the Quality of Data on Income: Recent Developments in Survey Methodology. Unpublished paper. University of Michigan, Department of Economics.
Juster, F.T., J. Lupton, J.P. Smith, and F. Stafford
  1999 Savings and Wealth; Then and Now. Paper presented at the Conference on Health and Retirement, October, Amsterdam.
Juster, F.T., and J.P. Smith
  1997 Improving the quality of economic data: Lessons from the HRS and AHEAD. *Journal of the American Statistical Association* 92:1268-1278.
Juster, F.T., J.P. Smith, and F. Stafford
  1999 The measurement and structure of household wealth. *Labour Economics* 6:253-276.
Kapteyn, A., R. Alessie, and A. Lusardi
  1999 *Explaining the Wealth Holdings of Different Cohorts: Productivity Growth and Social Security.* Working Paper. The Netherlands: Tilburg University.
King, M., and J. Leape
  1998 Wealth and portfolio composition: Theory and evidence. *Journal of Public Economics* 69:155-193.
Kitamura, Y., and N. Takayama
  2000 Household Wealth in Japan. Paper prepared for the Panel on a Research Agenda and New Data for an Aging World, Committee on Population, National Research Council.
Laibson, D.
  1997 Golden eggs and hyperbolic discounting. *Quarterly Journal of Economics* 112:443-477.
Lang, O.
  1997 Steueranreize und Geldanlagen im Lebenszyklus. Ph.D. dissertation, University of Mannheim, Germany.
Lusardi, A.
  1999 *Explaining Why So Many Households Do Not Save.* Working Paper. Hanover, NH: Dartmouth College.

Organization for Economic Co-operation and Development
   1998   *Resources During Retirement*. Working Paper AWP 4.3. Paris: Organization for
          Economic Co-operation and Development.
Poterba, J.
   1999   *Taxation and Portfolio Structure: Issues and Implications*. Working Paper. Cam-
          bridge, MA: Massachusetts Institute of Technology.
   2000   Stock market wealth and consumption. *Journal of Economic Perspectives* 14:99-118.
Poterba, J., and A. Samwick
   1999   *Taxation and Household Portfolio Composition: U.S. Evidence from the 1980s and 1990s*.
          Working Paper. Cambridge, MA: National Bureau of Economic Research.
Sheiner, L., and D. Weil
   1992   *The Housing Wealth of the Aged*. NBER Working Paper 4115. Cambridge, MA:
          National Bureau of Economic Research.
Smeeding, T.
   1997   *Reshuffling Responsibilities in Old Age: The United States in Comparative Perspective*.
          Luxembourg Income Study Working Paper, No. 153. Luxembourg.
Smith, J.P.
   1995   Racial and ethnic differences in wealth in the Health and Retirement Study. *Jour-
          nal of Human Resources* 30(Supplement):S158-S183.
   1999a Healthy bodies and thick wallets: The dual relationship between health and eco-
          nomic status. *Journal of Economic Perspectives* 13:145-166.
   1999b Inheritances and bequests. In *Health and Wealth: Theory and Measurement*, J.P.
          Smith and R.J. Willis, eds., pp. 121-149. Ann Arbor: University of Michigan Press.
   in   Why is wealth inequality rising? In *Increasing Income Inequality in America: The
   press Facts, Causes, and Consequences*, F. Welch, ed. Chicago: University of Chicago
          Press.
Smith, J.P., and T. Smeeding
   1998   *The Economic Status of the Elderly on the Eve of Social Security Reform*. Policy Report,
          November. Washington, DC: Progressive Policy Institute.
Thaler, R., and H. Shefrin
   1981   An economic theory of self-control. *Journal of Political Economy* 89:392-406.
Venti, S., and D. Wise
   1989   Aging, moving and housing wealth. In *The Economics of Aging*, D. Wise, ed.
          Chicago: University of Chicago Press.
   1990   But they don't want to reduce housing equity. In *Issues in the Economics of Aging*,
          D. Wise, ed. Chicago: University of Chicago Press.
   1991   Aging and the income value of housing wealth. *Journal of Public Economics* 44:371-
          395.
Wagner, G., R.V. Burkhauser, and F. Behringer
   1993   The English language public use file of the German Socio-Economic Panel. *Jour-
          nal of Human Resources* 28:429-433.
World Bank
   1994   *Averting the Old Age Crisis*. Washington, DC: The World Bank.
Yaari, M.E.
   1965   Uncertain lifetime, life insurance and the theory of the consumer. *Review of Eco-
          nomic Studies* 32:137-150.

5

Intergenerational Transfers

Trends in the ratio of workers to retirees are the tea leaves of policy making for aging populations. Armed with knowledge of age-related behaviors and age-defined benefits in a society, policy makers and commentators alike attempt to read shifts in the relative size of broad age groups for their public policy implications. As more people retire at ever earlier ages, their consumption must come from current output produced by those who work—by either transfer of assets (i.e., claims on output), private/private transfers, or collective wealth schemes (see Thompson, 1998). Of particular concern is whether the well-being of an expanding older population can be secured only at the expense of burgeoning public expenditures (see Chapter 4). Public costs are incurred through a variety of programs providing health care, housing, and financial security for retirees. Whether funded from general tax revenues or mandatory worker contributions, these programs are inherently structured transfers that redistribute resources from workers to elderly nonworkers in a society. Examples of such programs in the United States include Social Security, Medicare, and Medicaid. Comparably structured programs exist throughout Western Europe, Japan, and some other middle-income countries (e.g., Korea, Chile, and Mexico), with variations on the general theme seen in other countries as well (such as Singapore's Central Provident Fund). As noted above, however, publicly funded transfer programs are not the only source of support for the aged, even in developed countries. To varying degrees across societies and over time, the state, the marketplace, and the family have contributed to the support and care of older persons (Lee, 1994b; Soldo and Freedman, 1994).

Most of the other chapters in this volume address broad public policy concerns, such as meeting the health care needs of the aged or providing old-age financial security by combining individual savings, market annuities, and public pensions. In a departure from that approach, this chapter focuses on the whole of the family transfer system that disburses privately held resources across generations of kin for many of the same purposes served by public programs. While parents provide children with a range of in-kind services, such as shared food, housing, care services, and financial assistance, both during their lifetime and by bequest, adult children often provide elderly parents with comparable resource transfers. The extent of the latter transfers vary across countries: they are normative throughout Asia (Hermalin, 1997) and Southern Europe (Glaser and Tomassini, 1999); limited and largely responsive to parental health shocks or widowhood in the United States and the United Kingdom (Wolf, 1994a; McGarry and Schoeni, 1999); and rare in Scandinavian countries.[1] Regardless of cultural, institutional, and behavioral differences across countries, however, family transfers, including emotional and affective support, are important to the well-being of older persons.

The demographic forces that give rise to aging populations also transform the structure of the family. With declines in the rates of both fertility and old-age mortality, the number of living generations in a family increases (Watkins et al., 1987) even as the number of same-generation kin declines. In silhouette, the vertically extended family evolves from the pyramid created by regimes of high fertility and mortality to the narrow, elongated family structures observed in developed countries today (Bengtson and Silverstein, 1993). The elongated family structure concentrates obligations for elder care and support among fewer kin in descending generations of a family.

In most countries, the division of labor between the public and family transfer systems is rationalized by long-standing convention, rather than by concerns for efficiency or claims of specialized competency. As a result, interactions between the two broad types of transfer systems define many of the more important policy issues for an aging population. Specifying how transfers from one system affect the flow or volume of resources from the other, however, is seldom straightforward. Increasing inheritance taxes, for example, may "repay" public transfers in the aggre-

---

[1]In the poorest countries, public transfer programs are rare. Where they exist at all, such benefits are usually restricted to former government workers. Older persons have few options for transferring resources across their own life cycle through private financial markets or participation in private pensions. Surviving adult children are the singular means of insuring against the uncertainties of old age, and family transfers largely determine the well-being of older persons.

gate, but over time discourage family care for elderly kin. Alternatively, public care services may prompt a family to redirect its efforts to previously unattended areas of support; for example, adult children may reduce the frequency of their instrumental support but increase their affective support for frail parents. Under this scenario, the parent's overall quality of life might improve, but the net effect for the public sector would be to increase the total volume and cost of publicly financed care services.

Within-country studies can make only limited contributions to a policy agenda focused on the interactions between transfer systems or the efficacy and efficiency of the welfare produced for older persons under a given model. Even the richest of domestic datasets have limited utility for pursuing this agenda. There are several reasons for this. The first, and most obvious, is that with few exceptions (e.g., differences in the generosity of Medicaid benefits across U.S. states), transfer policies *within* a country are usually standardized. Most national policies dictate, for example, that all workers of a given age from a given sector with comparable work histories receive the same government-funded old-age pension. Cross-national research provides opportunities to relate variations in institutional arrangements to the distribution of attributes that determine benefit eligibility or benefit levels (e.g., sector of employment for government pensions) and the distribution of the old-age welfare produced (e.g., postretirement income security) in a population. In addition, within a given country, the legacy of a unique cultural heritage is imprinted on the division of labor between the state and family transfer systems. Because of this confounding, policy makers cannot reliably anticipate the responsiveness of family transfer behaviors to changes in the design of programs benefiting the older segment of the population.

This chapter considers how intergenerational transfer issues frame many of the important public policy questions in both developed and developing countries. We begin by posing a number of policy questions whose answers require novel ways of conceptualizing and producing relevant data. We then view intergenerational transfers from a macroeconomic perspective that focuses on flows of resources between generations. The discussion explores the directionality of wealth flows and considers how they may shift with changes in economic development. The third section addresses measurement issues involved in the collection of data on intergenerational transfers, examining the complexities of kin networks and suggesting which data should optimally be collected. The chapter then examines efforts to model and project family dynamics, including changes in such variables as kin availability, living arrangements, and changing family structures, factors that will assume increasing importance for policy making as societies age. Both micro- and macro-simulation procedures may be useful tools in gauging future policy needs.

Next we review research gaps in the area of family transfers, focusing in particular on the benefits and shortcomings of the macro and micro perspectives. Finally, we offer recommendations regarding new data and studies that might permit a synthesis of these two perspectives.

POLICY CONSIDERATIONS

The well-being of older persons depends to a large extent on the content and volume of an intricate set of transfer systems in which people are engaged during their lifetimes. Interactions between public and family transfer systems define many of the important policy issues for aging populations. Yet, as noted earlier, specifying how transfers from one system affect the flow of resources from the other is not straightforward. Along these lines, a number of important policy questions arise.

   1. *Do state-financed programs for the elderly drive out or reduce private/ family efforts?* If so, at what price to the family or the state? Alternatively, do state transfers magnify the effects of family transfers?

   2. *To what extent does the potential for bequests create incentives for transfers from adult children to elderly parents?* In countries with significant disincentives for bequests (e.g., hefty inheritance taxes), are adult child-to-parent transfers of space and time of the same magnitude, prevalence, and duration as in countries where bequests have the potential to repay late-life care and assistance transfers from children? Related to this is the question of whether parental wealth (ownership of land, property, savings) or prior investments in offspring "buy" family support in old age. Does parental wealth create comparable transfer incentives across cultures? To what extent are incentives for children to repay their parents for human capital investment sensitive to tax policies and to state-provided service systems?

   3. *Absent housing constraints, do older persons and their adult children universally buy more household privacy and autonomy as wealth increases?* (See Schoeni, 1998.) Does the state implicitly subsidize this preference by producing more in-home services for older persons or bearing the costs of a decaying housing stock?

   4. *What are the full costs of caregiving to the caregiver and to the state?* Providing services to elderly parents entails costs, both real and opportunity. These costs are usually estimated very crudely at a point in time with average market wages or replacement costs for a given service. But caregiving also may have longer-term costs that differ across countries. Depending on family leave, job protection, and pension policies, work interruptions for caregiving may not only reduce current wages, but also curtail lifetime earnings and reduce individual savings and accrual rates

in pension systems. Does the state eventually absorb the costs of family caregiving through later-life income replacement programs or public services? Alternatively, are the costs of caregiving offset by transfers from other kin to the caregiver (e.g., financial transfers from siblings) or, as Stark (1995) suggests, do caregivers as they age have stronger claims on services from their own children because of "patterning"?

5. *Are preferences for investing in the human capital of offspring so strong as to thwart policy initiatives to encourage greater savings in midlife or consumption of resources to buy care or financial security in late life?* For example, will the modest university fees now being levied in the United Kingdom appreciably reduce savings for old age? To what extent are preferences for human capital investment at the expense of individual consumption or savings culturally determined or responsive to policy? Assuming a constant rate of increase in life expectancy at age 60 or 80 and a continuation of current behavioral parameters, at what age would resource flows from young to old dominate under stylized versions of alternative transfer policies in developed countries?

6. *How do policies that affect early-life demographic decisions in turn affect late-life behaviors?* Demographic regimes and cohort histories imprint on family structure for subsequent decades and are a significant source of variation across countries (Henretta et al., 1997). For individuals, early-life choices ultimately constrain transfer options in later life. Beyond simple structural effects (e.g., childless women have a zero probability of living with offspring, while higher fertility increases the odds of coresidence), the effects of timing factors, such as age at marriage and at first and last birth, may operate through coincident life-cycle staging across generations of a family. Age of offspring at parental retirement, at death of first parent, or at own childbearing may encourage or discourage transfers to elderly parents and affect the magnitude of the transfer. Comparative research on the endogeneity of early-life demographic decisions (e.g., quality of the marriage pool, timing of fertility, childlessness) with late-life transfer outcomes should reveal variations in a range of policy variables within and across countries. A richer understanding of these issues requires a complex research agenda that incorporates distinctions among transfer currencies, providers and provider motivations, and the complete option set for both public and private transfers.

INTERGENERATIONAL TRANSFERS, ECONOMIC WELFARE, AND TRANSFER INSTITUTIONS

Policy makers have an array of options for broadening the resource base that supports older nonworkers. Among these are creating incentives that encourage individuals to transfer more of their own resources from mid- to late life through private savings, increasing the length of work life by penalizing early retirement, and encouraging transfers of financial assistance or help across generations of the family. Each of these options conveys costs and benefits for the elderly individual, his/her family, and the society.

Over the past two decades, economic demographers have developed simple and elegant methods for displaying the societal implications of alternative policy responses to an aging population. The key data inputs for such models are age-specific per capita or per household measures of aggregate consumption, earnings, transfers between and within families, tax payments, and public transfer receipts. These age-specific measures, summed across individuals of each age or households headed by persons of each age, yield familiar aggregate measures of consumption, labor income, and so on that appear in conventional national income accounts. The aggregate age-specific measures are derived from a variety of underlying sources, including survey data on consumer expenditures, labor earnings or intrafamily transfers, and administrative records of tax payments and beneficiary payments. (See, for example, Lee, 1994a, for a description of data sources used to construct such measures for the United States.) The main requirement is that the underlying data sources have information on age and household structure along with the relevant economic measures.

The intellectual origins of this line of research can be traced to a seminal paper by Samuelson (1958) that introduced the so-called "overlapping generations" model. This model uses a highly stylized demographic structure in which people live for two periods as "young" workers and "old" retirees. In any given period, the population is made up of the overlap of surviving members of the generation born during the last period, who are now old, and those born in the current period, who are now young. Arthur and McNicoll (1978) incorporated more realistic demography into this model by assuming that both time and age are measured as continuous variables, that the individual life span is finite and subject to age-specific mortality risks, and that new generations arrive over time as a continuous flow of births according to a given age-specific fertility schedule. In addition, they introduced savings and physical capital into the model, along with the assumption that the level of aggregate output depends on the aggregate quantity of labor and capital. More recently, Willis (1988) extended the model of Arthur and McNicoll to consider the role of intergenerational transfers through the family, state, and market in an age-structured model, and showed how various transfer policies may influence the national savings rate and the equilibrium rate of interest. In a series of papers, Lee and colleagues (Lee and Lapkoff, 1988; Lee, 1994b; National Research Council, 1997; Lee, 2000) have implemented this model empirically, and in conceptually related work, Auerbach et al. (1991) have developed a "generational accounting" model to assess public-sector intergenerational transfers.

Arthur and McNicoll (1978) address the question of whether a small increase in the rate of population growth raises or lowers per capita lifetime consumption in steady state.[2] We reverse their focus by asking about the economic effects of a decrease in the rate of population growth. This question is at the very core of the debate over the economic consequences of population aging and the efficacy of alternative policy responses. Standard neoclassical economic growth models of the type described by Solow (1956) and Diamond (1965) imply that low rates of population growth will always increase feasible consumption because of "capital deepening." That is, as the rate of population growth decreases, smaller shares of output need to be diverted away from consumption and toward investment to maintain a fixed amount of capital per worker. This beneficial effect of lower population growth was stressed by Coale and Hoover (1958) and many others in connection with discussions of policies aimed at reducing fertility in developing countries that were experiencing rapid population growth after World War II.

In a model that ignores the effects of age structure, lower rates of population growth always tend to raise per capita consumption because of the capital-deepening effect. This conclusion may not hold in an age-structured model because of an intergenerational transfer effect. Changes in the rate of population growth will produce such an effect whenever there are net aggregate transfers taking place between members of different age groups. These transfers may be in either direction, from young to old or from old to young, and they may occur in the institutional context of the family, state, or market. For example, transfers through the family may take the form of parental expenditures on children or old-age support provided by children for their parents; transfers through the public sector may involve tax-supported public education or pay-as-you-go social security programs; and implicit intergenerational transfers may take place through credit markets if lenders, on average, are either older or younger than borrowers.

Changes in the rate of population growth produce an intergenerational transfer effect because they induce a change in the age structure and, hence, alter the relative numbers of people who give or receive trans-

---

[2]The models discussed in this section employ a "comparative steady state" approach in which the long-run demographic and economic structure of a society whose population is growing at, say, 1 percent per year is compared with that of a society whose population is decreasing at a rate of 1 percent per year. Later, we briefly discuss some important questions associated with a transition in population growth from a higher to a lower level.

fers. On the one hand, a decrease in the rate of population growth increases the fraction of elderly in the population and therefore increases per capita lifetime consumption opportunities for members of each generation if the old tend to make net transfers to the young. For example, if parents transfer a given amount of resources to each child and there are fewer children because of a reduction in fertility, the resources available for consumption by adults will increase without reducing the amount consumed by each child. On the other hand, a decrease in population growth will reduce per capita lifetime consumption if net transfers are from the younger to the older generation.

It is important to distinguish between the effects of population aging on the potential economic welfare of the society as a whole and on particular programs within the public sector. For example, the fertility decline that is leading to population aging in the United States and other Western countries may have the long-run effect of increasing potential per capita lifetime consumption if the direction of net intergenerational transfers is from the older to the younger generation. In this case, the intergenerational transfer effect reinforces the capital-deepening effect. However, the effect of population aging is likely to cause increasing problems for public-sector transfer systems. In countries that finance old-age security through pay-as-you-go public pension schemes in which the direction of intergenerational transfers is from the younger to the older generation, it has become acutely obvious to policy makers that population aging may make it impossible to maintain such programs without increasing payroll taxes or reducing retirement benefits.

In the next section, we present some empirical findings to illustrate the direction and magnitude of transfer systems in countries at different levels of economic development and in various subsystems of transfers that operate through the family and the public sector.

The Direction of Intergenerational Transfers and Economic Development

Much of the demographic literature would lead policy makers to expect major shifts in the patterns of assistance among generations of kin as economic development progresses. Of particular note is Caldwell's (1976) theory that the direction of wealth flows reverses in the course of economic development. He argues that there are two types of societies: pre-transitional societies in which transfers from young to old are motivated by high fertility, and post-transitional societies characterized by levels of low fertility and net transfers from parents to children. This theory has been called into question on both theoretical and empirical grounds, most explicitly by Kaplan (1994:755) who argues:

In contrast to wealth-flows theory, models of fertility and parental investment derived from evolutionary biology expect that the net flow of resources will *always* be from parents to offspring, even when fertility is high. The logic underlying this expectation is that natural selection will have produced a preponderance of organisms that are designed to extract resources from the environment and convert those resources into descendants carrying replicas of their genetic material.

Careful empirical measures of age-specific consumption and production among primitive hunter-gatherers produced by Kaplan and other anthropologists indicate that individuals tend to produce more than they consume at every age. The implication is that net transfers are downward, from older to younger generations.

Empirical measures of net transfers in peasant societies are summarized in Figure 5-1 for several different societies, ranging from the hunter-gatherer tribes studied by Kaplan, to urban and rural areas of Cote d'Ivoire studied by Stecklov (1997), to measures for the United States calculated by Lee (1994a). The lower panel of the figure measures $A_c - A_y$, the difference between the mean age of consuming and the mean age of producing over the individual life cycle, using a clever geometric device of Lee's (1994a) invention. The tail of each arrow is located at the average age of production (A_y), and the head is located at the average age of consumption in the population (A_c). The length of the arrow is the number of years traversed by the average transfer. This distance measures the magnitude of the intergenerational transfer received or given as a proportion of the present value of lifetime income for a representative person in the society.[3] An arrow that points to the left indicates that the direction of net transfers is downward, from the older to the younger generation; an arrow that points to the right indicates an upward net transfer from the younger to the older generation. The vertical position of the arrows orders the society by the magnitude of the downward transfer.

The arrows in the lower panel of Figure 5-1 tell a clear and remarkable story. In all of the societies depicted except for the United States, net transfers are downward, as predicted by evolutionary theory, rather than upward, as predicted by Caldwell's wealth flows theory. Moreover, the magnitude of the transfers, as measured by the length of the arrows, is largest for the most primitive group, of intermediate length for the developing country, and small and of opposite sign for the most advanced country. Recall that the sign of ($A_c - A_y$) indicates the effect of higher population growth on the feasible level of per capita lifetime consumption, ignoring capital-dilution effects. The left-pointing arrows indicate

---

[3]This model assumes that the society is in a steady-state golden rule equilibrium with a constant rate of population growth equal to the rate of interest.

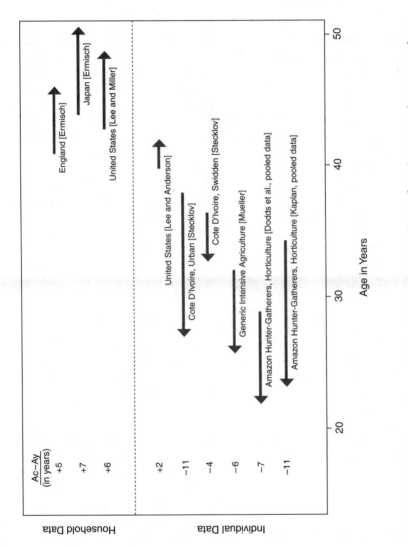

FIGURE 5-1 Direction and magnitude of intergenerational transfers: A cross-society comparison. SOURCE: Lee (2000). Reprinted with permission.

that a reduction in the rate of population growth would have a quite beneficial effect on per capita lifetime consumption for the hunter-gatherers and a smaller but distinctly beneficial effect in Cote d'Ivoire. The reason for this is that individuals within these two societies consume more than they produce at the beginning of life, but once they reach adulthood, they produce more than they consume until they die. Thus adults in these societies make investments in the next generation that are never repaid. In contrast, $(A_c - A_y)$ in the United States is positive, indicating that an increase in fertility would generate a positive intergenerational transfer effect that would be partially offset by a negative capital-dilution effect associated with the additional investment needed to equip more workers with a given amount of capital.

The direction of intergenerational transfers in the United States and other advanced countries differs from that in less developed countries and primitive societies for two main reasons. First, in the advanced countries, the elderly as well as children consume more than they produce, and they do so primarily as a consequence of reduced labor income. In short, unlike low-income societies, high-income societies provide for retirement transfers to fill the significant income gap that exists between the end of working life and death. Second, high-income societies are all experiencing very low rates of population growth and low mortality, so that the proportion of dependent young in these societies is far smaller than in high-fertility societies, while the proportion of dependent aged is much higher. These two factors tend to offset the fact that high levels of human capital investment in education and on-the-job training in the advanced countries result in a shift of individual productivity to later ages.[4]

Intergenerational Transfers in Developed Countries

The mechanisms by which intergenerational transfers take place through social, political, or economic institutions may be examined using modifications of the basic Arthur and McNicoll (1978) model as implemented empirically by Lee (1994a). By shifting the unit of analysis from the individual to the household, Lee explicitly introduces the family into the model. The arrows in the top panel of Figure 5-1 are based on household rather than individual measures of age-specific consumption and production for three advanced countries—England, Japan, and the United

---

[4]It should be noted, however, that Kaplan (1994) finds that male age-productivity profiles are positively sloped for a considerable period of time, reflecting, he argues, a considerable amount of learning required to become an efficient hunter. Thus, investment in human capital may be important even in very primitive societies.

States. In this panel, age refers to the age of the household head, and consumption and earnings are measured at the household level. Conceptually, the change in the unit of analysis from the individual to the household means that the measure of intergenerational transfers given by (A_c – A_y) accounts for only those transfers that take place *between* households. Age-differentiated transfers that take place *within* households in the advanced countries reflect primarily parents' private expenditures on their children, a downward transfer.[5] Within-household transfers also include the financial and time costs of assisting coresidential parents. These costs, which are upward transfers, are not included in the estimates shown in Figure 5-1, but are assumed to be relatively small when averaged over the entire population. Consequently, the magnitude of the between-family measure of (A_c – A_y) for the United States in the top panel of Figure 5-1 is even more positive than the corresponding measure of (A_c – A_y), at the individual level in the lower panel.

The difference in the direction of familial and public transfers for the United States in the 1980s is illustrated vividly in Figures 5-2 and 5-3, respectively. In addition to length and direction as in Figure 5-1, the arrows in these two figures vary in width, indicating the annual flow of resources associated with a given transfer, while the area of the arrow (length times width) indicates the total intergenerational transfer per household.

All components of familial transfers shown in Figure 5-2 are downward. Panel A measures interhousehold transfers due to bequests and inter vivos gifts. Bequests are given by household heads who average age 77 at death and are received by households headed by persons 52 years of age, a difference of 25 years. These transfers amount to a flow of $1,750 per year, and the total bequest transfer per household is $43,750 = (77 – 52)1750. Inter vivos gifts are much smaller, averaging $370 per year; are given and received at younger ages, 53 and 38, respectively; and total $5,550. Within-household transfers, measuring private childrearing and higher education costs per child, are shown in Panel B of Figure 5-2. Child costs are paid by parents who average 39 years of age to children who average 11 years of age. The flow value of child costs is $2,820 per year per child, and the total transfer is $78,960 per child. Transfers to pay the costs of higher education are from parents averaging 48 years of age to children averaging 20 years of age. They have a flow value of $215, and the total transfer is $6,020 per child.

---

[5]Within-household transfers also include the financial and time costs of assisting coresidential parents. These costs, which are upward transfers, are not included in the estimates shown in Figure 5-1, but are assumed to be relatively small when averaged over the entire population.

A. Interhousehold Transfers

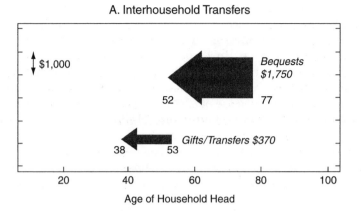

Age of Household Head

B. Within-household Transfers (per child)

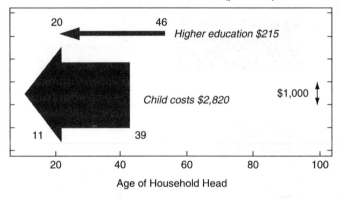

Age of Household Head

FIGURE 5-2 Familial transfers in the United States (data from the 1980s).
NOTE: The top panel describes flows of transfers between households; the bottom panel describes flows of transfers within households. The tail of each arrow is located at the average age of making each kind of transfer in the population, and the head of the arrow is located at the average age of receiving each kind of transfer in the population. The thickness of each arrow represent the per capita (or per household) flow of each kind of transfer, indicated by the number below each label. The area of each arrow equals the average net transfer of each kind expected to be received by the average person or household over the remaining lifetime, and is negative if the arrow points to the left.
SOURCE: Lee (1994b). Reprinted with permission.

In contrast with private familial transfers, the public transfers shown in Figure 5-3 are predominantly upward from younger to older generations. The largest public transfers in the United States are associated with the social security system. In Figure 5-3, workers who pay the social security payroll tax are in households whose head averages 41.2 years of age, while beneficiaries are in households in which the head averages 71.7 years of age. With a flow value of $2,270 per year, the total lifetime social security transfer is $69,235 per household. Health care costs are the other major source of public-sector intergenerational transfers. These transfers are received by households whose heads average 61.6 years of age and are funded by taxes paid by households whose heads average 42.8 years of age. The flow value of health costs is $1,862, and the transfer totals

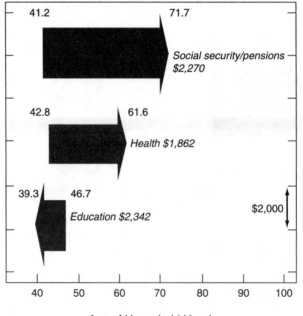

Age of Household Head

FIGURE 5-3 Public-sector transfers to and from households in the United States (data from the 1980s).
NOTE: See note to Figure 5-2. The tail of the arrow is located at the average age of paying taxes in support of each kind of transfer, and the head at the average age of receiving each kind of transfer, in each case based on the age of the household reference person. Data combine federal, state, and local transfers.
SOURCE: Lee (1994b). Reprinted with permission.

$35,005, about half the size of the social security transfer. Education is the only major public-sector transfer in a downward direction. While the flow value of $2,342 per year is comparable to the flow value of the social security transfer, the magnitude of the total intergenerational transfer, $17,330 per household, is much smaller because there is only a 7.4 year difference in the average age of household heads who pay education taxes (46.7 years of age) and heads whose households receive public education. On balance, net public-sector intergenerational transfers from the younger to the older generation in the United States outweigh private household transfers from the older to the younger generation, as shown by the right-pointing arrows for the United States in Figure 5-1.

Implications

The preceding discussion has several important implications for the direction and magnitude of net intergenerational transfers and the institutional mechanisms through which they flow. The net supply of saving from the household sector, measured at the point at which the rate of interest is equal to the rate of growth, is equal to the net intergenerational transfer through familial, public, and market mechanisms (Willis, 1988). Any transfer in an upward direction, such as the social security and health transfers depicted in Figure 5-3, reduces the net savings of the household sector, while any transfer in a downward direction, such as family expenditures on childrearing and higher education shown in Figure 5-2 or public expenditures on education shown in Figure 5-3, increase the supply of savings. Thus, the willingness of the older generation to finance investment in the human capital of their children, either privately as parents or publicly as taxpayers, also enhances the society's accumulation of physical capital by increasing the supply of savings and reducing the equilibrium rate of interest. On the other hand, Feldstein (1974) argues that programs such as social security and Medicare that generate upward transfers through the public sector tend to reduce the supply of savings, raise the rate of interest, and reduce the accumulation of physical capital in a society.

Interesting and important behavioral questions underlie the accounting relationships depicted in Figures 5-1 through 5-3. In particular, the ultimate impact of a change in a public transfer program depends on the motivations and behavior of individuals and families. For example, Feldstein's argument that pay-as-you-go social security programs reduce savings assumes that households follow a model in which savings serve to smooth consumption over the life cycle. A tax during working years followed by a benefit during retirement years reduces the variability of life-cycle income, thereby decreasing the need for savings. In the life-cycle model employed by Feldstein, individuals care only for their own consumption. Barro (1974) shows that Feldstein's conclusions may be reversed if parents are altruistic toward their children. To maintain a balance between their own utility and that of their children, altruistic parents offset public social security transfers from the younger generation by equal and opposite private transfers to their children, thus neutralizing the effect of social security on saving.[6] It has been difficult to determine the empirical effect of public transfers on national savings and the aggregate capital stock, largely because of a lack of comparable international data on savings behavior that could exploit cross-national variations in public policy to identify these effects.

Public transfers also create a potential divergence between the private and social costs of childbearing. As noted earlier, the sign of $A_c - A_y$, measured at the individual level, indicates whether higher population growth will raise or lower potential lifetime consumption. In the case of the United States, as discussed above, the arrow based on individual data in the bottom panel of Figure 5-1 indicates that a small increase in the birth rate would have a slightly positive effect on permanent per capita lifetime consumption. Under the usual assumptions of economic models of fertility, households have children up to the point at which the marginal cost of children of given quality is equal to the monetary value of the utility gain from an additional child.

The arrows in Figure 5-2 depicting familial transfers in a downward direction indicate the net private cost of children to parents, which, according to the theory, are balanced against the utility gains from children. While a reduction in fertility would increase the consumption of the adult household members, the loss of utility would be at least as great as the gain in utility from increased consumption. The arrows in Figure 5-3 show that public transfers are largely upward, from the younger to the older generation. This implies that an increase in the birth rate would allow workers to pay lower taxes per capita, holding per capita public transfers to the older generation constant. This social benefit, however, creates no private incentive to increase fertility. Thus, an extra birth by a given household will benefit others because of the social security taxes the child will pay as an adult. An insignificant fraction of this benefit, however, accrues to the biological parents, who make fertility decisions and bear the private costs of children. The estimated size of this external

---

[6]Kohli (1999), studying the redistribution of aggregate income in the former East Germany after reunification, argues that a portion of public transfers to the elderly is "channeled back" to younger kin. While potentially inefficient, Kohli argues that rerouted transfers have a greater welfare effect than that produced by direct public transfers to younger persons.

benefit to childbearing in the United States is about $200,000 per birth (National Research Council, 1997). This analysis suggests that many of the public policy issues associated with population aging are a consequence of providing goods, services, and income for the aged through unfunded public transfer mechanisms. These mechanisms may distort savings, but such distortions could be eliminated by shifting to funded pension and health insurance programs requiring increased real saving.

COLLECTION OF DATA ON INTERGENERATIONAL TRANSFERS

The preceding discussion underscores the fact that the nature and direction of intergenerational transfers may differ greatly from one social context to another. Each society develops a set of mechanisms, including formal and informal elements, that define the timing and content of support, the appropriate participants, and their mutual obligations. The depth and complexity of these systems allow for wide variation in the facets that are measured and in the research methods employed. For example, in economic terms alone, an older person no longer in the labor force may have income because of accumulated wealth and savings, income from a government or private pension, and/or income or material support from one or more children or other relatives. To capture these flows requires attention to several dimensions, among them the source of the income, the amount, and the nature of the provider (amount of assets, type of pension or social security arrangement, characteristics of the children). To complicate matters, it is also possible that the older person in question will be extending material support to others (e.g., to a parent or child), necessitating similar detail on the economic supports provided.

When this potentially complex matrix of exchanges and their characteristics is multiplied by other important types of support—the provision of physical assistance or assistance with household duties, emotional support and companionship—the limits of subtlety of survey questionnaires and reasonable interview length are quickly approached. It is probably not too much of an exaggeration to say that there are as many approaches to appraising intergenerational transfers as there are questionnaires, as each research team achieves a unique compromise among the constraints and challenges inherent in the situation.

The goal of this section is to enumerate the main dimensions of intergenerational transfers and to suggest several reasonable strategies for obtaining the salient information on each. We follow Soldo and Hill (1993) by defining intergenerational transfers as a generic term used to describe the redistribution of resources within an extended family structure, incorporating both inter- and intrahousehold exchanges. This focus on the family does not diminish, of course, the need to collect detailed information on the supports received from the community, the state, and friends and neighbors. Not only are these sources major providers of certain types of support in some countries (such as pension and social security income in industrialized nations), but the existence of these sources can also have an effect on the likelihood and amount of support forthcoming from family members (Schoeni, 1992).

Outlining an Intergenerational Support System

If we conceive of intergenerational transfers as a series of exchanges between an indexed elderly person or couple (i.e., the focal point of the investigation) and his and/or her family network, the major components of this exchange system include who is involved, what is exchanged (and sometimes where), the quantity of the items exchanged, and when the exchange takes place. In addition, one often wishes to know how important the exchange is to the recipient and how much of a burden it represents to the provider, as well as the motivations behind it. Though this listing is straightforward, operationalizing these dimensions can be complex and presents the analyst with a number of difficult options. The scheme shown in Box 5-1 portrays the components of a support system in more detail as a starting point for identifying their implications for survey questionnaires.

The top panel in Box 5-1 highlights the need to properly identify the focal elderly unit and the kin network with which exchanges are carried out, and shows the three major "currencies" of transfer—space, money, and time. The second panel lists the salient dimensions of each exchange, providing a partial checklist of attributes that might be measured for either individual transfers or classes of transfer. These include such basic characteristics as the parties to the exchange, the purpose of the transfer, and the magnitudes involved, as well as less obvious aspects, such as the form, timing, and impact of the transfer.

Mapping the Kin Network

The starting point in describing an intergenerational support system is defining the kin network of reference and measuring its characteristics. Though technically this stage may not involve actual exchanges, it is vital in several respects. Mapping the number, location, and characteristics of kin serves as the denominator against which the frequency and nature of exchanges can be gauged. Certain types of assistance (e.g., physical assistance) are difficult to provide at a distance, and it is important to distinguish those elderly who do not receive such types of assistance because of the lack of potential caregivers from those who do not receive that assis-

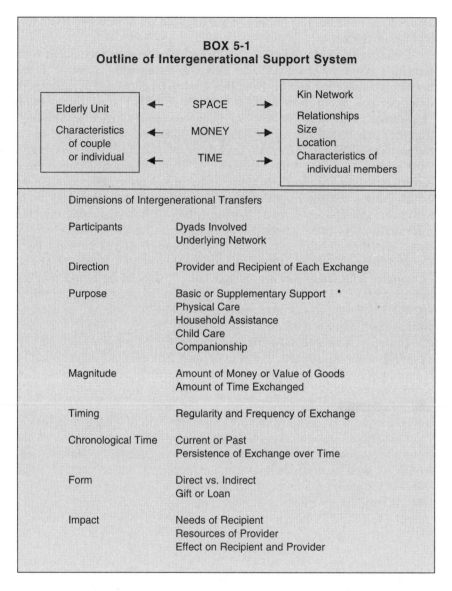

BOX 5-1
Outline of Intergenerational Support System

Elderly Unit		Kin Network
Characteristics of couple or individual	← SPACE → ← MONEY → ← TIME →	Relationships Size Location Characteristics of individual members

Dimensions of Intergenerational Transfers

Participants	Dyads Involved Underlying Network
Direction	Provider and Recipient of Each Exchange
Purpose	Basic or Supplementary Support • Physical Care Household Assistance Child Care Companionship
Magnitude	Amount of Money or Value of Goods Amount of Time Exchanged
Timing	Regularity and Frequency of Exchange
Chronological Time	Current or Past Persistence of Exchange over Time
Form	Direct vs. Indirect Gift or Loan
Impact	Needs of Recipient Resources of Provider Effect on Recipient and Provider

tance for other reasons. In addition, knowledge of the kin network is essential for testing competing hypotheses about the motivations and social dynamics of exchanges, such as the differences in assistance provided by or received from sons and daughters (Lee et al., 1994). From a practical standpoint, identifying the kin network in detail often makes it easier to record the exchanges that take place with specific members and serves to remind the respondent of the relevant set of possible providers and beneficiaries.

Defining the kin network is not straightforward, as the salient relationships may vary across societies and over time within societies. It has been noted that data on kin structures tend to be anchored in samples of older persons rather than younger individuals. That is, we often obtain "top-down" instead of "bottom-up" views of family structure, although the latter may be equally useful (Hagestad, 2000). Another key decision is the amount of detail to collect about each member and whether this should vary with the nature of the relationship. Current practice ranges from recording summary numbers, perhaps by broad geographic location, to establishing a detailed matrix that enumerates each member and his or her characteristics separately.[7] We argue below that reasonably detailed information should be collected about parents and children of the respondent. Whether siblings and other kin should be treated in the same fashion will depend on the culture and on the degree to which contact and exchanges with these kin are customary. It should be noted that for elderly respondents who are currently married and coresiding with their spouse, information will often be needed about key relatives of each, as well as about children that may not be jointly theirs.

A major decision is how to treat members within the household versus those residing outside. We recommend that detailed information be collected about each household member, regardless of his or her relation to the elderly respondent. Since there can be more than one married child and set of grandchildren coresiding, as is often the case in some developing countries, it is useful to distinguish the parent of each grandchild in the household. And since elderly parents may be coresiding with the indexed respondent, one will usually wish to ascertain the state of their health, as well as other characteristics common to all household members—information that is particularly useful in assessing ongoing or potential caregiving burdens. Another important concern is how long each member has lived in the current household, which together with information about the elderly respondent's own moves, can reveal whether the

---

[7]A variety of grid-like survey instruments have proven useful in recording the multiplicity of potential exchanges (see, e.g., Hermalin, 2000). Where feasible, computer-assisted interviewing, either in person or by telephone, opens up many possibilities for keeping track of various classes of individuals. For example, a grid of coresident and noncoresident family members can be called up whenever questions on exchanges arise, and the pertinent information recorded. With paper questionnaires, considerable ingenuity must be employed to ensure that the interviewer has all of the relevant information on hand at each stage.

respondent joined an existing household or when others joined a household established by the respondent. Similarly, discussion of household dynamics can lead to questions about who is the head of the household (in economic as well as nominal terms) and about ownership of the home and land, all central to an understanding of the nature of transfers involving space.

Moving beyond the household multiplies the number of decisions concerning the kin to include and the information to collect. Experience from Asian surveys (see Ofstedal et al., 1999) suggests a detailed strategy for the closest kin, with more summary measures reserved for distant relations. Two data considerations are particularly critical: the geographical location of each of the children and any surviving parents, and the relevant characteristics of these network members. For children, one wishes to know not only their basic sociodemographic characteristics, but also information about the stage of family building (e.g., number of children and age of oldest child) and occupation of the spouse. In terms of geography, it may be desirable to obtain even more detail, such as the distance or time to reach each child (or vice versa) and the usual means of transportation. And in some countries, information on family members living outside the country can be valuable in light of important remittances often made by overseas contract workers to family households.

Information on the spatial network of children forms the backdrop for understanding the frequency of contact between the elderly respondent and his or her noncoresident children. The frequency and nature of contacts reflect in part the intergenerational exchange of time, another important currency in measuring transfers. As before, the amount of detail will vary with the particular situation. It may be most useful to measure the frequency of personal visits (ranging from "every day" to "have not seen for a long time") and the frequency of contacts by phone and letter. In other instances, one may also want to distinguish whether the visit takes place in the home of the elderly person(s) or that of the child (i.e., who visits whom).

In addition to this range of information about noncoresident children, the health, location, and frequency of contact should be obtained for noncoresident parents of the indexed respondent (and spouse). This information can be collected as a subset of the questions asked of noncoresident children or as part of a separate inquiry about parents, including important information about deceased parents (such as age at death, cause of death, and where living when died).

For other relatives beyond children and parents, it is often necessary in the interest of time to obtain summary information, which can still provide insights into the size and strength of the kin network. During development of the 1989 Taiwan Survey of Health and Living Status of the Elderly, for example, it was expected that siblings might be a strong source of support (Hermalin et al., 1996). Consequently, the location of and contact with siblings were mapped in some detail but still in a summary fashion, while information about other relations was curtailed even further. In the U.S. Health and Retirement Survey (HRS), by contrast, detailed information was obtained about four siblings of the respondents with at least one living biological parent, a sample selection table being employed when there were five or more siblings (Soldo and Hill, 1995).

In addition to mapping the kin network, attention should be given to carefully defining the elderly unit in question. If the elderly respondent is single, widowed, or divorced, little confusion is likely to arise in tracing the exchanges between the respondent and his or her network. When the respondent is currently married, however, care must be exercised as to whether the questions are intended to cover the couple or the particular respondent. Although visits and transfers of money or goods are likely to be for the benefit of the couple, this will not always be the case. If the intent is to measure exchanges in which the couple is involved, this should be made clear from the structure of the questionnaire. In practice, one will usually seek a mix of respondent and couple responses. In asking about the receipt of physical assistance or assistance with household duties or about specific forms of companionship or emotional support, the focus is almost always on the respondent. But questions about financial support or more general patterns of visiting are often formulated with the couple in mind. Similar caution is needed in tracing what the elderly unit does for others. Should the focus be on what the couple does or what the particular respondent does in terms of financial assistance, taking care of grandchildren, assisting children, and so on?

Measuring and Recording Exchanges

In the previous section we indicated how information on the transfer of space through living arrangements can be gathered in the course of obtaining details about household structure. Here the emphasis is on exchanges of money (or its equivalent) and time. Broadly speaking, there are two strategies for obtaining this information: one is person-centered and involves asking whether exchanges of certain types have occurred with named individuals or classes of individuals; the other is exchange-centered and involves asking whether exchanges of specific types occurred, and if so, obtaining the names or classes of the individuals involved (assistance from governmental and nongovernmental organizations can be ascertained separately). Few survey instruments are entirely of one type or another, so both strategies are likely to be found in the same protocol. Another decision in survey design is whether to concentrate the exchange questions in one section or to decentralize them by topic—pursuing, for example, questions on physical assistance in a section on health and questions on financial assistance in a section on income. Again, these strategies are often mixed, with some exchanges being grouped and others dispersed.

A person-centered structure in a survey of elderly individuals requires inquiry about exchanges with each coresident and noncoresident child, even if no such exchanges have taken place. This approach therefore reduces the chance that a given exchange will be overlooked and provides a convenient way of recording the information and connecting it to the characteristics of the children. On the negative side, insofar as there are relatively few exchanges of a given type, it can be time-consuming and tedious to go through a long list of possible participants (e.g., parents, parents-in-law, grandchildren as a class, siblings as a class, and all other relations).

With the exchange-centered approach, the respondent is not probed about each possible provider, but since these questions come after the kin network details, the range of potential providers should be well in mind. Focusing on the exchange puts more pressure on ensuring that the persons named as giving and receiving assistance are recorded properly, so that the nature of the transfer can be aligned with their personal characteristics.

Any survey instrument that seeks to quantify transfers needs to establish a respondent's need for different types of assistance and the sufficiency of the assistance received. Measuring need is a critical aspect of understanding intergenerational transfers since we expect the existence of need and its extent to be a prime determinant of the provision of support. There are different strategies for establishing need, and the approach used can vary with the type of support involved. One tactic is to assume that those receiving assistance have a need, and hence to focus on identifying the suppliers and the sufficiency of the assistance received. This is not necessarily the best strategy, but its use is prompted by concern that a direct question on whether a respondent has certain needs could be met with denial, foreclosing the possibility of obtaining information about associated transfers.

Understanding the transfer of money or its equivalent has a number of dimensions in addition to ascertaining recent exchanges. Special gifts or loans that occurred in the past to help a child or other relative pay educational expenses, open a business, travel, or meet special needs (such as medical expenses) can be important for understanding current patterns of exchange. They enter into the testing of various hypotheses about

motivations for transfer, including reciprocity vs. altruism and investment in human capital for old-age support, that are associated with several economic theories (Lillard and Willis, 1997).

Exchanges of money or time within the household often pose more
measurement challenges than interhousehold exchanges because the
former exchanges can occur in a number of ways. For example, rather
than providing money, those living with the elderly respondent may pay
the major expenses of the household (also possible, of course, to some
degree for those living at a distance). To capture these variations, it is
desirable to direct some questions to household financial arrangements.
This involves, for example, identifying each household member with income, measuring total household income, determining how household
expenses are met (e.g., through pooling of income versus specific member
contributions), identifying non-household members who cover expenses,
and assessing the adequacy of income for respondent and spouse in relation to household expenses. Such questions complement the more standard ones on sources of income for respondent and spouse and the importance of each source. And, as highlighted in Chapter 4, attention
should also be paid to joint ownership of assets and transfers of assets to
children and others, particularly in cultures where some division of property often takes place upon retirement or well in advance of death.

Transfers of time often are considered from the perspective of the
elderly as recipient, for example, assistance that the respondent might
receive with various activities of daily living. Yet it is also important to
account for time an elderly respondent gives to others for a wide variety
of purposes. Increasingly, older parents provide child care for their grandchildren to assist working couples, and they often provide companionship as well as care to their own elderly parents. Understanding still
another aspect of time transfers involves identifying the nature of emotional support and companionship received by the respondent (such as
satisfaction with the willingness of family members to listen to worries
and problems, accompaniment in outside-the-home activities, the degree
to which respondents feel loved and cared for, and the degree to which
family members can be counted on for care during illness) and identifying the specific persons most likely to provide each type of support.

As with money, transfers of time for household-related activities
sometimes require special attention. For example, it is not always easy to
distinguish assistance an older person receives with household chores
because of a physical or cognitive limitation from assistance provided as a
result of customary divisions of labor. Likewise, to get a sense of the
assistance an elderly respondent provides to others through household
activities versus assistance received, it is useful to obtain a picture of the
division of labor for major household tasks. A further consideration is

assessment of the caregiver burden, in terms of time and resources expended, on those providing assistance for others. This information is difficult to capture unless the caregivers are interviewed as well.

Summary of Key Measurement Issues

The intent of the above discussion is not to propose a model questionnaire, but to suggest reasonable strategies for obtaining the salient information about intergenerational transfers within the confines of a survey. As more attention is focused in this area, it is likely that consensus will emerge as to the most efficient means of pursuing the critical variables. A summary of the key strategies is as follows:

- Map the relevant kin network both spatially and in terms of sufficient characteristics of each member.
- Identify the specific individuals within the kin network who are providing each type of support (including elderly providers), and record the information so that these individuals can be linked with their characteristics.
- If an elderly respondent is currently married, make clear whether the supports received or provided apply to the individual or to the couple.
- For supports that are likely to involve a number of network members, identify the main provider by measuring the quantity of support from each or having the elderly recipient identify the key provider.
- For transfers of money, identify large transfers over the lifetime in addition to current exchanges.
- Pay special attention to intrahousehold transfers of money and time (in terms of household duties) since these exchanges can take a number of forms.
- Do not overlook the assistance received and provided in the form of emotional support and companionship.
- For the major dimensions of support an elderly respondent may receive, try to ascertain the need for and sufficiency of that support.

Having touched on the topics in Box 5-1 in the context of a household survey, we should stress that several important dimensions of intergenerational relations go beyond the confines of single cross-sectional surveys. One of these, the persistence of transfers and patterns of exchange, requires panel designs to trace whether given forms of assistance continue over time and, in particular, whether the specific exchange partners remain the same or vary as an older person ages. With life expectancy increasing throughout the world, there will likely be a series of transitions in the level and manner of the support provided, most obvious perhaps in terms of living arrangements. Hence, methods of measuring these transitions and the duration of various types of exchanges will become of increasing importance. Another dimension that requires alternative data collection strategies is that of understanding the direct and indirect trade-offs that occur among those providing support. If one child supports a parent with activities of daily living, for example, is that child in turn receiving any financial or other form of assistance from his or her siblings? Understanding such trade-offs and how these decisions evolve requires going beyond interviews with elderly recipients by fully involving members of the network in appropriate data collection efforts.

Although it would be desirable to develop and use comparable survey instruments in many countries, national needs and differing study goals will likely contribute to variation in the near future. At this point it may be more important for analysts to reach agreement on topics and goals and allow some variation in methods. Surveys that capture a reasonable proportion of the complexities inherent in intergenerational transfers should greatly increase the value of the analysis within each country, and soon enhance the potential of comparative research across countries and cultures.

ASSESSING FAMILY DYNAMICS AND THEIR IMPLICATIONS FOR FUTURE TRANSFER PATTERNS

Understanding and mapping the complexities of kin networks and transfer patterns is an important step in policy development. Determining how best to use such information to project future trends is the new policy frontier in many countries. The aging of populations worldwide goes hand in hand with changes in family household structure (see Wolf, 1994b, for a review). A fairly substantial (though by no means complete) literature exists with regard to the living arrangements of older persons and will not be reviewed here. (See, for example, Kendig et al., 1992; Blieszner and Bedford, 1996; Palloni, 2000; and the bibliographies therein.) Suffice it to say that living arrangements tell only part of the story of elderly well-being. Indeed, much past work has focused on the *form* of living arrangements while ignoring the *function* (Hermalin, 1997). That is, coresidence of an elderly individual with a child and/or grandchildren may or may not be a positive experience for any of the parties involved. Objective measures of living arrangements should not be used to hypothesize about subjective measures of well-being or the quality of relationships among coresident family members. This is why it is crucial to understand the nature of transfer mechanisms that operate within households, among families, and in broader community and social contexts.

In industrialized countries with well-developed state support mechanisms, elderly persons depend upon spouses and children for emotional and psychological support and occasionally for financial aid as well. In the developing world, where pension and formal social security systems are not widely available, the elderly depend almost exclusively on family support. Past research has established that family care is an integral part of long-term care throughout the world and has a substantial impact on caregiving arrangements for the elderly (Angel et al., 1992; Kendig et al., 1992; Wiener and Hanley, 1992; Soldo and Freedman, 1994). While these basic patterns are unlikely to disappear, they will be altered by a host of factors ranging from secular trends in fertility and marital status, to changing economic and health status, to strong normative shifts relative to traditional familial obligations and the value of independent living.

In the United States and many other developed nations, cohorts who will become the elderly of the 21st century were on the leading edge of the "family revolution," characterized by large increases in the prevalence of divorce and out-of-wedlock childbearing and an overall decline in marriage and remarriage. The future elderly are less likely than their current counterparts to be married (Goldscheider, 1990). Clearly, planning for aging societies needs to take into account how ongoing demographic changes will alter the nature of families and households and affect intergenerational transfers (Zeng, 1988). How many elderly persons likely will live alone, with a spouse only, or with children or other relatives or be institutionalized in the future (Grundy, in press)? To what extent will people have to care for both parents and young children? What are the implications of these changes for caregiving needs and the health service system (Freedman, 1996)? Long-term care costs in the United States, for example, have doubled during each decade since 1970, reaching an annual level of $106.5 billion in 1995. Home health care costs grew 91 percent from 1990 to 1995, in contrast with 33 percent for institutional care costs (Stallard, 1998). Thus the mix of home-based and institutional care has been shifting rapidly toward home health care, especially for the oldest old (Cutler and Meara, 1999). Changes in family structure strongly affect caregiving needs, the long-term care service system, and health-related policy making (Himes, 1992).

Research on methodology for household and family projection addresses such questions as the above. Projection models may be grouped into three categories: those based on characteristics of household heads (headship rates); those based on household structure and living arrangements as gleaned from census or large-scale survey data (macrosimulation); and those based on kin networks, marital status transitions, and other variables often derived from in-depth survey data (microsimulation). As described below, each approach has its benefits and drawbacks.

In the global context, projecting numbers of households and their family characteristics is most frequently done on the basis of information about heads of household, as these represent the most common reference points in censuses and surveys. In many if not most countries, such data are the only available information from which to proceed and are useful in formulating at least a rough forecast of future numbers of households. However, methods based on projecting households according to the characteristics of the household head have several serious shortcomings. In surveys and censuses, the household head is often an arbitrary and vague choice (the concept of household head can vary from area to area within a country, and may change over time). A second major disadvantage is the unclear (or indirect) linkage of headship rates to underlying demographic events. This poses major problems for projection models, as it becomes difficult to incorporate demographic assumptions about future changes in fertility, marriage, cohabitation, union dissolution, and mortality (Murphy, 1991; Mason and Racelis, 1992; Burch and Skaburskis, 1993). Consequently, information produced by projections using the headship-rate method (typically with little or no information on specific household types) often is inadequate for planning purposes (Bell and Cooper, 1990). However, the most problematic feature of the headship-rate method is that it lumps all household members other than heads into an extremely heterogeneous group of "nonheads." This categorization obviates the study of family life courses and intergenerational transfers between children and other nonheads.

To address the need for more detailed and realistic information on family structure and behavioral patterns, the study of population aging is increasingly concerned with mapping and modeling kin availability. The development and refinement of microsimulation approaches to kinship modeling (e.g., the SOCSIM model [Wachter, 1987; Hammel et al., 1991]; the KINSIM model [Wolf, 1994b]; and the MOMSIM model [Ruggles, 1993]) have made important contributions to the study of kinship patterns and family support for elderly persons. Compared with the macrosimulation approach discussed below, microsimulation methodology offers three major advantages: it can consider a large set of life dimensions with many covariates simultaneously; it can easily and explicitly retain relationships among individuals; and it provides rich output, including probabilistic and stochastic outcome distributions. However, these advantages come at a cost. Three kinds of random variations in microsimulation have been discussed in detail in the literature (see, for example, Van Imhoff, 1999). One is due to the nature of Monte Carlo random experiments, wherein different runs produce different sets of outcomes.

Second, the starting (base) population in a micromodel is a sample from the total population, and thus is subject to classic sampling errors, especially for relatively small subgroups, such as persons of very advanced age. Third, microsimulation, which includes many explanatory variables and complex relationships among individuals, increases the stochastic fluctuations and measurement errors (specification randomness) to which the model outcomes are subject.

Keilman (1988), Van Imhoff and Keilman (1992), and Ledent (1992) review dynamic household models based on the macrosimulation approach, which has been used with some success in various nations (see, e.g., Keilman and Brunborg, 1995, for an application in Norway). Macrosimulation models do not have the problems of the inherent random variation of Monte Carlo experiments and sampling errors in the starting population. The specification randomness is present in a macromodel, but it is likely to be less serious than in a microsimulation model (Van Imhoff and Post, 1998). However, most macromodels (e.g., the LIPRO model, well known in Europe) require data on transition probabilities among various household types, data that are not available from conventional sources such as vital statistics, censuses, and ordinary surveys. Such stringent data demands are an important factor in the slow development and infrequent application of these models. Therefore, it is important to develop a dynamic household simulation/projection model that requires only conventional demographic data obtainable from vital statistics, censuses, and household surveys.

We now turn to several examples of the usefulness of simulation approaches. Several microsimulation studies have explored the implications of various schedules of unchanging demographic rates for kinship distributions; these include the LeBras (1973), Smith (1987), and Wolf (1988) studies of kinship and family support in 16 developed countries. In the latter study, three simulation variants were produced. The base scenario used fertility and mortality schedules prevailing in the 1970s as constants, while the other two incorporated substantial declines in mortality and fertility, respectively. Results indicated that continued demographic changes in developed countries would increase the proportion of elderly without living offspring. Among those elderly persons with living offspring, the average age of those offspring is approaching (or in some cases has reached) the elderly age threshold. The most important change, propelled by declining mortality rates, is a rise in the proportion of the population with a living mother.

The first detailed kinship forecasts to incorporate an observed pattern of changing demographic rates in microsimulation were produced in the early 1980s (Hammel et al., 1981). Reeves (1987) introduced divorce into the model and presented forecasts of kin for the U.S. population through the year 2020, quantifying the relative leverage of divorce, fertility, mortality, and marriage assumptions over various estimates. Using data from the U.S. National Survey of Families and Households and other resources, Wolf (1994a) simulated the lifetime pattern of coresidence with an aged parent and its sensitivity to demographic change. He suggested that the "coresidence expectancy" of an American adult and his or her elderly parent is quite small, but is fairly sensitive to certain types of demographic change, such as declining female mortality. Recently, Tomassini and Wolf (2000) conducted a study of the effect of persistent low fertility in Italy on shrinking kin networks for the period 1994-2050. Throughout the simulation period, some 15 to 20 percent of Italian women aged 25-45 are the only living offspring of their surviving mothers and thus are potentially fully responsible for their mothers' care. The majority of women have just one sibling with whom they could share parental care.

Wachter (1997, 1998) took another innovative step by simulating both biological kin and stepkin. Figure 5-4 shows the sharpness of the anticipated rise and fall in average numbers of biological children and the increasing numerical prominence of stepchildren among the U.S. white population aged 70 to 85 between 1980 and 2030. By 2030, the growth in numbers of stepchildren due to divorce and remarriage wholly compensates for the net decline in average biological children after 1980. Figure 5-5 shows the predicted patterns in average numbers of biological grandchildren and biological plus stepgrandchildren for the same population and age group as in Figure 5-4. It is clear that there is a multiplier effect from the proliferation of stepchildren over two generations, and by 2030, stepgrandchildren represent more than one-third on average of all grandchildren. Stepchildren and stepgrandchildren can therefore be expected to make a large contribution to the overall pool of younger relatives for the elderly of the future.

Benefiting from methodological advances in multistate demography (Land and Rogers, 1982; Willekens et al., 1982; Schoen, 1988), Bongaarts (1987) developed a nuclear-family-status life-table model that has been applied to the United States to estimate the length of life spent in various family statuses (Watkins et al., 1987). One finding from this study is that not only have the years spent with at least one parent over age 65 risen (from fewer than 10 years under the 1900 regime to nearly 20 years under the 1980 regime), but, as a result, so has the proportion of adult lifetime spent in this status (from 15 to 29 percent). The same model applied to Korea (Lee and Palloni, 1992) suggests that declining fertility means there will be an increase in the proportion of Korean women with no surviving son. At the same time, increased male longevity means the proportion of elderly widows will also decline. Thus from the elderly woman's point of view, family status may not deteriorate significantly in the coming years.

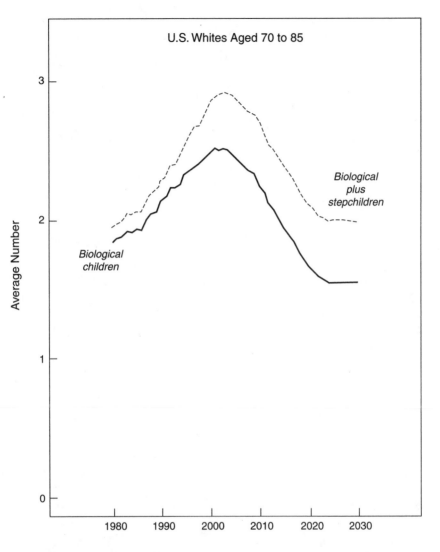

FIGURE 5-4 Living biological and stepchildren for whites aged 70-85 in the United States: 1980 to 2030.
NOTE: Based on the output of Berkeley SOCSIM simulations, averages of 40 replications.
SOURCE: Wachter (1998).

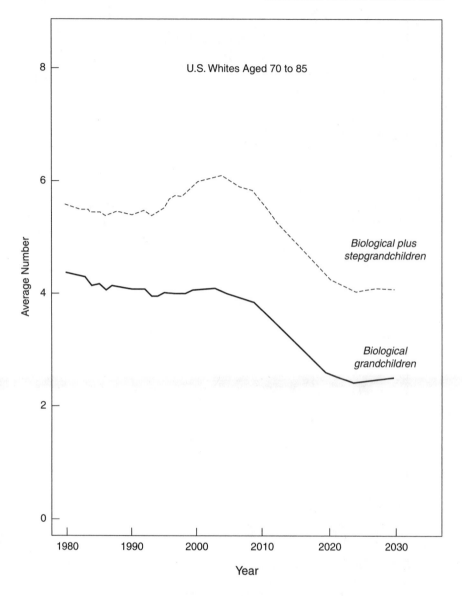

FIGURE 5-5 Living grandchildren for whites aged 70-85 in the United States:
1980 to 2030.
NOTE: Based on the output of Berkeley SOCSIM simulations, averages of 40
replications.
SOURCE: Wachter (1998).

From society's perspective, however, the demand for support of elderly women is likely to increase. The momentum of rapid population aging means the fraction of the overall population that is elderly women (especially sonless and childless widows) will increase among successive cohorts. Given the strong trend toward nuclearization of family structure in Korea and the traditional lack of state involvement in socioeconomic support, the future standard of living for a growing number of elderly widows in that nation is tenuous. A similar prospect looms in Taiwan and Japan (Hermalin et al., 1992; Jordan, 1995).

Zeng (1991) extended Bongaarts' model into a general family-status life-table model that includes both nuclear and three-generation family households. The life-table models of Bongaarts and Zeng are female-dominant one-sex models and assume that age-specific demographic rates are constant. Building on these family-status life-table models, Zeng et al. (1997, 1998) developed a two-sex dynamic projection model that permits demographic schedules to change over time. Application of this model to the situation in China showed that the family household structure and living arrangements of the Chinese elderly would change dramatically during the first half of the 21st century; for example, by 2050 the percentage of elderly living alone would be 11 and 12 times larger than that in 1990 in rural and urban areas, respectively. The same model used to project family households and living arrangements in Germany from 1996 to 2040 (see Figure 5-6) implies large increases in the numbers of German elderly living alone or with spouse only (Hullen, 2000).

In summary, microsimulation models are especially useful for projecting kinship patterns given their ability to account for complex interrelationships among members of extended families, including stepkin. These models are less powerful for national or regional family household projections for countries (regions) with middle and large population sizes because of sampling errors in the base populations. Macrosimulation models are appropriate for projecting household composition and living arrangements for entire populations of a country or region since they can fully use census information to construct the starting population with little sampling bias. To date, however, it is virtually impossible to project complex kinship networks using macromodels.

RESEARCH GAPS AND IMPLICATIONS FOR DATA COLLECTION

As implied by the discussion in this chapter, there are two parallel literatures on transfer systems. Macro intergenerational models of demographic and economic processes of the sort described by Lee (1994a, 1997) and Kotlikoff (1992) can be used to relate shifts in the composition of a

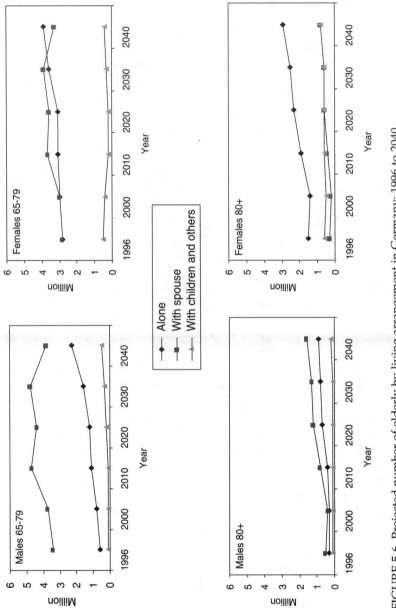

FIGURE 5-6 Projected number of elderly by living arrangement in Germany: 1996 to 2040. SOURCE: Hullen (2000). Reprinted with permission.

population (Wolf, 1994a) or policies of a country directly to changes in the cost or structure of transfer systems. To date, these complex aggregate models have been used primarily to identify net costs to state transfer systems, although, as discussed earlier, it is possible and desirable to apply generational accounting methods to all transfer systems, including the family. The other literature is oriented toward the analysis of micro-phenomena.

Macromodels

Driven by heroic assumptions, macromodels of family transfers require information on the age structure of a population at a point in time and observed schedules of fertility and mortality rates. As noted above, census materials in combination with macro administrative data on national expenditures are inputs into a variety of generational accounting models. Even these ambitious data arrays, however, are inadequate for describing market options and variations in their price and supply. Such models also need to be supplemented with new, well-conceived measures of individual preferences and expectations of family and other relevant transfer systems. Further, geographic information system technology should be useful for plotting the locations of potential providers against that of the older reference person and for introducing variation in the locations of and access to alternative providers.

While behavioral parameters are largely ignored in the estimation of macrolevel generational accounting models, they play a large role in the interpretation of data derived from these models. Best known are the implications of pay-as-you-go social security systems for aggregate savings behavior, which turn out to depend on whether individuals tend only to consider welfare from their own life-cycle consumption (Feldstein, 1974) or also to consider altruistically the welfare of their children and other descendants (Barro, 1974). In the former case, saving is reduced by a social security program, while in the latter case, the "Ricardian equivalence theorem" implies that public transfers from younger taxpayers to older retirees will be offset by private transfers from parents to their children, leaving net saving unchanged.

Other theoretical models of family transfers and family behavior may produce still other implications. For example, Cox (1987) shows that intergenerational transfers within families that are motivated by exchange (e.g., money exchanged for caregiving) rather than altruism may cause social security programs to either increase or decrease saving, depending on the (implicit) price elasticity of demand for the services provided by children to their parents. In another variant, Becker and Barro (1988) argue that Ricardian equivalence will not hold even in an altruistic model when fertility is treated as a choice variable. In the context of developing countries, Parish and Willis (1993) and Lillard and Willis (1997) suggest that family transfers may play a significant role in parental investment in the human capital of their children in the presence of borrowing constraints. Parents may divert retirement savings toward investment in their children's human capital in expectation of old-age support from those children.

Micromodels

Unfortunately, it has been difficult to conduct empirical tests of hypotheses about the effects of public transfer programs and policies on savings or other family behaviors, including fertility, human capital investment in the young, and monetary and time transfers by children to their parents or vice versa. For reasons discussed above, macrodata are inadequate for the task of testing behavioral hypotheses and estimating policy effects. Microdata are more useful, but there is a lack of relevant microdatasets. Microlevel data on savings and intrafamily transfers tend to be available only in a limited number of countries, and at the moment only in the United States among developed countries.[8] There are a number of high-quality datasets that measure family transfers (often in conjunction with other life domains) in developing countries, especially in Asia.[9] Among these are the Malaysian Family Life Survey (MFLS), the Indonesian Family Life Survey (IFLS), and several bodies of data from Taiwan and other Asian countries.[10] Although most analyses of transfers in developing countries focus on a single country, Frankenberg et al. (2000) show that a cross-national comparison of Malaysia and Indonesia can be quite illuminating when care is taken to collect microdata in comparable ways across countries. It is worth noting that both MFLS and IFLS were designed and carried out by the same organization (RAND), with many of the same researchers being involved in designing the two surveys.

Several panel studies in the United States now provide fairly com-

---

[8]The English Longitudinal Survey of Aging will contain transfer information similar to that in HRS.

[9]A Mexican longitudinal survey, modeled after HRS and modified to deal with differences in culture and economic structure between the United States and Mexico, is expected to commence in the near future. It will contain extensive transfer information.

[10]These include the Taiwan Family and Women Survey (Lee et al., 1994); the Study of Health and Living Status of the Elderly in Taiwan (Weinstein and Willis, 2001); and a number of datasets from Taiwan, the Philippines, Thailand, and Singapore that are part of a collaborative project, Rapid Demographic Change and the Welfare of the Elderly, involving the University of Michigan and institutions from these countries (see Hermalin, 2000).

plete coverage of the full option set for family transfers. This is accomplished either by interviewing multiple generations within the same family (e.g., the National Longitudinal Survey, the Panel Study of Income Dynamics, and a small subsample of the National Survey of Families and Households) or by having respondents enumerate individual kin and provide proxy reports of the relevant sociodemographic and economic attributes of each (e.g., the National Long Term Care Survey and HRS). By linking reports of transfers given or received to the potential individual exchange partners, these datasets provide opportunities to test hypotheses about donor motivation, reciprocal transfers over time within a given family, substitution of state transfers for family transfers, and net costs and benefits to donors and recipients over time. In combination with economic data on privately held resources (net worth), eligibility for all types of state transfer programs, and current and future benefit levels, these studies provide the data needed to examine a broad range of policy issues. Such richly detailed data come at a high price, however, and complex models are required to reap their analytic potential.

These datasets can be used to describe transfers and test certain hypotheses. For example, analyses of data from HRS and the Asset and Health Dynamics Among the Oldest Old Survey by McGarry and Schoeni (1995, 1998) show that the net direction of monetary transfers in the United States is from parents to children for parents throughout the entire age range over age 50. As another example, Altonji et al. (1992) used data from the Panel Study of Income Dynamics to test the altruism hypothesis and found convincing evidence to reject some of its stronger implications. However, since almost all Americans are in the social security system, it is not possible to determine the effect of the program on savings, retirement, or intrafamily transfers using U.S. data alone. There are two approaches to data collection that could be used to estimate the effects of public programs on these variables. One would be to collect comparable microdata across countries whose public transfer programs differ. Highly developed countries in western Europe and elsewhere would be the best candidates for this approach. The other approach would be to collect data from a given country in which public programs change over time. Taiwan provides a good example because it is beginning to introduce a number of public programs into a society that previously had almost no such programs. And, crucially, there exist high-quality microdatasets for Taiwan that were collected before the change in policy regime, as well as ongoing data collection efforts that are scheduled to continue into the future.

RECOMMENDATIONS

5-1. An aggregate intergenerational accounting framework should be used to measure transfer streams and assess the costs of policy options. There is substantial variation in the mix of public- and private-sector inputs into the well-being of persons of different ages. Charting the volume, timing, and costs of different transfer streams is necessary to identify the effects of population aging within a country, as well as the costs of alternative policy options. Administrative data on age-specific tax and benefit receipts, essential inputs to the accounting framework, must be available as needed. Further, the value of nonmonetary transfers (e.g., family care of the elderly) must be captured and incorporated into the framework through redesigned survey mechanisms, time-use diaries, and related techniques.

5-2. Survey instruments that capture a full accounting of the nature and structure of intergenerational transfers should be developed. Exchanges among family members, whether living together or apart, represent the major intergenerational transfer system in developing countries and a key component in industrialized countries as well. It is essential to obtain a full accounting of the nature and structure of these transfers, including their content in terms of time, space, and money; the parties to the exchange; the persistence of the arrangements; and the underlying preferences and options shaping the observed patterns.

5-3. The use of cohort analyses and innovative simulation studies should be expanded. In both developing and industrialized countries, demographic, social, and economic changes are likely to have major impacts on public and private transfer systems through their effects on preferences, resources, and the size and structure of the kin network. Rising educational levels, for example, are likely to change the preferences of the future elderly for privacy and the types and amount of leisure desired, inter alia. While not all such changes can be anticipated, cohort analyses and simulation studies should be widely employed to illuminate trends in family size, marriage and divorce patterns, household arrangements, educational levels, and urban-rural residence. The implications of the emerging patterns should be considered in longer-term planning for older populations.

5-4. Prospective studies should be developed to explore the responsiveness of the family system to changes in policies and socioeconomic circumstances. To fashion sound policies and programs, it is important to understand the interrelationships among intergenerational transfer systems, particularly the responsiveness of the family system to new policies. This goal is complicated by the fact that policies may have unintentional effects on exchanges of family resources. Careful prospective studies that are attentive to the way family members substitute for or complement nonfamilial resources, as well as to the family accommodations that take place in response to changing circumstances, can delineate key patterns and help guide policy formation.

5-5. Comparative analyses of prospective studies in developed and developing countries should be promoted. The important factors that bear on the combination of intergenerational transfer systems and their interrelationships generally display little variation within a country. However, the mix of transfer programs and their salience vary considerably between developed and developing countries and within each group as well. Cross-national research presents clear opportunities to relate variations in institutional arrangements to transfer incentives and behaviors. This variation provides a continuum of experience whose study can greatly enhance understanding of the role of various factors and their likely responsiveness to policy and program changes.

REFERENCES

Altonji, J.G., F. Hayashi, and L.J. Kotlikoff
  1992 Is the extended family altruistically linked? Direct tests using micro data. *American Economic Review* 82(5):1177-1198.
Angel, R.J., J.L. Angel, and C.L. Himes
  1992 Minority group status, health transitions, and community living arrangements among the elderly. *Research on Aging* 14(4):496-521.
Arthur, B.W., and G. McNicoll
  1978 Samuelson, population and intergenerational transfers. *International Economic Review* 19(1):241-246.
Auerbach, A.J., J. Gokhale, and L.J. Kotlikoff
  1991 Generational accounts: A meaningful alternative to deficit accounting. In *Tax Policy and the Economy*, D. Bradford, ed., pp. 55-110. Cambridge, MA: MIT Press for the National Bureau of Economic Research.
Barro, R.J.
  1974 Are government bonds net wealth? *Journal of Political Economy* 28(6):1095-1117.
Becker, G.S., and R.J. Barro
  1988 A reformulation of the economic theory of fertility. *Quarterly Journal of Economics* 103(1):1-25.
Bell, M., and J. Cooper
  1990 Household Forecasting: Replacing the Headship Rate Model. Paper presented at the Fifth National Conference of the Australian Population Association, November, Melbourne.
Bengston, V.L., and M. Silverstein
  1993 Families, aging and social change: Seven agendas for 21st-century researchers. In *Annual Review of Gerontology and Geriatrics. Focus on Kinship, Aging and Social Change*, G.L. Maddox and M.P. Lawton, eds., pp. 15-38. New York: Springer.
Blieszner, R., and V.H. Bedford
  1996 *Aging and the Family*. Westport, CT: Greenwood Press.

Bongaarts, J.
  1987   The projection of family composition over the life course with family status life
         tables. In *Family Demography: Methods and Their Applications*, J. Bongaarts, T.K.
         Burch, and K.W. Wachter, eds., pp. 189-212. Oxford: Clarendon Press.
Burch, T.K., and A. Skaburskis
  1993   Projecting Household Headship: Exploration and Comparison of Formal and
         Behavioural Approaches. Project Summary for Research Division, Canada Mort-
         gage and Housing Corporation.
Caldwell, J.C.
  1976   Toward a restatement of fertility decline. *Population and Development Review* 2:
         321-366.
Coale, A.J., and E.M. Hoover
  1958   *Population Growth and Economic Development in Low Income Countries.* Princeton,
         NJ: Princeton University Press.
Cox, D.
  1987   Motives for private income transfers. *Journal of Political Economy* 95(3):509-546.
Cutler, D.M., and E. Meara
  1999   *The Concentration of Medical Spending: An Update.* NBER Working Paper 7279.
         Cambridge, MA: National Bureau of Economic Research.
Diamond, P.A.
  1965   National debt in a neoclassical growth model. *American Economic Review* 55:116-
         1150.
Feldstein, M.
  1974   Social security, induced retirement, and aggregate capital formation. *Journal of
         Political Economy* 82(5):905-927.
Frankenberg, E., L.A. Lillard, and R.J. Willis
  2000   Money for Nothing? Altruism, Exchange and Old Age Security in Southeast Asia.
         Unpublished working paper. RAND, Santa Monica, CA.
Freedman, V.A.
  1996   Family structure and the risk of nursing home admission. *Journals of Gerontology.
         Psychological Sciences and Social Sciences* 51(2):S61-69.
Glaser, K.F., and C. Tomassini
  1999   Proximity to Children: A Comparison of Britain and Italy. Paper presented at the
         Annual Meeting of the Population Association of America, March, New York.
Goldscheider, F.K.
  1990   The aging of the gender revolution: What do we know and what do we need to
         know? *Research on Aging* 12(4):531-545.
Grundy, E.
in press   Co-residence of mid-life children and their elderly parents in England and Wales:
         Changes between 1981 and 1991. *Population Studies.*
Hagestad, G.O.
  2000   Intergenerational Relations. Paper presented at the United Nations Economic
         Commission for Europe Conference on Generations and Gender, July, Geneva.
Hammel, E.A., C. Mason, K.W. Wachter, F. Wang, and H. Yang
  1991   Rapid population change and kinship. The effects of unstable demographic
         changes on Chinese kinship networks. In *Consequences of Rapid Population Growth
         in Developing Countries, 1750-2250*, pp. 243-271. New York: Taylor and Francis.
Hammel E.A., K.W. Wachter, and C.K McDaniel
  1981   The kin of the aged in A.D. 2000; The chickens come home to roost. In *Aging:
         Social Change*, S.B. Kieseler, J.N. Morgan, and V.K. Oppenheimer, eds., pp. 11-39.
         New York: Academic Press.

Henretta, J.C., E. Grundy, and K. Glasser
  1997 Parents and Children of Mid-life Adults: U.S.-Britain Comparisons. Paper presented at the Conference on Family, Households, and Kin: Social and Spatial Aspects of Change, King's College, June-July, London.
Hermalin, A.I.
  1997 Drawing policy lessons for Asia from research on aging. *Asia-Pacific Population Journal* 12(4):89-102.
  2000 *Challenges to Comparative Research on Intergenerational Transfers.* Comparative Study of the Elderly in Asia, Research Report no. 00-56, August. Ann Arbor: University of Michigan Population Studies Center.
Hermalin, A.I., M.B. Ofstedal, and L. Chi
  1992 *Kin Availability of the Elderly in Taiwan: Who Is Available and Where Are They?* Comparative Study of the Elderly in Asia, Research Report no. 92-18. Ann Arbor: University of Michigan Population Studies Center.
Hermalin, A.I., M.B. Ofstedal, R. Freedman, M.-C. Chang, and C. Roan
  1996 *Methodological Considerations in Aligning Independent Surveys of Parental Support from Older and Younger Generations, with Illustrative Data from Taiwan.* Comparative Study of the Elderly in Asia, Research Report no. 96-38. Ann Arbor: University of Michigan Population Studies Center.
Himes, C.L.
  1992 Future caregivers: Projected family structures of older persons. *Journal of Gerontology: Social Sciences* 47(1):S17-26.
Horowitz, A.
  1985 Family caregiving to the frail elderly. In *Annual Review of Gerontology and Geriatrics*, C. Eisdorfer, ed. New York: Springer.
Hullen, G.
  2000 Projections of German population living aarrangements and household and family structure. Paper presented at the Joint Meeting of the Committee for Regional Statistics of the German Statistical Society and the Working Group on Population Statistical Methods of the German Society on Population Science, Nurnberg, Germany (September 26-27). Bundesinstitut für Bevölkerungsforschung.
Jordan, M.
  1995 Japan Nearing Crisis in Care of Elderly. *The Washington Post*, October 31:A8.
Kaplan, H.
  1994 Evolutionary and wealth flows theories of fertility: Empirical tests and new models. *Population and Development Review* 20(4):753-791.
Keilman, N.
  1988 Dynamic household models. In *Modelling Household Formation and Dissolution*, N. Keilman, A. Kuijsten, and A. Vossen, eds. Oxford: Clarendon Press.
Keilman, N., and H. Brunborg
  1995 *Household Projections for Norway, 1990-2020. Part I: Macrosimulations.* Oslo: Statistics Norway.
Kendig, H.L., A. Hasimoto, and L.C. Coppard
  1992 *Family Support for the Elderly. The International Experience.* Oxford: Oxford University Press.
Kohli, M.
  1999 Private and public transfers between generations: Linking the family and the state. *European Societies* 1:81-104.
Kotlikoff, L.J.
  1992 *Generational Accounting.* New York: Macmillan.

Land, K.C., and A. Rogers, eds.
  1982   *Multidimensional Mathematical Demography.* New York: Academic Press.
LeBras, H.
  1973   Parents, grandparents, bisaieux. *Population* 1:9-37.
Ledent, J.
  1992   Vers des perspectives de familes/ménages sur la base d'un modèle de type mul-
         tidimensional. Unpublished manuscript. INRS – Urbanisation, Montreal,
         Canada.
Lee, R.D.
  1994a The formal demography of population aging, transfers, and the economic life
         cycle. In *Demography of Aging.* Committee on Population. L.M. Martin and S.H.
         Preston, eds., pp. 8-49. Commission on Behavioral and Social Sciences and Edu-
         cation. Washington, DC: National Academy Press.
  1994b Population age structure, intergenerational transfers, and wealth: A new approach
         with applications to the U.S. *Journal of Human Resources* 29(4):1027-1063.
  1997   Population dynamics: Equilibrium, disequilibrium and consequences of fluctua-
         tions. Chapter 19 in *Handbook of Population and Family Economics*, M.R. Rosenzweig
         and O. Stark, eds. Amsterdam: Elsevier Sciences.
  2000   Intergenerational transfers and the economic life cycle: A cross-cultural perspec-
         tive. Chapter 2 in *Sharing the Wealth: Demographic Change and Economic Transfers
         Between Generations*, A. Mason and G. Tapinos, eds. Oxford: Oxford University
         Press.
Lee, R.D., and S. Lapkoff
  1988   Intergenerational flows of time and goods: Consequences of slowing population
         growth. *Journal of Political Economy* 96(31):618-651.
Lee, Y.-J., and A. Palloni
  1992   Changes in the family status of elderly women in Korea. *Demography* 29:69-92.
Lee, Y.-J., W.L. Parish, and R.J. Willis
  1994   Sons, daughters and intergenerational support in Taiwan. *American Journal of
         Sociology* 94:1010-1041.
Lillard, L.A., and R.J. Willis
  1997   Motives for intergenerational transfers: Evidence from Malaysia. *Demography*
         34(1):115-134.
Mason, A., and R. Racelis
  1992   A comparison of four methods for projecting households. *International Journal of
         Forecasting* 8:509-527.
McGarry, K., and R.F. Schoeni
  1995   Transfer behavior in the Health and Retirement Study: Measurement and the
         redistribution of resources within the family. *Journal of Human Resources* 30
         (Supplement):S184-S226.
  1998   Transfer behavior within the family: Results from the Asset and Health Dynam-
         ics Survey. *The Journals of Gerontology: Social Sciences* 52B (Special Issue):82-92.
  1999   Social Security, Economic Growth, and the Rise in Independence of Elderly Wid-
         ows in the 20th Century. Paper presented at the United Nations Economic Com-
         mission for Europe Conference on the Status of the Older Population: Prelude to
         the 21st Century, December, Sion, Switzerland.
Murphy, M.J.
  1991   Modelling households: A synthesis. In *Population Research in Britain*, Supplement
         to *Population Studies* (45), M.J. Murphy and J. Hobcraft, eds.

National Research Council
    1997   *The New Americans. Economic, Demographic, and Fiscal Effects of Immigration.* Panel
            on the Demographic and Economic Impacts of Immigration. J.P. Smith and
            B.Edmonston, eds. Commission on Behavioral and Social Sciences and Educa-
            tion. Washington, DC: National Academy Press.
Ofstedal, M.B., J. Knodel, and N. Chayovan
    1999   *Intergenerational Support and Gender: A Comparison of Four Asian Countries.* Com-
            parative Study of the Elderly in Asia, Research Report no. 99-54. Ann Arbor:
            University of Michigan Population Studies Center.
Palloni, A.
    2000   Programmatic and Policy Aspects of Population Ageing and Living Arrange-
            ments. Paper prepared for the United Nations Population Division Technical
            Meeting on Population Ageing and Living Arrangements of Older Persons: Criti-
            cal Issues and Policy Responses, February, New York.
Parish, W.L., and R.J. Willis
    1993   Daughters, education and family budgets: Taiwan experiences. *Journal of Human
            Resources* 28:861-898.
Reeves, J.
    1987   Projection of number of kin. In *Family Demography: Methods and Their Applica-
            tions,* J. Bongaarts, T.K. Burch, and K. Wachter, eds. Oxford: Clarendon Press.
Ruggles, S.
    1993   Confessions of a microsimulator. *Historical Methods* 26:161-169.
Samuelson, P.
    1958   An exact consumption-loan model of interest with or without the social contriv-
            ance of money. *Journal of Political Economy* 66(6):467-482.
Schoen, R.
    1988   *Modeling Multi-group Population.* New York: Plenum Press.
Schoeni, R.F.
    1992   *Another Leak in the Bucket? Public Transfer Income and Private Family Support.* Re-
            search Report no. 92-249. Ann Arbor: University of Michigan Population Studies
            Center.
    1998   Reassessing the decline in parent-child old-age coresidence during the twentieth
            century. *Demography* 35:307-313.
Smith, J.E.
    1987   The computer simulation of kin sets and kin counts. In *Family Demography: Meth-
            ods and Their Applications,* J. Bongaarts, T.K. Burch, and K. Wachter, eds., pp. 249-
            266. Oxford: Clarendon Press.
Soldo, B.J., and V.A. Freedman
    1994   Care of the elderly: Division of labor among the family, market, and state. In
            Demography of Aging. Committee on Population. L.G. Martin and S.H. Preston,
            eds., pp. 146-194. Commission on Behavioral and Social Sciences and Education.
            Washington, DC: National Academy Press.
Soldo, B.J., and M.S. Hill
    1993   Intergenerational transfers: Economic, demographic and social perspectives. *An-
            nual Review of Gerontology and Geriatrics* 13:187-216.
    1995   Family structure and transfers measures in the health and retirement study. *Jour-
            nal of Human Resources* 30 (Supplement):S108-S137.
Solow, R.
    1956   A contribution to the theory of economic growth. *Quarterly Journal of Economics*
            70:65-94.

Stallard, E.
   1998   Retirement and Health: Estimates and Projections of Acute and Long-term Care
          Needs and Expenditures of the U.S. Elderly Population. Paper presented at the
          Society of Actuaries' Retirement Needs Framework Conference, December, Or-
          lando, Florida.
Stark, O.
   1995   *Altruism and Beyond: An Economic Analysis of Transfers and Exchanges within Fami-
          lies and Groups.* Cambridge: Cambridge University Press.
Stecklov, G.
   1997   Intergenerational resource flows in Cote d'Ivoire. *Population and Development
          Review* 23(3):525-553.
Thompson, L.H.
   1998   *Older and Wiser: The Economics of Public Pensions.* Washington, DC: Urban Insti-
          tute Press.
Tomassini, C., and D. Wolf
   1999   Shrinking Kin Networks in Italy Due to Sustained Low Fertility. Papers in
          Microsimulation, Series Paper no. 5, December. Syracuse, NY: Syracuse Univer-
          sity Center for Policy Research. [To also be published in the *European Journal of
          Population.*]
Van Imhoff, E.
   1999   Modelling Life Histories: Macro Robustness Versus Micro Substance. Paper pre-
          sented at the International Workshop on Synthetic Biographics: State of the Art
          and Developments, June, San Miniato, Italy.
Van Imhoff, E., and N. Keilman
   1992   *LIPRO 2.0: An Application of A Dynamic Demographic Projection Model to Household
          Structure in The Netherlands.* Netherlands: Swets and Zeithinger.
Van Imhoff, E., and W. Post
   1998   Microsimulation methods for population projection. *Population: An English Selec-
          tion* 10(1):97-138.
Wachter, K.W.
   1987   Microsimulation of household cycles. In *Family Demography: Methods and Their
          Applications*, J. Bongaarts, T.K. Burch, and K.W. Wachter, eds., pp. 215-227. Ox-
          ford: Clarendon Press.
   1997   Kinship resources for the elderly. *Philosophical Transactions of the Royal Society:
          Biological Sciences*, Series B352:1811-1818.
   1998   Kinship Resources for the Elderly: An Update. Available: http://
          www.demog.berkeley.edu/~wachter/ [February 28, 2001].
Watkins, S.C., J.A. Menken, and J.Bongaarts
   1987   Demographic foundations of family change. *American Sociological Review* 52:346-
          358.
Weinstein, M., and R.J. Willis
   2001   Stretching social surveys to include bioindicators. In *Cells and Surveys. Should
          Biological Measures Be Included in Social Science Research?* Committee on Popula-
          tion. C.E. Finch et al., eds., pp. 250-275. Commission on Behavioral and Social
          Sciences and Education. Washington, DC: National Academy Press.
Wiener, J.M., and R.J. Hanley
   1992   Caring for the disabled elderly: There's no place like home. In *Improving Health
          Policy and Management: Nine Critical Issues for the 1990's*, S.M. Shortell and U.
          Reinhardt, eds. Ann Arbor: Health Administration Press.

Willekens, F.J., I. Shah, J.M. Shah, and P. Ramachandran
   1982   Multistate analysis of marital status life tables: Theory and application. *Population Studies* 36(1):129-144.
Willis, R.J.
   1988   A theory of the equilibrium rate of interest: Life cycles, institutions and population growth. In *Economic Consequences of Alternative Population Patterns*, R.D. Lee, W.B. Arthur, and G. Rodgers, eds., pp. 106-138. Oxford: Oxford University Press.
Wolf, D.A.
   1988   Kinship and family support in aging societies. In *Social and Economic Consequences of Population Aging*. New York: United Nations Department of International Economic and Social Affairs.
   1994a Co-residence with an aged parent: Lifetime patterns and sensitivity to demographic change. In *Ageing and the Family*. New York: United Nations Department of International Economic and Social Affairs.
   1994b The elderly and their kin: patterns of availability and access. In *Demography of Aging*. Committee on Population. L.G. Martin and S.H. Preston, eds., pp. 146-194. Commission on Behavioral and Social Sciences and Education. Washington DC: National Academy Press.
Zeng, Y.
   1988   Changing demographic characteristics and the family status of Chinese women. *Population Studies* 42:183-203.
   1991   *Family Dynamics in China: A Life Table Analysis*. Wisconsin: University of Wisconsin Press.
Zeng Y., J.W. Vaupel, and W. Zhenglian
   1997   A multidimensional model for projecting family households—with an illustrative numerical application. *Mathematical Population Studies* 6(3):187-216.
   1998   Household projection using conventional demographic data. *Population and Development Review* 24 (Supplementary issue):59-87.

6

The Health of Aging Populations

As the length of life and number and proportion of older persons increase in most industrialized and many developing nations, a central question is whether this population aging will be accompanied by sustained or improved health, an improving quality of life, and sufficient social and economic resources. The answer to this question lies partly in the ability of families and communities, as well as modern social, political, economic, and health service delivery systems, to provide optimal support to older persons. However, while all modern societies are committed to providing health and social services to their citizens, these systems are always in flux, guided by diverse and evolving national and regional policy formulations. Health, social, and economic policies for older persons vary substantially among industrialized nations. Analysis of these variations through appropriate cross-national research may assist greatly in the formulation of effective policies aimed at enhancing the health status, as well as the social and economic well-being, of elderly populations.

Among the most important policy concerns relevant to health and longevity are the future fiscal viability of pension, health, and social insurance systems, both public and private, and the implications of these systems for savings and investment rates (see Chapter 3). How long people continue working, paying taxes, and saving will feature prominently in the consequences of population aging. Many people already work less than half a lifetime because of extended periods of schooling and training in early life, earlier retirement, and enhanced longevity, posing a challenge to the sustainability of systems designed to support older persons. If the trend toward increased longevity continues without a parallel extension in working life, the stress on these systems could be even greater.

As discussed elsewhere in this volume, labor force participation, investment and saving behavior, and provision of health services are complex phenomena that are interrelated at both the individual and societal levels (Quinn and Burkhauser, 1994; Smith, 1999). For example, incentives provided by government and employers play important roles in determining labor force participation. Reducing the implicit tax on continuing work beyond the normal age of retirement and reducing the costs of hiring (and possibly retraining) older workers have the potential to encourage longer working lives (see Chapter 3). Yet in designing such incentives, policy makers need to know how long they can reasonably expect people to keep working. Just how physically and mentally capable are older people? What is the trajectory of health and function as people age? Can their productivity be maintained and enhanced at older ages, and at what cost? Does the type of productivity and engagement change with age? How can health care services be provided in such a manner as to maintain optimal health and function? Most basically, policy makers must make difficult decisions about the allocation of limited resources to preserving and improving health. How is good health achieved at a reasonable cost? Should more resources be directed toward behavioral change and other health promotion and disease prevention programs, including health enhancement in early life, or should more be dedicated to the treatment of patients with advanced diseases? How much should be invested in the development of new health care technologies, service delivery enhancements, and professional training?

A focus on national-level health status and its temporal trajectory is critical for several reasons. Health status is one of the most important indicators of well-being, and it predicts a large proportion of societal expenditures on health and social services for the elderly. Health status is also reciprocally affected by social and political policies and programs. Further, health status is malleable through high-quality health promotion and disease prevention programs, as well as effective medical services. National programs and policies that may appear to be devoted to health and health services for older persons often have important implications for and complex interactions with other economic sectors. Table 6-1 provides examples.

This chapter is devoted to the centrality of health status and change in informing health, social, and economic policy formulation. We first outline the key issues to be addressed by research on the health status of the elderly. We then present a conceptual model of the determinants of health

TABLE 6-1 Relationship of Public-Sector Programs and Policies to
Health Services for Older Persons

Sector	Relation to the Provision of Health Services for Older Persons
Housing	• Provision of suitable-quality housing, both in the community and within institutions, to sustain health. • Reconstruction of housing to accommodate disabled older persons.
Public Health	• Creation of prevention and health promotion programs that affect older persons.
Education	• Training of all levels of health professionals and ancillary workers in special skills related to the problems of older persons.
Manufacturing	• Provision of increasingly complex mechanical and electronic devices for the treatment and rehabilitation of older persons.
Urban Design	• Location of housing for older persons so as to optimize access to health, nutritional, recreational, and social services. • Opportunities for generativity and engagement by older persons.
Transportation	• Provision of public transportation and facilitation of personal transport to enhance mobility and its social outcomes.

status to provide a framework for the ensuing discussion. Next we review the basic measures of health status, presenting selected examples of
basic international patterns and trends. This is followed by a brief look at
the characteristics of national health systems. Data sources for cross-
national research on the health status of the elderly are then considered,
as well as the pitfalls and strengths of such research. Finally, we offer
recommendations for strengthening research in this domain.

KEY ISSUES

National health policy decisions with respect to older persons are
becoming increasingly complex for several reasons. As noted in Chapter
2, the numbers of the elderly and oldest old have increased dramatically
in most industrialized nations. Countries that already have a substantial
elderly population face increasing proportions in the coming decades,
with all the accompanying social and economic demands. In addition,
nations must prepare for the growing numbers of disabled younger persons who are now surviving to older ages because of improved health
care. Policy decisions related to the provision of health services for the
elderly have become complex from technological, fiscal, and ethical perspectives. Also, as noted above, health services are intimately tied to the

provision of social services and economic support, including housing, nutrition, institutional care, and related activities. Preventive and rehabilitative services have added not only to the costs of care, but also to the potential for improved function, mobility, and social engagement. Health care for older persons is thus different from that provided to other age groups in several respects: greater resource demands; the intertwining of professional health services with social services; the frequent occurrence of important ethical conundrums; a higher prevalence of physical and mental disabilities; and, perhaps not as obvious in policy formulation, less scientific evidence for use in determining effective preventive and medical interventions. In this context, the following issues merit special emphasis.

1. What is the importance of health status for retirement preferences and patterns? How are health status and retirement age related? Have recent trends in reduced age-specific rates of disability translated into increased and longer labor force participation?

2. What impact does health have on families? How has the changing health status of older persons altered the productivity and economic status of families and households? How do families make economic provisions to care for unhealthy parents, and what are the effects on labor force participation? How does the changing health status of older persons, in particular the onset of infirmity, affect the capacity to be a caregiver for an ill or disabled spouse or other family member? What economic provisions do families make for long-term care of older persons, whether in the community or within chronic care institutions? How do these provisions dovetail with public and voluntary assistance and care programs?

3. How important is health to wealth and economic status? What evidence is there that health status directly affects individual wealth, assets, and economic productivity? What is the role of the health care system in the prevention, treatment, and rehabilitation of illnesses, and how does this work to maintain personal economic status? How do health shocks affect future economic status and personal and family wealth in accordance with underlying socioeconomic status?

4. How do economic status and educational levels affect the health of individuals across the life course? By what mechanisms and to what degree does economic status lead to better health status? At what ages do the effects of economic status have the greatest impact on health status? How does the distribution of wealth, income, and economic productivity within a nation serve to preserve, enhance, or depress health status independently of individual and family socioeconomic characteristics? How does the provision of health services affect long-term health outcomes?

The formulation of health service delivery policies and systems for older persons requires a continuing flow of information, including quantitative data on the above and other issues related to population health status and directions, as well as the resources expended in the health care system. In particular, the ability to draw on international experiences in health and health care can greatly enhance the potential of such policies and systems. Moreover, cross-national research can enable the creation of evaluative mechanisms that would often not be feasible in any one country because of the homogeneity of medical practices and administrative cultures. Such research can also help address the above issues by providing a range of observations of change over time and, perhaps, early indications of emerging health trends. And comparative work can improve our understanding of how particular diseases and conditions are expressed as disability in a variety of work, social, policy, and living environments, thus providing insight into which adjustments in those environments may be most cost-effective.

CONCEPTUAL MODEL OF THE
DETERMINANTS OF HEALTH STATUS

As noted above, the determinants of health are complex and comprise multiple policy domains. One basic but important conceptual model that can be used to illustrate the breadth of these determinants is shown in Figure 6-1. This construct represents the health of all demographic groups in a society, although the emphasis here is on the health of older persons. The determinants are presented in a set of concentric circles, with the community population at the center. Outermost, and often difficult to quantify, are the general social, economic, cultural, and environmental (physical-chemical) conditions that have important long-term health effects. The next circle contains society's basic social, health, and economic institutions, which sustain or impair a healthy existence. The next circle emphasizes the critical role of social and community interactions and exchanges, whereby individuals make their collective decisions. The circle next to the core highlights the importance of individual behavioral choices (e.g., cigarette smoking, risk-taking behaviors) in the determination of health status.

One drawback of a two-dimensional representation is the absence of time. Other models highlight more fully such issues as the role of infancy and childhood and the environment on health outcomes in later life. Nevertheless, the model in Figure 6-1 is useful in many respects. For example, it highlights the intimate interaction between the economic and employment environments and health discussed above (see Annex 6-1 for a specific policy example). As a corollary, the model places the role of

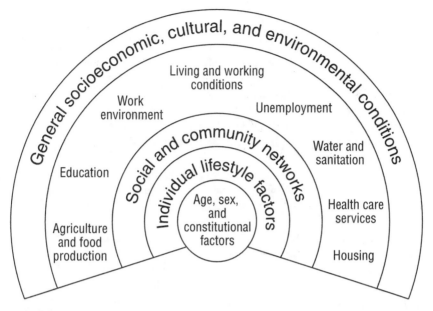

FIGURE 6-1 A conceptual framework for determinants of health status.
SOURCE: Dahlgren and Whitehead (1991). Reprinted with permission.

professional health services in an important but not dominant role among
the institutional forces that mediate health status. The model quite appro-
priately also emphasizes the role of basic public health determinants,
such as the physiochemical environment and the provision of safe and
adequate food and sanitary services. In addition, the model reflects an
appreciation of individual responsibility for health status, both in the
selection of behaviors and in the collective decisions made by individuals.
Finally, the model shows that policy interventions in one institution or
domain may or may not have the desired effect because of the multiple
sectors involved. Thus, policy outcomes may be enhanced only through
multiple intervention points; conversely, interventions in one sector may
have unpredicted outcomes in others.

MEASURING HEALTH STATUS

During the 20th century there were great changes in patterns of population health status and survivorship in both the industrialized and developing worlds. Among industrialized nations, the early part of the century saw the greatest improvement in mortality among infants, children,
and pregnant women. These improvements continue to the present time.

Later in the century, however, substantial reductions in mortality among older adults occurred in nearly all developed countries as a result of declines in deaths primarily from heart disease, but also from other major causes. Moreover, there has been a shift among older persons to surviving, and even thriving, with prevalent chronic illnesses such as various heart conditions and arthritis. Population surveys have also indicated that the age-specific prevalence of physical disability has declined in some countries (Jacobzone et al., 1998). Developing countries have lagged behind their more industrialized counterparts in terms of mortality decline and the overall epidemiological transition from a preponderance of infectious and parasitic diseases to one of chronic and degenerative diseases. As noted in Chapter 2, however, the overall gap between more and less developed countries has narrowed considerably.

The last third of the 20th century also saw a significant expansion in the ways population health status can be characterized, particularly by supplementing mortality data with emerging measures of personal clinical signs and symptoms, diseases and conditions, and functional disabilities. The potential availability of more specific types of health data has greatly increased the set of quantitative tools for health policy and planning, particularly as regards older persons, whose rates of disease and disability are higher than those of other demographic groups.

Identifying the trajectories of important health measures is central to forecasting health care needs and generating policies for older persons. Yet, defining "health" and the health status of individuals is not an easy matter. Even under optimal circumstances and without resource constraints, it is challenging to fully assess the physiological state of individuals, to understand the nature and determinants of personal or social behavior, and to predict the range and intensity of the outcomes of environmental challenges (e.g., from the workplace or elsewhere in the community). Nor is it easy to predict what effects various medical services or interventions will have on individuals. With the newer and more precise measures of health status now available, however, much can be accomplished.

Health status can be characterized from varying perspectives depending on the goals and uses of the information. For example, personal health can be assessed by subjective self-report, more objective physiological and biochemical measurement, or standardized indicators of diseases and disabilities present. In fact, all of these perspectives are important and complementary. Further, health status may be characterized according to major domains such as physical health (e.g., the function of the heart and lungs), mental health (e.g., the presence of depressed mood), and physical and social functional health (e.g., the ability to climb stairs or work at a particular occupation). Health may also be thought of in its temporal, longitudinal dimensions. For example, how is health status changing, or did an individual live or die? Changes in health status may be reflected as well in the intensity of health care resource utilization, such as pharmaceutical, institutional, or rehabilitative care. This temporal perspective is critical and leads to an emphasis on longitudinal, cohort data sources.

While there are no wholly standardized approaches to characterizing health status, there are several meaningful ways in which individual health is assessed and described. These data may not be available from many areas in a computerized or otherwise readily retrievable format, but can usually be obtained by abstracting clinical records or surveying patients, health professionals, administrators, and/or populations within a geographic area. Annex 6-2 describes in detail the health status measures most commonly used for survey and administrative data collection in the categories of clinical signs, symptoms, and syndromes; morbidity (i.e., discretely defined medical conditions); self-rated health; functional status and disability; physiological and pathological measures; mortality data and derived measures; and aging and mental illness.

CHARACTERIZING HEALTH CARE SYSTEMS

As noted in the model of health determinants discussed above, both personal behaviors and many public health measures bear on health status. Health promotional activities aimed at older persons may or may not involve direct contact with the formal health care system; examples of the latter activities include education programs and provision of good preventive nutrition, safe transportation to enhance mobility, and assurance of adequate housing. Thus the efficacy and net impact of many basic public health programs, with their incumbent costs, can be assessed only by using population survey information in addition to the data derived from clinical sources. Moreover, decreased use of toxic substances and increased exercise and structured leisure activities, and even paid and unpaid work, are associated with enhanced function, decreased occurrence of physical and emotional illness, and higher quality of life among older adults. Effective national and regional policies for health promotion among older persons therefore require that important deficits in these areas be identified. Population surveys may be the only means of acquiring accurate information on such issues as cigarette and alcohol consumption, perceived elder abuse, the availability and use of exercise and other leisure and recreational programs, and levels of mobility and social interaction.

Also central to national health policy for older persons is the ability to provide community-based preventive services, generally delivered in the context of primary care. The presence of such services has been used in the United States and elsewhere as a benchmark of the general quality of care (Bloom et al., 2000). Included are such activities as provision of appropriate immunizations and screening for early and treatable conditions, such as colon and breast cancer, high blood cholesterol, high blood pressure, and depression. Explicit geriatric screening and management programs are recommended for falls, early cognitive impairment, physical disability, and inappropriate use of medication. Provision of these services leads to a higher quality of life and helps maintain or enhance function in the elderly. Even in the presence of overt illness, a systematic approach to the complex functional and medical problems of older persons, often referred to as geriatric assessment, can help maintain useful function. Some preventive activities may be recommended by health professionals but executed by others. An important example is environmental screening of residences to prevent falls and enhance mobility, such as by providing ramps rather than stairs and handrails at appropriate locations.

Coordination of public and clinical policies relevant to health promotion and disease prevention among the various sectors involved is essential if these policies are to have the desired positive effects on the health status of older persons. International comparisons of preventive service delivery programs may help identify those with the most desired outcomes and indicate which individual programs may be applied usefully in many nations. For example, standardized specific blood cholesterol levels predict very different heart disease rates in different countries (Kromhout, 1999), possibly leading to different priorities for prevention programs. Again, the most effective means of obtaining the information necessary for such cross-national research is representative household surveys of older persons.

All national health systems are extremely complex in structure, function, and administration. This complexity and diversity makes their classification difficult, a difficulty that is exacerbated by the fact that all health systems are constantly evolving in accordance with ongoing political and economic forces. This complexity also makes policy initiation and assessment, regardless of how broadly construed, extremely challenging. At the same time, however, most modern health care systems, particularly within developed countries, face common forces and challenges: rapid and costly technological innovation; the increasing infusion of business practices to contain the costs of delivering care; growing consumer demands for care that is uniformly distributed geographically and socioeconomically; the provision of effective quality assurance programs; the need to identify funding for the breadth of health services demanded by communities, to balance the needs of primary and specialty care programs, and to respond to complementary and alternative medical practices; and, in many cases, the decentralization of authority in previously monolithic systems.

A variety of classification systems have been proposed and applied in the comparative study of health systems, but no generally accepted taxonomy has emerged. A broad range of health system typologies is reviewed by Mechanic and Rochefort (1996); these typologies variously emphasize such dimensions as political organization and control, economics and fiscal management, population demands and utilization, the role of market forces, universality of coverage, cultural influences on professional practice, the degree of professional dominance, and adherence to various social movements and principles.

Because of the higher rates of morbidity and disability that occur with increasing age, older people make substantial use of formal health services. Such services consume an enormous amount of resources, and a central policy issue for all countries is how to expend available resources in a way that will yield the best health outcomes feasible by the most efficient means. Again, cross-national comparative research is one important avenue for addressing this issue by examining international variations in organization, financing, delivery, and evaluation of elder health services. To illustrate, Figure 6-2 highlights the international variation in per capita nursing home utilization across 20 countries, and Figure 6-3 shows variation in spending for health services across the G7 nations. One of the most important macroanalytical policy questions is the relationship of health system organization, administration, and financing to health status and outcomes. Little work has been done in this area, but cross-national analyses offer the best approach to understanding how major components, such as the level of investment in new technology, affect health outcomes.

There are many units of analysis for characterizing health systems, depending on the issues being addressed. Table 6-2 lists examples of analytic variables commonly used to describe health systems at either the national or regional level. These variables involve a substantial amount of conceptual complexity, and several issues should be considered when using them. As noted earlier, health status is determined only in part by the units of health service delivered. Health systems offer numerous preventive care and public health services in ways that are difficult to quantify. In all age groups, but particularly among older persons, there is a substantial amount of self-care, as well as varying levels of alternative and complementary health care practices, including self-medication with herbs and the use of alternative practitioners, that may have an impact on health outcomes. Further, both preventive and clinical care may impact health outcomes and quality of life only in future decades, and this latency

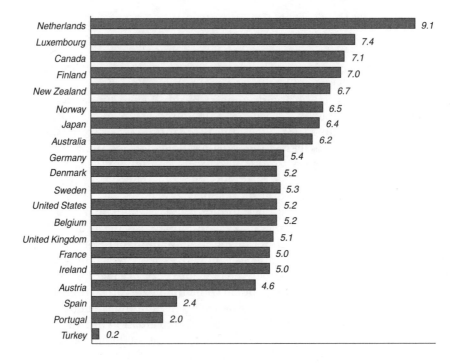

FIGURE 6-2 Percent of elderly population in residential care: Circa 1991.
SOURCE: Organization for Economic Co-Operation and Development (1996).

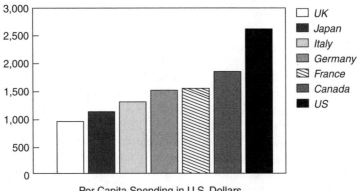

FIGURE 6-3 Medical spending in the G7 countries: 1990.
SOURCE: Cutler (1999).

TABLE 6-2 Selected Units of Analysis for Characterizing Health Systems

Category	Variables
Type of Formal Care: Location/Institutional Nature	• Acute general hospital • Intermediate care facilities • Long-term institutional care (e.g., mental health, mental retardation, rehabilitation, infectious disease) • Community-based, primary care facility • Home-based care • Pharmaceutical/dental/mental health services • Emergency care facilities
Basic Funding Mechanisms	• Fee-for-service • Personal insurance, with or without copayments • Employer insurance, with or without copayments • Government-provided insurance, with or without copayments, including taxation systems • Mixed payment systems and other contractual systems
Community-Based Care Typologies	• Clinical public health services • Health education programs • Workplace health programs and services • Health-oriented recreational and leisure programs • Informal care, including family and self-care • Complementary and alternative care modalities
Health Care Utilization Measures	• Episodes of attendance at various units of health care • Access to care based on distance to provider(s) • Access to care based on consumer satisfaction, including culturally acceptable care
Patient-Centered Measures	• Continuity of care over time and different medical services • Cultural appropriateness of care • Presence of patient education programs

may be difficult to assess in analytical studies. In fact, many of the fundamental professional activities of health systems may be critically important to patients and their families, but would not be expected to result in objective, quantitative health outcomes; examples include ensuring that illness is not present, providing prognostic information, assisting with care administration issues, and delivering family-friendly hospice care. Despite these conceptual challenges, however, cross-national studies offer the best opportunity to determine how various health system structures and funding and management mechanisms affect health outcomes.

Regardless of how sophisticated, modern, and comprehensive health services may be in a nation, utilization of those services is often uneven and may vary by socioeconomic status, ethnicity, geographic location, and many other factors. Equally important, there may be selective factors related to illness characteristics and personality among individuals that dictate special behaviors within the health system, confounding the study of health outcomes. Moreover, all health care systems have adverse effects, which can diminish the net positive effects of health outcomes. Common examples include hospital-acquired infections, misapplication of therapies, and the unintended adverse effects of medications and devices. It is important to identify these adverse effects, as many are remediable. Finally, there is variation within national health systems in the quality of care and quality assurance programs. For example, substantial small-area variation in medical/surgical procedure utilization rates and health outcomes has been demonstrated within many modern health systems. In addition, some services may be less sophisticated in rural or frontier areas or in other geographical locations. This variation highlights the need for comprehensive, large-area or national data with which to conduct suitable research.

EXISTING HEALTH DATA ON OLDER PERSONS: TYPES, AVAILABILITY, AND QUALITY

The data required to conduct cross-national research on the health status of the elderly may come from many sources, and it is not always possible to anticipate in advance what variables will be needed. Moreover, elderly populations have a number of special characteristics that make their health data needs different from those of other groups:

• Health events on average occur at a more rapid rate among the elderly than in other age groups, increasing the need for longitudinal (panel) data on cohorts of elders.
• Older persons have many clinical signs, symptoms, and functional impairments that need to be given special attention since they are not included within traditional administrative data systems that focus on morbidity.
• Since older persons commonly have multiple medical conditions and functional impairments, there is a need to develop summary measures of comorbidity and health status in order to deal efficiently with the available health and administrative data. Considering the conditions and impairments of the elderly in isolation will, in some instances, impede global policy development.
• Successful health service delivery for older persons benefits from data on their physical and social environments. Knowledge of the social environment is critical for the large number of elders who have limitations in mobility or self-care; it is also essential for ensuring that pre-

scribed medical regimens are delivered correctly in both home and community settings. Data on the physical environment are important as well for minimizing falls, injuries, and the progression of disability and, in some cases, for preventing deaths from climate-related causes.

• Cognitive and mental impairments are common among the elderly, particularly among the oldest old. Such impairments can lead to a lack of social support and interchange, failure to follow medical treatment plans, inability to perform self-care, and increased need for structured supervision and institutionalization. Thus, acquisition of data on the population occurrence and correlates of mental impairments becomes critical for shaping elder health and health care policy. Because some of these impairments preclude direct interviewing of those involved, techniques for acquiring proxy data are necessary.

• Compared with other age groups, older persons have much higher rates of institutional residence and use of long-term care services in the home and community. A comprehensive national population perspective on this large and growing group requires data on the health status of these persons and the nature of the long-term and institutional care being provided.

The remainder of this section reviews the various sources of health data on the elderly, along with ways in which these data could be made more useful for cross-national research and policy formulation.

Sources of National Health Data

A broad range of data on health and health status is available in most developed nations and increasingly in developing nations as well. These data must be approached cautiously and their limitations recognized. Table 6-3 (adapted from Andrews, 1999) summarizes health data sources and their potential limitations.

As Table 6-3 illustrates, a number of barriers may exist to the successful application of these potentially rich data sources. First, in many instances there may simply be insufficient or inappropriate data gathered or available, and the data collected may be of limited accuracy. There is also little standardization in the collection and representation of administrative data across nations, a limitation that may extend to computer software and formats. Information may not be available in a timely manner, often being delayed by several years. Policy and decision makers may misunderstand the relevance of information for research applications, and those conducting research studies and surveys may misunderstand the policy process, although the imposition of political perspectives on the conduct of research may be detrimental to all. Political, fiscal, and ethical

TABLE 6-3 Sources of Health Data and Their Potential Limitations

Source	Potential Limitations
Census Data	Infrequent collection; generally little health content
National Household Surveys	Target population, sample size, periodicity, comprehensiveness, survey design
Mortality Vital Records	Age accuracy among elders, analytical access
Morbidity Information	Accuracy, access, geographic coverage, variation in format and vocabulary/coding
Health Administrative Data	Timeliness, lack of analysis, format variation
Special Research Studies	Relevance, quality, presentation, national coverage, availability for analysis
Health Care Evaluations	Availability, timeliness, accuracy
Outcomes Research	Varying conceptual frameworks, availability, utility, legal implications
Longitudinal Cohorts/Panels	Design, costs, timeliness, relevance
Qualitative Studies	Design, coverage, relevance
Market Research	Target population, relevance, accuracy
Institutional Sources	National coverage, costs, data access, identification of all relevant populations, type of data

SOURCE: Adapted from Andrews (1999).

considerations may not permit easy distribution of the data to appropriate analysts. Finally, there may be inadequate analytical methodology to summarize and interpret complex and large datasets. Thus concerted administrative and political effort is required to collect the data necessary to exploit the opportunities of cross-national research.

International Repositories of Health Data

Availability and access are key limitations for many of the health data sources listed in Table 6-3. While some datasets will inevitably have limited distribution, others would be usefully provided in repositories or catalogued for administrative and research analysts. No single central repository now exists for health information from population surveys or health system administrative data relevant to older persons. Important catalogues are being compiled, however, by such organizations as the United Nations (Agree and Myers, 1998), the Organization for Economic Cooperation and Development (OECD) (Gudex and Lafortune, 2000), the European Union (Hupkens, 1997), and the U.S. National Institute on Aging (2000). In addition, the Interuniversity Consortium for Political and Social Research at the University of Michigan operates a National Archive of Computerized Data on Aging (HtmlResAnchor http://www.

icpsr.umich.edu/NACDA/index.html) that is increasingly international in scope. The efforts of these organizations will continue to be important in identifying the data needed for cross-national research.

The Concept of the Graduated Minimum Dataset

The diverse practical needs of health care organizations and agencies that address aging issues, both within and among nations, pose a challenge to achieving the data comparability required to answer many fundamental questions that transcend local populations. Each unit builds administrative data systems and collects data consistent with its unique needs and perceptions of utility. A common problem that results is loss of the capacity to gain analytical power by comparing local experiences with those in other populations or regions.

National governments may deal with this issue by developing minimum and/or core datasets with precise definitions for each data element. Doing so enables common approaches to data reporting on vital and health statistics and to analysis across population groups, elements of service systems, and utilization and costs of care. In the United States, the National Center for Health Statistics, working with other agencies in the Department of Health and Human Services and with the advice of the National Committee on Vital and Health Statistics, establishes minimum datasets, data elements, and data definitions used uniformly throughout the Department of Health and Human Services. While these activities contribute importantly to common nomenclatures and data standards, special data repositories are needed for information thus collected in developed and, where possible, developing countries. The World Health Organization has worked and continues to work toward this end.

Most countries continue to standardize the vocabulary of health services administration. For example, the United States is moving toward a standard long-term care dataset with the following categories: demographic items, health status items, service items, and procedural items. Demographic items include sex, birth date, race, ethnicity, marital status, usual living arrangements (type and location), and court-ordered constraints if any. Such a list could be expanded substantially (for example, to include educational level attained, income from various sources, entitlements received, and religion and religious participation). The list can be altered in response to political, social, or economic forces, as well as agreed-upon international nomenclature where possible.

Variations in data collection across countries greatly compound the difficulties of obtaining comparable information. Even small variations in definition, question formulation, and mode of data collection may significantly alter responses and impair comparability. Moreover, understanding and interpretation of data elements may vary among cultural settings. It is essential to facilitate valid comparisons by easing the data collection burden on countries and regions that have many fewer information gathering resources than the richest Western countries, and by providing a basis for meaningful national comparisons across surveys, administrative data systems, and other sources of health and aging data.

The concept of the graduated minimum dataset could be applied to facilitate health research and policy analysis relevant to aging by providing basic descriptive data on individuals, disease and disability measures, long-term care programs and facilities, health service utilization, and related data elements. Since all nations cannot be expected to invest the same level of resources in data collection, a hierarchy of data collection modules, ranging from easily collected basic data elements to increasingly elaborate datasets, would be an appropriate universal approach. Such a hierarchy might have five to ten levels—from a bare minimum of descriptive statistics to rich and comprehensive data elements such as those found in the Health and Retirement Survey and the Medicare Current Beneficiary Survey. Each such level would have clear definitions of elements, precise wording, and defined response categories. The choice of data elements would be supported by reliability and validity studies justifying their inclusion. Any administrative authority could decide how extensive its data collection would be, but whatever the level selected, the data collected could be made comparable to those from other collection efforts. The value of such a system is that the administrative authority could add any data items needed to meet local purposes without undermining the comparability of the data collection efforts across geographic units. A feasibility study of a small number of aging-related measures, such as those related to disability, could be conducted to test this approach and assess the implementation issues that need to be resolved.

Linking of Health Data

Assessing the health of older persons requires the compilation of data from many sources, such as personal and family surveys, vital records, health care administrative records from various providers, and other health-relevant sectors of society. Moreover, since multiple conditions and impairments are common among older persons, they may seek medical and social services from a variety of providers. The value of data linkage for improved policy formulation has been well-documented (National Research Council, 1988). The use of primary institutional records increases the accuracy of the information available for analysis and complements information that can be gained only from interviews. At the same time, however, there are several potential impediments to record linkage, including costs, privacy concerns, and the logistics of assembling data from multiple sources.

OVERCOMING OBSTACLES TO CROSS-NATIONAL RESEARCH ON THE HEALTH STATUS OF THE ELDERLY

As noted earlier, cross-national comparisons can be useful in a number of ways in addressing issues related to the health status of elderly populations. A cross-national perspective encompasses a broad range of variations that can yield important qualitative insights into alternative institutional arrangements, policies, and programmatic interventions not available for study in one country. Cross-national comparisons can also provide some sense of the generalizability of observations made in specific national and cultural contexts. To the extent that similar patterns and trends are observed across nations that vary in social structure and culture, as well as in health and welfare approaches, one can have greater confidence that generalizations formulated have merit. Box 6-1 provides an example of how a key issue—deinstitutionalization of elders—could be illuminated by cross-national research.

At the same time, one must recognize the complexity involved in comparing national health systems with varying histories, organizational arrangements, cultural influences, and statistical systems. It is essential that when making such comparisons, the analyst understand thoroughly the contexts being compared and the special measurement, definitional, and linguistic features of each system to ensure that comparable units are being evaluated. Even apparently simple concepts can be difficult to compare across systems. As an example, physicians have varying functions in different national health care systems. General practitioners in the United Kingdom and other European nations, for instance, are exclusively community practitioners, while in the United States they typically provide some amount of in-patient and institutional care.

In addition to cultural variations, there are many factors that may limit or confound cross-national research and must be considered to maximize the credibility of the findings of such studies. For example, underlying population health status may vary across nations; this variation may lead to different outcomes of the same health policy or intervention. There may also be differences in the nature, selection, representativeness, or completeness of population samples and health administration databases, possibly leading to spurious analytic findings. Variation in the accuracy and completeness of clinical and vital records information can confound cross-national comparisons as well. Concepts of health states, individual diseases and conditions, and disability may likewise vary across nations and cultures, and such variations may not be fully captured using inter-

BOX 6-1
Deinstitutionalization of Elders

With continuing increases in longevity, many more people are surviving to advanced ages, when the prevalence of chronic illness and disability increases significantly. In the past, persons surviving with substantial disabilities typically were dependent on family members for their care or were institutionalized in mental hospitals, old-age homes, and other types of custodial institutions (Grob, 1991). Currently, national patterns of family care, the use of custodial institutions, and the mix of long-term care alternatives and services vary substantially (see, e.g., Ribbe et al., 1997; Mechanic and McAlpine, 2000). Thus it would be useful to have a better statistical description of cross-national variations in long-term care and how these services change over time.

Future cohorts of elders with high levels of disability face two competing care approaches likely to affect their later years. One approach, which promotes increasing rates of institutionalization, responds to the limited capacities of family members as caregivers as a result of decreased family size, female labor force participation, high divorce rates, increased geographic mobility, and three- and four-generation families with growing care needs and care-giving burdens. A competing approach is focused on deinstitutionalizing dependent populations, including the elderly, those with mental illness, those with developmental disabilities, and others Vladeck, 1980; Mechanic and Rochefort, 1992), making institutional care less likely than demographic predictions would have suggested. In the United States, for example, nursing home rates per 1,000 population for the age groups 65-74, 75-84, and 85+ all declined between 1985 and 1995, resulting in less nursing home demand than was anticipated (Bishop, 1995). Decreasing disability by age may partly explain the decline, but other factors are likely to be salient as well.

One important factor is the growth of home-based care. Much more medical and long-term care is provided in the home and homelike settings as a result of changes in technology and financial coverage, as well as the growth of organizational infrastructures needed to provide such care (Kane et al., 1998). These settings include life-care communities, assisted-living facilities, supervised housing, board-and-care and rooming-home residences, adult day care, foster care, and integrated community programs. There is increasing interest among public authorities who deal with the elderly, families, and elders themselves in maintaining as much independence as possible and providing needed care in the least restrictive setting. The extensive medicalization of long-term care characteristic of the American health care system has become less common in many western European countries, where old-age homes based on a social model and community care programs have been more fully developed. Cross-national comparative research is therefore needed to assess the relative costs and health outcomes of these alternative approaches.

Such research is challenged, however, by the fact that health data systems are based largely on medical institutions, and few adequate data sources exist that can be used to quantify and characterize newly emerging institutional alternatives. We presently lack clear and consistent definitions of the relevant modalities or minimally adequate sampling frames for studying them. Some useful trend data are available from billing records for home health services, but even very large population sample surveys have too few individuals within each of these care alternatives to provide any reliable information on developing trends. Such problems are compounded in cross-national efforts, in which the designations used may vary a great deal from one setting to another. To address this problem, better descriptive information is needed about the most prevalent long-term care programs in various nations, the range and mix of services they provide, the characteristics of the populations they serve, levels of disability, financing sources, and the intensity of the medical and social services provided (National Research Council, 1988; National Research Council, 1992). It is unlikely that truly comparable data will be acquired in the foreseeable future, but a database providing insight into long-term care alternatives and how they function in varying community and cultural settings could serve as important background for policy formulation on this issue in many nations.

national disease coding systems. Differences in styles of clinical practice and healer-patient interaction and in the use of alternative practitioners may preclude full comparability of summary diagnostic information. And variations in health service organizational modes, financing, and budgeting may make it difficult to capture resource levels or allocations for comparable units of service delivery. Given these variations, the failure to find certain effects of national health systems on a particular health or programmatic outcome may be due to the noncomparability of the study units as well as to the possibility that no effect is actually present.

At the same time, there clearly is increased comparability among nations in the clinical/administrative and survey data being collected. In the future, cross-national research is likely to be facilitated by increased international exchange of scientific information, as well as by advances in survey instruments and measurement techniques; health care evaluation methodology; clinical training and achievement norms; database computerization and management; and regulatory standards for drugs, devices, and other medical interventions. These advances will be enhanced by the growth of international companies and industries that address the provision of clinical services in many parts of the world.

RECOMMENDATIONS

6-1. Designers of government-sponsored nationwide surveys should enhance basic health information on older persons and strengthen the foundation for standardized measures that can be applied to cross-national comparisons. Health status information on older persons should, at a minimum, include the frequency and rates for (1) deaths and their major causes; (2) important acute and chronic medical conditions and their major manifestations; (3) measures of important self-reported health status; (4) population levels of physical, social, and mental function; (5) preventive and health promotional behaviors; and (6) important disabilities. In addition, minimum health care information for older persons should include (1) utilization rates for important types of health services, including institutional and home-based care; (2) personal and family expenses for formal health services; (3) rates of use of medications and devices; (4) major cultural influences on the concept of health and the use of health services (such as gender, ethnicity, geographic residence, and socioeconomic status); and (5) the use of informal and alternative and complementary health care services, including self-care practices and assistance from families and other nonprofessional sources.

6-2. *The concept of a graduated minimum dataset should be implemented as a means of facilitating health research and policy analysis relevant to aging populations.* To provide basic descriptive data on individuals, disease and disability measures, long-term care programs and facilities, and health service utilization, countries should adopt systematic data collection procedures. All nations cannot invest the same level of resources in data collection; thus a hierarchy of data collection modules ranging from easily collected basic data elements to increasingly elaborate datasets would be an appropriate universal approach. Such a hierarchy might have five to ten levels—from a bare minimum of descriptive statistics to rich and comprehensive data elements such as those found in certain OECD countries.

6-3. *All countries should facilitate the linkage of population-based and administrative health information with other important economic, social, and health service data.* Despite logistical and other challenges, linking population survey data to medical, vital, and administrative records, as well as other social and economic data sources, can expand the value of the data for determining population health status and conducting programmatic and policy planning and evaluation (e.g., for assessing levels and changes in disability rates, estimating the effects of insurance coverage on health system expenditures, and providing supplementary information on medical program functions).

6-4. *Longitudinal data on the health of older persons should be collected to enable identification of the risk factors, causes, and preventive interventions for disease and disability.* Panel (cohort) studies should also include economic, behavioral, and social domains to make it possible to identify those groups and individuals at special risk for illness and their respective consumption of health care resources, and to determine whether health outcomes differ according to variations in health care interventions, programs, and policies.

6-5. *Cross-national panel studies should be used to clarify the relationship between health system organization, administration, and financing on the one hand, and health status and outcomes on the other.* Data from longitudinal, population-based surveys, linked to administrative records and with comparable questions across countries, are essential in comparing health across countries and attributing changes in health to particular factors. Moreover, comparative work can improve our understanding of how particular diseases and conditions are expressed as disability in a variety of family, social, and residential environments, thus providing insight into which policies and interventions are most efficacious.

ANNEX 6-1
THE ROLE OF SOCIAL INEQUALITY IN
THE HEALTH OF ELDERS

In all societies, health and functioning vary according to socioeconomic position. The magnitude of these differences and their causes vary over time both within and among societies. To develop policies that can effectively ameliorate these differences requires an understanding of their causes. Policy responses to socioeconomic differentials in health and functioning will ideally cover a wide range of determinants, including medical care and social services. There are likely to be socioeconomic differences in the provision of, access to, and response to these services.

Social inequalities in health affect older as well as younger people. Annex Figure 6-1 shows mortality by employment grade among British civil servants who were part of the first Whitehall study (Marmot and Shipley, 1996). The figure shows clearly that mortality rates follow a social gradient. The implication for monitoring and for policy is that this is not a clear case of poor health among those who are materially deprived and better health for everyone else; the social gradient in health runs the social gamut from top to bottom. While Annex Figure 6-1 is confined to mortality, social inequalities in morbidity loom large among the elderly, and the implications for policy are perhaps even more challenging here. A particular problem in many industrialized countries is the large numbers of elderly women living alone and hampered by disability. Their situation is worsened by factors related to social position, with implications discussed below.

Annex Figure 6-1 also shows that the relative difference in mortality from top to bottom is less at older than at younger ages. This raises two further issues: the appropriate measure of disease burden and the appropriate measure of social classification. Although the relative difference in mortality may be less at older ages, the absolute difference is greater because overall mortality rates are higher. Although relative differences are usually taken as a guide to the strength of causal factors, absolute differences are a better indicator of the social importance of the total burden of disease and suffering.

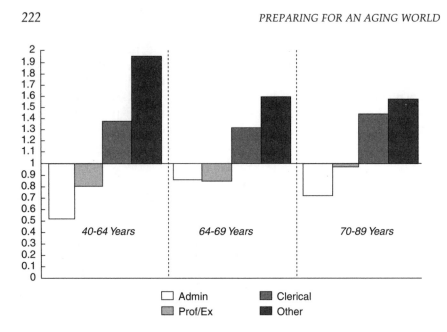

ANNEX FIGURE 6-1   Relative mortality (all causes) by grade of employment, Whitehall men, 25-year follow-up.
SOURCE: Marmot and Shipley (1996).

Classification of Socioeconomic Position

Some countries have had a long tradition of measuring socioeconomic position. The theoretical basis for the various measures that have been used is sometimes explicit, more often implicit, and sometimes nonexistent. Measures based on education, income, occupation, or some combination of these are commonplace and often atheoretical. It has been argued that a sounder theoretical basis for socioeconomic classification would yield better understanding of the determinants involved. One approach to this end is to conceive of three different modes of social stratification: one based on degree of material deprivation, one based on social power relations, and one based on general social standing (Bartley and Marmot, 2000).

Measures of material deprivation are appropriate for assessing health differences among those living under conditions of absolute poverty. Such measures are less appropriate where health follows a social gradient, such as in the Whitehall studies (Marmot and Shipley, 1996; Marmot et al., 1991). In such cases there are clear social inequalities in health among people who are not materially deprived. Other concepts must therefore come into play. A second approach that does potentially relate to the whole social gradient is based on power relations in the workplace. Occupations are defined in terms of power and autonomy, a perspective that has its origins in the Marxist concept of class. This approach is the basis for the Eriksson-Goldthorpe scheme, which in turn provided the framework for the new British socioeconomic classification that will be used nationally for the 2001 census. A third approach, that of general social standing, has features in common with Weber's concept of status, based on patterns of consumption and lifestyle. The status group shares the same level of prestige or esteem and, in addition to common forms of consumption and lifestyle, limits its interactions with members of other groups.

It is impossible to give a blanket prescription for the most appropriate measures of socioeconomic position in different cultures. As measures are developed and applied, it would be valuable to attempt to relate them to theoretical concepts such as the three sketched above.

A measure that is appropriate for social classification among people of working age may be less appropriate for those beyond working age. In many countries, occupation is used as a basis for social classification. There is ample justification for this approach in that work is central to peoples' lives (Marmot and Feeney, 1996). Occupation is a major determinant of income, which in turn affects life chances. Also, the work career is an important part of socialization and achievement of social identity outside the family. It offers opportunities for both fulfillment and frustration of life's goals. Self-esteem, social approval, personal attitudes, and behavioral patterns are all influenced by occupational level. Finally, occupation itself and conditions in the workplace may be important determinants of social inequalities in health.

The degree to which occupation continues to provide a reliable indicator of these four elements in people beyond working age will vary. Additional methods of social classification will be needed. This will especially be the case for older women, particularly those single, widowed, or divorced. Other socioeconomic measures that have been used include education; income; housing tenure; characteristics of area of residence; and, in Britain, household access to a car. The issue of appropriate classification bears on the question of why social inequalities in health may be of lesser magnitude in women than in men. In the past, the social status of married women was better defined by their husband's occupation than by their own. While this situation may still obtain in some circumstances and populations, it is being challenged by dramatic social changes (Bartley et al., 1999). Close attention must be paid to the most appropriate measures that will allow comparison of social inequalities in health within and between genders.

Data Needs for Understanding Determinants of Social Inequalities in Health and Well-Being

Any feature of social or personal life, of biology, and of services may influence social inequalities in health. At the request of the World Health Organization, the International Center for Health and Society at University College London organized research findings on the social determinants of health under 10 headings (Wilkinson and Marmot, 1998).

- Social gradient through the life course
- Stress
- Early life
- Social exclusion
- Work
- Unemployment
- Social support
- Addiction
- Food
- Transport

While these categories were intended as a guide to policy makers, they may also serve as a template for research (Marmot and Wilkinson, 1999). One area that does not appear obvious from this list is the quality of housing and the physical and social environment of neighborhoods. These may be thought of as falling under social exclusion, but, as with health itself, their quality is likely to follow a social gradient. A fuller understanding of the appropriate determinants of socioeconomic differences in health and functioning generally requires longitudinal, representative population surveys. Such surveys are essential for establishing causal associations and assessing the magnitude of causes operating in all directions. In other words, longitudinal data are important for determining the degree to which levels of health and functioning determine social and economic position, as well as for assessing the magnitude and nature of the social determinants of health.

A Policy Response: The British Independent Inquiry into Inequalities in Health

In the late 1970s, Britain took the lead internationally in marshalling the evidence on inequalities in health with a government-sponsored inquiry that became known as the Black Report (Black et al., 1988). The Black Report stimulated research on this subject in Britain and internationally, but had little detectable effect on policy. In 1997, the new Labor government in Britain set up an independent inquiry into inequalities in health under the chairmanship of a former chief medical officer, Sir Donald Acheson (Acheson, 1998). The Acheson Inquiry summarized the evidence on the determinants of social inequalities in health and made 39 recommendations. Importantly, these recommendations were organized by stages of the life course to focus on elders as well as other age groups. The government is currently in the process of acting on these recommendations.

ANNEX 6-2
COMMONLY USED MEASURES OF HEALTH STATUS

The measures of health status commonly used for survey questionnaires and administrative data collection can be grouped into seven categories: clinical symptoms, signs, and syndromes; morbidity, or discretely defined medical conditions; self-rated health; functional status and disability; physiological and pathological measures; mortality data and derived measures; and aging and mental illness. The measures used in each of these categories are reviewed in turn below.

Symptoms, Signs, and Syndromes

Illness-related observations and perceptions are by clinical definition called symptoms, signs, or syndromes.

Symptoms are bodily perceptions that people interpret as being abnormal. Many types of symptoms exist, such as knee pain, headache, fatigue, itching skin, decreasing movement of a joint, sleeplessness, or a depressed mood. These are by nature subjective and may result in differing individual interpretations and subsequent behaviors. For example, one person may seek medical attention for a given symptom, while another may not. Symptoms are particularly common among older persons, and because of this and the frequent lack of objective confirmatory evidence, they make medical diagnosis among elders complex and challenging. Knowing the prevalence rates for important symptoms may assist in understanding the demand for medical care. Symptoms may or may not be harbingers of important underlying medical problems, but substantial resources are often spent in further diagnosis and treatment. Cross-cultural studies of symptoms have been conducted to evaluate differences and similarities in implications for health care provision in such areas as jaw arthritis (Suvinen et al., 1997) and tooth pain (Moore et al., 1998).

Signs are objectively detectable evidence of an abnormality that may be seen both by the individual and the health care professional. Examples include skin rashes, warmth or redness of a body part to the touch, audible wheezing sounds, and inappropriate behaviors in a particular social setting. Signs are also very common among older persons. As with symptoms, they may or may not be indicative of a serious underlying medical problem and may or may not lead to seeking medical care.

When characteristic patterns or clusters or signs and symptoms occur in an individual, they may be called a *syndrome*. An example is a cold or influenza, with which there is a characteristic pattern of cough and running nose, headache, fever, muscle aches, and weakness. In general, syndromes are common but do not always imply a particular underlying disease; for example, in a few instances, the "flu syndrome" might actually reflect tuberculosis or an immune deficiency. Most important, syndromes, like signs and symptoms, represent a significant factor in medical care. Most "flu syndromes" are caused by viral infections and lead to high utilization of medical services. Thus providing data on the frequency of these syndromes in both geographic and patient populations becomes essential for the formulation of health care policies. Knowing their occurrence rates and demands on health care resources across cultures and nations can assist in understanding approaches to their efficient management.

Morbidity, or Discretely Defined Medical Conditions

The term "morbidity" in the present context refers to the named medical conditions that health professionals, administrators, and patients and their families use to define and communicate health information. Most morbid conditions, such as diabetes mellitus, stroke, lung cancer, and myocardial infarction (heart attack), have consensual definitions that apply in most instances. However, there can be important variations in disease vocabulary and usage within a language group or country, in addition to important international variations. The result is less precision and accuracy of information obtained from medical records, and the attendant need to perform standardized relabeling (coding) of diagnostic designations for clinical and administrative purposes. While there can be variation in the extent and severity of any clinical condition, disease names provide considerable information on the biological and clinical effects of a particular condition within both individuals and populations, including the average extent of bodily pathology, usual treatment patterns, and prognosis. Clinical care resource consumption can be inferred from a disease name within a given country and health care system. Despite the current limitations of morbidity designations and their classification, then, familiarity with disease names and taxonomy is critical for deriving and quantifying information for policy, research, and administrative purposes.

In addition, accurate, consensually defined disease names frequently form the basis for assessment of clinical evidence, development of practice guidelines, and quality assurance activities (Grimshaw and Russell, 1993; Muir Gray, 1997) for both national and international applications.

The policy relevance of morbidity data for older persons is clear. The development, maintenance, and evaluation of programs that provide resources for the prevention, treatment, or rehabilitation of various diseases require detailed knowledge of the occurrence, severity, and functional impact of those conditions. Such information can often be acquired from health care data, and its acquisition is becoming easier as a result of computerization of clinical encounter records in both ambulatory and institutional settings. However, obtaining a population view of morbidity occurrence may require population sample surveys, since health system coverage may not coincide with geographic regions and applies only to actual users. Population surveys can add this critical perspective, but information obtained from older lay persons in this manner may be incomplete or only partially valid. Some persons may not fully understand or be able to name their own conditions, and some conditions may not have been clinically evaluated. For example, adult-onset, non-insulin-dependent diabetes remains undetected in at least a third of older Americans. As a result, morbidity rates should be acquired from combined population and institutional sources for maximum validity and policy value.

Older persons often have multiple medical conditions, any of which may alter the nature of the others. Thus comparing the diagnosis, treatment, or outcomes of a particular condition, either within a country or region or cross-nationally, often requires adjustment for other diseases and conditions, or "comorbidity." For example, the presence of comorbid conditions in addition to the disease under consideration can affect quality-of-life scale scores (Xuan et al., 1999), promote the progression of disability (Fried et al., 1999), enhance prediction of hospital lengths of stay (Roe et al., 1998), and generally alter health outcomes after hospitalization (Elixhauser et al., 1998). Comorbidity scales can be applied both to population survey data and to health care administrative datasets (Katz et al., 1996).

The universal approach to organizing morbidity and clinical diagnoses into an internationally acceptable taxonomy is the International Classification of Diseases and Conditions (ICD). The ICD, currently in its 10th edition, is promulgated by the World Health Organization (WHO). It contains several thousand medical conditions and rubrics and is intended to reflect both the complexity of and progress in understanding health and disease. The ICD has enjoyed application in all Western-style health systems, having been adapted and translated for many general applications. However, while the ICD is critical for analyzing community disease information, some limitations should be noted:

• The ICD is a mix of anatomy, physiology, disease behavior, and causation that can only reflect the existing state of disease understanding.

• Some types of clinical information are not available in disease names, such as individual functional status (see below) or the physiological severity of a condition.

• As noted above, there is little ability to deal with the multiple conditions that frequently occur among older persons (comorbidity) and how these conditions affect the disease of interest.

• Rubrics often do not map easily onto other taxonomic systems.

• Because of scientific uncertainty, partial understanding of the nature of many diseases, and the growing relationship between diagnostic rubrics and health system reimbursement, the ICD often reflects political, economic, and intellectual controversy.

• The ICD does not deal easily with the preventive, legal, and administrative aspects of clinical practice.

Because of these and other limitations, alternative and ancillary disease nomenclature and taxonomic systems have been developed. One example is the Systematized Nomenclature of Medicine (SNOMED) system (Lussier et al., 1998), which uses a multiaxial approach to the designation of a given condition. Separate information is provided for different domains, such as anatomical locale, physiological impact, and putative causes of the condition. Several other taxonomies have been developed as well, such as the ICD-O, a detailed catalogue of cancer types, severity, and disease extent; E-Codes, an exhaustive coding system for environmental exposures associated with human disease; and N-Coding, a detailed taxonomy of bodily injuries.

Collaborative international studies of morbidity occurrence have been conducted to assist program planning for health services. An important example is the WHO program on Multinational Monitoring of Trends and Determinants in Cardiovascular Disease (MONICA). Coronary disease is the most common cause of death among elders in most countries. Through MONICA, coronary disease events have been monitored regionally in 16 European countries and Australia, Canada, China, New Zealand, and the United States since 1981. In a recent large-scale cross-national analysis (Tunstall-Pedoe et al., 2000), incremental enhancements to the quality of coronary care in various geographic areas were correlated with short-term heart attack survival (the "case-fatality ratio"). This ecological analysis, done separately for men and women, produced evidence that greater improvement in coronary care (a higher "treatment score") is associated with a larger decline in the case-fatality ratio, indicating improved survivorship. While further assessment is needed, this type of cross-national study supports the value of investing in improved coronary care facilities across a broad range of approaches to such care.

Self-Rated Health

Items measuring self-rated health are frequently found in surveys of many kinds. An example is a question asking respondents to characterize their overall state of health using categories such as excellent, good, fair, or poor. Such evaluations may or may not correspond to that which would be provided by a physician.

The person-centeredness of such questions make them extremely useful for a number of purposes in health research. First, self-related health is used in measures of health, psychological well-being, and health-related quality of life, concepts that are usually ill-defined but nearly always include some element of physical well-being and functioning. These are matters for which the individual is certainly the best source of information. Second, self-rated health can be used as a screening tool to identify high-risk groups and risk factors; poor self-rated health is consistently associated with low socioeconomic status and high levels of other illness risk factors in both national and international studies. Third, self-rated health can be used as an outcome in the evaluation of medical interventions as an important addition to the usual mortality and morbidity outcomes; treatments with similar effects on length of life may have different implications with respect to the quality of those years. Fourth, self-rated health can be used as a predictor of illness behavior, retirement, or the long-term use of medication and other health care services; studies of retirement decision making have often included this measure as the only indicator of health status (Bjorner et al., 1996). Finally, the most compelling reason for including self-rated health on surveys is its apparent predictive power with respect to mortality. In 1982, a Canadian study showed that self-ratings of health given by a representative sample of elderly residents of Manitoba in 1971 were better predictors of mortality by 1977 than either their medical records or self-reported conditions. A 1997 review found 27 published studies of representative samples from 13 countries reporting analyses of self-rated health and mortality; in 23 of these studies, self-rated health was a significant predictor of mortality for males and/or females even after other measures of health status had been taken into account (Idler and Benyamini, 1997). Another review conducted 2 years later found 19 studies that included an additional 4 countries; only 2 of these studies reporting no significant association between self-rated health and mortality risk (Benyamini and Idler, 1999).

The number of such studies and the consistency of their findings is impressive for several reasons. The very appearance of so many studies in such a short time (a span of 17 years, with most appearing after 1990) is noteworthy in itself, especially considering that the data reported are from longitudinal studies, many of which had been planned and were begun years earlier. The implication is that some question eliciting a global evaluation of health was used in the interviews for these studies because it had been deemed useful for some other purpose and subsequently was found to be related to mortality risk in secondary analyses. This large body of findings also presents two paradoxes. One is that the interviews on which the analyses were based were conducted in the language of the respondents, and few if any attempts were made to standardize the questions or the response categories. A second is that the countries involved vary a great deal in the proportion of respondents that evaluate their health in the poorest category ("poor," "bad," "extremely bad," "very sick," "worse health compared with others," or "not healthy"). This variation renders the near uniformity of the findings all the more surprising, since cultural as well as linguistic meanings of health differ greatly from one country to another, as do the more objective morbidity and mortality rates. Indeed in many of the studies, poor self-related health predicts mortality with effect sizes and significance levels similar to those associated with smoking. These findings underscore, as few others could, the validity of lay perspectives on health and the usefulness of a holistic approach to defining health. Respondents to surveys are supplying their own meanings of health, which may include some or all of WHO's broad definition of human health (a "complete state of physical, mental, and social well-being"). Self-ratings of health thus provide a simple, direct, and economical way of capturing perceptions of health using criteria that are as broad and inclusive as the responding individual wants to make them.

Functional Status and Disability

The functional characterization of older persons along physical, cognitive, and social dimensions is extremely important in directing health policy. Functional disability is uniquely common among older persons, and there is substantial potential for its prevention. Age-related increases in physical and cognitive disability are often a direct result of chronic medical conditions such as heart disease, stroke, vascular disease, arthritis, Parkinson's disease, cancers, and dementia. Yet they are also related to social and environmental factors. Decreases in social interaction and engagement can be a result of both physical and cognitive changes, as well as a loss of friends and family to mortality and migration and a decline in social roles, including productive work. Decreases in social engagement can in turn worsen the outcomes of physical disability and cognitive impairment.

Physical Disability

Physical disability results in a decreased ability to perform roles essential to remaining independent and productive and maintaining a home. It is estimated that in the United States, more than 20 percent of older adults have limitations in their ability to perform major daily activities as a result of underlying disease (Manton et al., 1997). The aspects of physical disability most frequently considered are the ability to perform tasks essential to living independently in the home (e.g., meal preparation or bill paying) or to self-care (e.g., bathing and dressing). However, a broad spectrum of more demanding activities, such as paid work, voluntary activities, and recreation, are also affected.

Disability and dependency rates among older adults, as well as use of long-term care, vary substantially among regions and cultures and by socioeconomic status and social structure. Understanding rates of disability within and among countries and regions, as well as the health, health care, social, and economic factors that may affect these rates, helps provide a basis for planning for future chronic care needs. Moreover, disabled older adults require the most intensive and costly general health care and community services. The size of the disabled population, therefore, has a tremendous impact on current and overall future health care needs.

As noted, there is increasing evidence of the potential for preventing disability. Such measures include the primary prevention of disabling diseases and tertiary prevention to minimize their progression and impact. It may also be possible to decrease disability through social approaches (e.g., altering the social factors that affect function) and through environmental modifications. Moreover, newly developed methods can be used to screen for individuals at risk of disability or its progression, so that appropriate interventions can be undertaken. It may be noted that the potential for all of these various approaches to reduce disability argues for continuous national tracking of disability levels through representative surveys and related methods.

Cognitive Impairment

The loss of cognitive function increases with age in all populations studied. This cognitive loss, in turn, leads to important clinical and functional consequences termed dementia. In the majority of industrialized countries, the most important dementing illness is Alzheimer's disease.

As with physical function, rates of dementia prevalence vary among communities, cultures, and nations (Jorm and Jolley, 1998). Rates among those aged 85 and older in industrialized countries may be as high as 50 percent. A key factor associated with dementia is a loss of independence in one or more aspects of everyday function. This association between functional impairment and subsequent dementia suggests that cognitive impairment mediates selected age-related transitions in physical function (Carlson et al., 1999).

Social Function

Social function denotes the extent of individual engagement with family, friends, and society. Individual social networks vary in the type, quality, and frequency of interactions with others. Engagement with society takes many forms, including participation in social, religious and political institutions and paid and volunteer work. Such engagement frequently provides a sense of productivity and of making a contribution to society. Ongoing participation in structured activity, such as paid or volunteer work or managing a household (Glass et al., 1999; Musick et al., 1999), has been shown to decrease the risk of mortality. Positive social networks have also been associated with decreased risk of disability with regard to basic self-care activities (activities of daily living), as well as other health outcomes. Conversely, social disengagement has been shown to predict cognitive decline and disability (Bassuk et al., 1998). However, it should be acknowledged that a better health status may also allow more active and productive social function.

Assessment of Functional Status

An individual's ability or limitation in performing the tasks of daily life is commonly assessed through self-reports or through functional performance testing in the home or clinic. Functional measures can be used to describe specific limitations in discrete areas, such as using a spoon or remembering numbers. Other measures can be used to describe the cumulative impact on an individual of one or more chronic conditions, cognitive impairments, and physiological changes associated with aging, as well as social, environmental, and psychological modifiers of these conditions. Thus, functional status and disability measures serve both to assess the net impact of disease and aging on the individual and to express the ability of the individual to care for him- or herself and to manage a household.

Disability measures essentially describe a syndrome rather than one or more specific diseases; for example, someone may have difficulty walk-

ing across a room because of arthritis, a neurological condition, cardio-
pulmonary disease, or many other factors. While chronic diseases have
an important impact on functional levels, not all persons with a particular
disease have measurable functional decrements, and not all will become
disabled from their disease.

Physical function typically is assessed with reference to activities in
which physical movement predominates, such as basic self-care activities
(including bathing, dressing, and toileting); more complex, instrumental
activities (including cooking, shopping, and recreational exercise); and
mobility (moving from one place to another) and other basic physical
movements (including reaching, kneeling, and fine hand movements). It
should be noted here that in some instances, these measures may be
heavily influenced by living environments and social role expectations.

Cognitive function is usually assessed through special cognitive-psy-
chological testing of basic cognitive processes performed by the human
brain, such as memory, calculation, visuo-spatial abilities, and reasoning,
although impairment may sometimes be inferred from declines in the
performance of instrumental activities. Measurement of a decline in particular cognitive functions generally cannot be used to diagnose a specific
disease and must be accompanied by thorough clinical evaluation. Formal psychological testing also is used to assist in determining mental
illness.

Finally, assessment of social function is usually performed by query-
ing individuals, families, and others to determine the nature of social
networks—type; quality, positive or negative; and frequency of interaction. Types of social engagement (frequency of participating in social or
productive activities) are also determined.

Functional status measures are increasingly collected in clinical practice. In contrast with information on morbidity (diseases) encountered in
the health care system, however, the information on such measures is
often not coded or easily retrieved from administrative datasets or clinical
records. Sometimes, functional status can be inferred from various diagnostic rubrics (e.g., dementia) or from clinical interventions (e.g., physical
rehabilitation), but drawing such inferences is challenging. An increasing
number of population surveys with health and economic goals contain
functional status measures, often in longitudinal perspective, and offer
considerable analytical potential for policy applications. Some recent examples from various countries are shown in Annex Box 6-1.

There are numerous measures of functional status, and while they
can be used in cross-national research for understanding the causes of
various levels and changes among the elders of many nations, the number
of comparisons could be large. One way to deal with this problem is to
apply summary measures of several individual functional attributes, us-

---

ANNEX BOX 6-1
Examples of National and Regional Surveys of Older
Populations Using Functional Status Measures

Australia: Australian Longitudinal Study of Ageing
Bangladesh: Matlab Health and Socioeconomic Survey
Europe: European Longitudinal Study on Aging (11-county study)
Indonesia: Health and Aging Dynamics in a Low-Income Population
Israel: Cross-Sectional and Longitudinal Aging Study
United States: Survey of Asset and Health Dynamics Among the Oldest Old,
    Established Populations for Epidemiologic Studies of the Elderly, Longitudinal
    Study of Aging and Supplement on Aging II, National Long-Term Care Survey,
    Women's Health and Aging Study, Cardiovascular Health Study
International Comparisons: Luxembourg Income Study (data from more than 25
    countries for 1 or more years, including disability status of head of household
    and spouse)

---

ing survivorship methods or "health expectancy measures" (Robine et al., 1999) to create a disability profile employing the time to onset of disability among the population of each age in the context of general survivorship. An example of the application of this approach is shown in schematic form in Annex Figure 6-2. Age-specific prevalence rates provide important information and have been determined for representative population samples in many countries. Annex Figure 6-3 shows gender- and age-specific prevalence rates for severe disability in four countries. Interestingly, there are clear differences among countries in trends by age that require further exploration.[1] Such cross-national differences offer special opportunities to explore environmental, cultural, and biological explanations. Given that analyses of declines in age-specific levels of physical disability (Freedman and Martin, 1998; Manton et al., 1993; Crimmins et al., 1997) do not go far in explaining such trends, there is a clear need for international contrasts to provide and test causal hypotheses. Also of interest is the extent to which the more recent epidemiological transition

---

[1]Documenting and exploring these differences has been the goal of REVES (International Network on Health Expectancy and the Disability Process), a group of international researchers that has been meeting regularly since 1989. Estimates of healthy life expectancy are now available for at least 49 countries worldwide, and time series exist for 15 of these nations (Robine, 1999). To date, however, harmonization of concepts among countries has proven elusive, and differences in definitions and methodologies among countries preclude strict cross-national comparison.

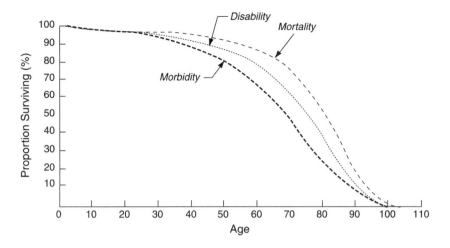

ANNEX FIGURE 6-2 A general model of health status and change (observed mortality and hypothetical morbidity and disability survival curves for U.S. females in 1980).
SOURCE: World Health Organization (1984). Reprinted with permission.

in poorer countries will lead to different patterns of disability change as mortality decline proceeds.

Physiological and Pathological Measures

For at least 150 years, the acquisition of bodily materials and the measurement of human physiological functions have been part of medical practice for purposes of diagnosis and assessment of the efficacy of treatment. Rapid advances in such measures in clinical practice have been limited only by the availability of the necessary resources and the ability of patients to accept the diagnostic burden. In the Western tertiary care setting, many technologically complex determinations are being performed, including complex metabolic investigations, noninvasive imaging of body organs, and assessment of complex organ functions (e.g., of the brain and heart). Genetic determinations are also becoming an increasingly important part of clinical practice. More traditional and routine blood and urine evaluations are extremely common as well, and literally hundreds of specific determinations are available for evaluating disease processes.

Several important policy questions relevant to older persons stem from these laboratory assessments. Does the increasing availability of

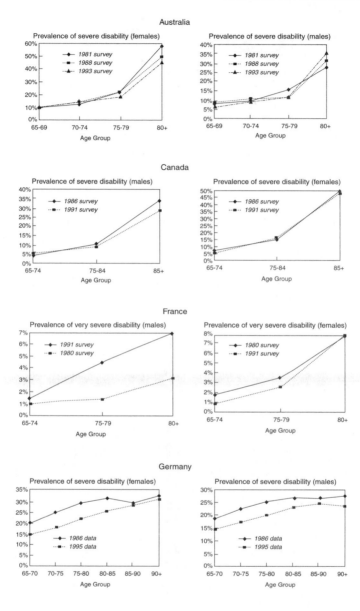

ANNEX FIGURE 6-3 Trends in the prevalence of severe disability among the elderly in four countries.
NOTES: Australia: severe handicap, households and institutions; Canada: HALS survey, households and institutions, severe disability; France: households, confined to bed; Germany: households, microcensus, severe disability.
SOURCE: Jacobzone et al. (1998).

these sophisticated measures contribute to improved health outcomes among older persons? How should these complex and expensive tests be applied more efficiently both geographically and to individual patients? Does their use lead to secondary medical care activities that improve health status? Do long-term adverse health effects occur because of improper medical decision making based on these tests? Several of these questions can be addressed in cross-national investigations since there is considerable regional and national variation in access to and funding and application of such procedures, enabling useful and important outcome studies. However, cross-national evaluation of the outcomes of various medical tests and procedures requires assurance that these tests and procedures have similar properties and interpretation to allow comparative studies.

An additional and important issue is the application of laboratory testing procedures to surveys of geographically defined older populations. Such application has generally lagged behind clinical use because of difficulties in test portability for community studies, lesser acceptance of such testing among those without overt clinical conditions, and impeded access to persons having substantial functional impairment or residing within an institutional setting. Several approaches to this problem have been devised, including inviting survey participants to regional clinical testing centers; creating more acceptable portable testing and specimen-collection devices; and limiting the testing in various ways, for example, to tests for risk factors for important chronic conditions of older persons (e.g., blood pressure or blood cholesterol or sugar levels), use of simple physical testing devices (e.g., those for respiratory function or muscle strength), physical performance tests that reflect common functions (e.g., self-care activities of daily living), and tests for blood determinants that reflect more complex constructs (e.g., levels of environmental contaminants or genetic determinations).[2] It may be noted that new testing procedures for population health assessments are continually being evaluated and should always be considered.

Mortality Data and Derived Measures

Mortality data, despite certain weaknesses in accuracy and as measures of population health, have been widely applied to guide health policy, in part because of their universal availability from industrialized countries. As noted in Chapter 2, recent advances in both the socioeco-

---

[2]For two recent discussions of new testing procedures and their relevance to population-based studies, see United States Agency for International Development (2000) and National Research Council (2001).

nomic and health spheres, along with changes in individual and group lifestyles, have ensured a notable increase in life expectancy among the elderly. A 60-year old European, North American, or Japanese woman may expect to live another 20-25 years and her male peer another 18-20 years. As recently as 20 years ago, men and women of the same age lived 2 to 4 years less. Much of this recent gain in survivorship has been due to declines in mortality from heart disease. It is expected that survivorship among older persons, particularly the oldest old, will continue to increase, and this increase may trigger higher health and welfare costs. Costs could increase in particular for the prevention and care of chronic degenerative diseases, for assistance for the disabled, and for care associated with other disabling diseases that afflict the oldest old. These potential changes argue for the collection of data needed to estimate trends in future total mortality and specific diseases.

Despite generally decreasing mortality rates, there are disparities among various groups within industrialized countries; mortality rates are lower among women, married persons, and those of higher social class. There are also substantial regional and national variations, necessitating the collection of region-specific health data and the formulation of health and social policies that allow flexibility in managing this variation. To study elderly mortality and survival patterns, data are needed for total mortality (deaths from all causes) and for particular causes, classified according to specific features; data are also needed for characterizing the population at risk of dying.

Mortality data typically come from death certificates of national vital record systems. Currently, however, there is substantial variation in the quality of the data, and information may be missing for certain geographic jurisdictions, impeding understanding of mortality trends for policy purposes. Just how this variation in quality affects analytical studies depends on the goals and policy questions involved. Annex Table 6-1 summarizes options for comparing mortality rates among various older populations, either cross-sectionally or longitudinally. Options are shown for both group or collective mortality findings and individually followed mortality as part of the lifetime history of health and disease.

Availability of General Mortality Information

Mortality data by gender and age have been available for 48 European and non-European countries since World War II. Only a few countries possess longer time series. Some central statistical offices supply data that are also classified according to year of birth, thus facilitating the study of mortality for different cohorts. Usually, deaths and the relative population exposed to the risk of dying are classified for individual ages

ANNEX TABLE 6-1 Options for Comparing Mortality Rates

Type of Data	Approaches	Data Needs	Measures and Methods
Collective	Cross-sectional	Deaths by age, gender, and calendar year; population at risk	Rates by age, age-standardized cancer ratio, proportional mortality ratio,
		Deaths by cause and year, population at risk, and competing events	standardized mortality rates, probability, life table, life table by cause
	Longitudinal (by cohort)	Deaths by age and year of birth, population at risk	Rates by age and cohort, probability and life tables by cohort
Individual	Longitudinal biographies	Death records, data on individual survival, linkage data	Survival analyses, Kaplan-Meier models, Cox models, etc.
		Follow-up data	Analysis of life histories, biographies (hazard models)

through age 99 and as a single group for those aged 100 and over, although most countries have recently made efforts to publish data for individual ages for the latter segment of the population as well.

Kannisto (1994) has constructed a database that comprises a mortality series for persons aged 80 and over for a set of industrialized countries that publish such data annually. The data have been subjected to a number of tests of their plausibility and internal consistency. On the basis of these tests, countries have been classified into four quality categories: those with good-quality data (Czechoslovakia, Denmark, England and Wales, Finland, France, Germany, Hungary, Iceland, Italy, Japan, Luxembourg, the Netherlands, Norway, Scotland, Sweden, and Switzerland); those with acceptable-quality data (Australia, New Zealand-non Maori, and Portugal); those with acceptable data under certain conditions (Estonia, Ireland, Latvia, Poland, and Spain); and those whose data should be used with caution (Canada, New Zealand-Maori, and the United States).

The database was constructed from data on deaths arranged into cohort survival histories. Once mortality measures by age are available, life tables can be constructed and analyses of elderly survival performed. Amalgamation of data on life expectancy, diseases, and disabilities will make it possible to derive measures that incorporate healthy and disabled life expectancy.

Quality of Vital Records

It is well known that mortality estimates at old ages may be hampered by various problems (Coale and Kisker, 1986, 1990; Kannisto, 1994, 1996; Thatcher et al., 1998). For example, age misreporting is usually found both in death registration and in censuses and other surveys. The most common manifestations of the data quality problem are implausible age-specific mortality fluctuations and abnormally low mortality estimates at older ages (Preston et al., 1997). Two common problems are the tendency to report age in round numbers (the nearest 5 or 0) and age exaggeration among the oldest old. Other problems in the quality of data on occupation, education, and surviving kin have been described.

Causes of Death

While causes of death have been registered throughout the industrialized world dating back to the beginning of the 20th century, it is only recently that certain quality changes have been introduced in standardized registration procedures. Death certificates are the responsibility of medical doctors, according to WHO guidelines. The certificate is divided into two sections. The first lists the diseases leading to death, and the second details other conditions, so-called *associated causes*, which may have contributed to the death event. In the first section, the doctor must list the direct cause of death, known as the *immediate cause*; followed by the pathology immediately preceding this, or the *intermediate cause*; and lastly the originating or *initial* or *main cause*. A death certificate may contain indications regarding more than one cause, thus making it possible to trace back the whole process leading to death, at least in theory. Death is taken to be the end result of a chain of diseases, whose advent and development may be linked to other preexisting diseases. Published mortality analyses tend to emphasize the *main cause*, which, particularly when dealing with the elderly, is often difficult to identify. To shape policies targeted at the prevention and treatment of selected diseases, it would be highly useful to have available all the information contained in the death certificate. Having these data is crucial to identifying certain diseases, such as diabetes, that may not appear among the principal causes on the certificate but play a leading role in mortality levels. Indicators of mortality by multiple causes (Nam, 1990) may also be defined if the necessary data are available.

It should be noted that there are several sources of error in certification of the causes of death. Physician certifiers may make errors in diagnosis, or there may be inadequate clinical information available. Sometimes, ill-defined descriptors of older persons, such as "senility" or "heart attack," are entered when no specific clinical information is available. There may also be errors in coding of reported death events by vital registrars. However, quality control in this area is increasing, and this source of error is diminishing.

Individual Data and Mortality Differentials

The study of mortality differentials has provided a number of explanatory hypotheses and offered the possibility of moving from description of the differences observed to identification of their root causes. Many studies have involved analyzing mortality differences according to socioeconomic status, usually encompassing cross-sectional analyses of older populations (e.g., Mare, 1990; Martelin, 1995). However, the impact of social status may be cumulative throughout the life course. Mortality at old age can depend on living conditions during childhood, adolescence, and adulthood, and thus a longitudinal approach may be valuable. Such an approach involves a more complete overview of the entire process as it occurred during the individual's lifetime (Sahli et al., 1995). Death is considered the final event in a life history composed of a succession of various passages spanning a variety of situations and experiences, gradually culminating in an illness (or accident) and then death (Caselli et al., 1987). Data from health, census, and other sources are linked to derive a lifetime picture of social, economic, medical, and other influences.

Cross-National Mortality Contrasts

Cross-national comparisons of the mortality of older persons can be instructive. Annex Figure 6-4 shows the probabilities of death for men and women aged 80-99 (the oldest old) in five countries—Sweden, Japan, France, Italy, and Australia—during the last half of the 20th century. In addition to the clear decline over the study interval and the almost universal finding of higher mortality probabilities in men than in women, three observations stand out. One is that gains in survivorship are happening even among the oldest segments of the world's elders. Another is that the relative survivorship gains among women have been greater than those among men. Finally, the dispersion of the gains is greater among

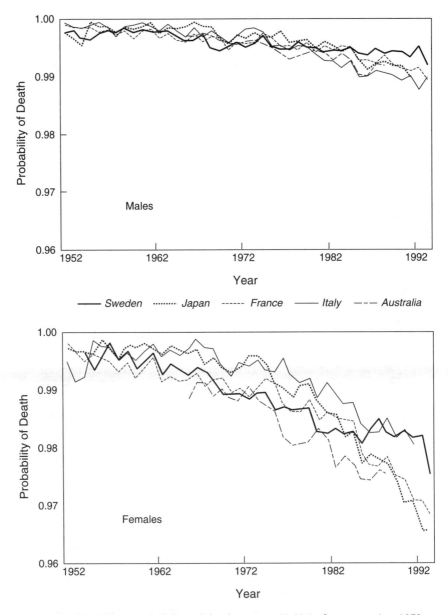

ANNEX FIGURE 6-4 Probability of death at ages 80-99 in five countries: 1952 to
1994.
SOURCE: Prepared by the panel based on data from the Max Planck Institute for
Demographic Research, Rostock, Germany.

women than among men. The latter two findings should prompt cross-national research into national differences in changing survivorship.

Aging and Mental Illness

Psychiatric disorders are significant contributors to physical, social, and emotional dysfunction and disability among the elderly, but it is only recently that such problems have drawn significant attention (Wells et al., 1989). All of the important mental conditions of young adulthood and middle age, including depression, mania, schizophrenia, personality disorders, addictions (including alcoholism), phobias, anxiety, and panic disorders, occur in older persons. Moreover, with increased survivorship and longevity among older persons, dementia and Alzheimer's disease have become quite common. The dementing illnesses themselves are often accompanied by additional psychiatric symptoms that require medical treatment. These symptoms are among the most important reasons for institutionalization or community-based long-term care. Various approaches to institutionalization of elders with mental and physical disability were discussed earlier in Box 6-1.

A particularly important and common condition of older persons is depression, a disorder that illustrates the difficulties of determining the population burden and health service needs associated with psychiatric illness. Early epidemiological studies of mental illness indicated lower rates of depression among the elderly than among younger population subgroups, but there is much reason to doubt the validity of such estimates. Older people are more reluctant to admit to depressive symptoms than younger persons and are more likely to express their symptoms in somatic terms. Most of the instruments measuring depression in community settings, however, depend substantially on psychological items that elderly persons are less likely to endorse. Prevalence estimates of depression among the elderly can vary as much as 15-fold depending on the definitions used, populations studied, and research approaches (Gurland et al., 1996). An important difficulty in assessing and treating depression among older persons involves their different life circumstances as compared with younger persons. Elders have more physical illness and take more medications, making it more difficult to differentiate depression from other health states. In addition, older persons who suffer decrements in function and who lose spouses and friends experience depressive symptoms that they and health professionals commonly view as part of the aging process itself. Researchers often have difficulty differentiating reactions to the losses of normal aging from depression per se. Depression among the elderly is common in primary care practice, and doctors caring for this population tend to be skeptical of the psychologically oriented epidemiological instruments. New efforts are being made to derive valid measures of depression in elderly populations and to provide more appropriate treatment (Unutzer et al., 1999).

Depression exemplifies the problems of determining the care burden of mental illness among older persons. Among elders, mental conditions are often associated with important medical illnesses, but receive lower priority in clinical diagnosis and treatment. In addition, as noted, many mental problems are mistakenly considered to be part of normal aging and not given appropriate attention, particularly in the primary care setting. Also, administrative and clinical records related to treating mental illness, while sometimes in the mainstream of medical systems, are often kept in separate locations with separate access restrictions. Thus, population rates of mental illness may not be attainable from clinical or administrative records, and the use of population surveys for this purpose should be considered. It is ironic that surveying for mental illness requires a substantial participant burden, as the instruments are often long and detailed. This constraint has limited the number of community- and population-based assessments available for planning and evaluation. Thus it is not surprising that even among industrialized countries, clinical services for the prevention and treatment of mental illness are often lacking because of their costs and competing clinical priorities. There are also substantial differences among cultures in the behavioral manifestations and lay and professional interpretations of mental symptoms and conditions. This variation makes international comparisons particularly hazardous, and necessitates extreme care and documentation of clinical events when conducting such research studies.

REFERENCES

Acheson, D.
    1998   *Independent Inquiry into Inequalities in Health Report.* London: The Stationery Office.
Agree, E.M., and G.C. Myers
    1998   *Aging Research in Europe: Demographic, Social and Behavioral Aspects.* Geneva: United Nations Economic Commission for Europe.
Andrews, G.
    1999   A Research Agenda on Ageing for the Twenty-first Century. Draft report of an Expert Consultative Meeting, 1-3 February, Vienna.
Bartley, M., and M. Marmot
    2000   Social class and power relations at the workplace. In *The Workplace and Cardiovascular Disease, Occupational Medicine: State of the Art Reviews* 15(1), P.L. Schnall, K. Belkic, P. Landsbergis, and D. Baker, eds. Philadelphia: Hanley and Belfus.
Bartley, M., A. Sacker, D. Firth, and R. Fitzpatrick
    1999   Understanding social variation in cardiovascular risk factors in women and men: The advantage of theoretically based measures. *Social Science and Medicine* 49:831-845.

Bassuk, S.S., L.F. Berkman, and D. Wypij
  1998 Depressive symptomatology and incident cognitive decline in an elderly community sample. *Archives of Geriatric Psychiatry* 55:1073-1081.
Benyamini, Y., and E.L. Idler
  1999 Community studies reporting association between self-rated health and mortality: Additional studies, 1995 to 1998. *Research on Aging* 21:392-401.
Bishop, C.E.
  1995 Where are the missing elders? The decline in nursing home use, 1985 and 1995. *Health Affairs* 18:146-155.
Bjorner, J.B., S. Tage, O-G.K. Kristensen, G. Tibblin, M. Sullivan, and P. Westerholm
  1996 *Self-Rated Health: A Useful Concept in Research, Prevention, and Clinical Medicine.* Stockholm: Swedish Council for Planning and Coordination of Research.
Black, D., J.N. Morris, C. Smith, P. Townsend, and M. Whitehead
  1988 *Inequalities in Health. The Black Report: The Health Divide.* London: Penguin Books.
Bloom, S.A., J.R. Harris, B.L. Thompson, F. Ahmed, and J. Thompson
  2000 Tracking clinical preventive service use: A comparison of the health plan employer data and information set with the behavioral risk factor surveillance system. *Medical Care* 38:187-94.
Carlson, M.C., L.P. Fried, Q.L. Xue, K. Bandeen-Roche, S.L. Zeger, and J. Brandt
  1999 Association between executive attention and physical functional performance in community-dwelling older women. *Journals of Gerontology, Series B, Psychological Sciences and Social Sciences* 54(5):S262-270.
Caselli, G., J. Duchene, and G. Wunsch
  1987 L'apport de la démographie à l'explication de la mortalité différentielle. In *L'explication en Sciences Sociales. La Recherche des Causes en Démographie.* Chaire Quetelet '87, Institut de Démographie, Louvain-la-Neuve: Université Catholique de Louvain.
Coale, A.J., and E.E. Kisker
  1986 Mortality crossover: Reality or bad data? *Population Studies* 40:389-401.
  1990 Defects in data on old-age mortality in the United States. *Asian and Pacific Population Forum*, Spring.
Crimmins, E.M., Y. Saito, and S. Reynolds
  1997 Further evidence on recent trends in the prevalence and incidence of disability among older Americans from two sources: The LSOA and the NHIS. *Journals of Gerontology* 52:S59-S71.
Cutler, D.
  1999 Data Needs for Studying the Health Care System. Paper prepared for the Panel on a Research Agenda and New Data for an Aging World, Committee on Population, National Research Council.
Dahlgren, G., and M. Whitehead
  1991 *Policies and Strategies to Promote Social Equity in Health.* Stockholm: Institute for Futures Studies.
Elixhauser, A., C. Steiner, D.R. Harris, and R.M. Coffey
  1998 Comorbidity measures for use with adminstrative data sets. *Medical Care* 36:8-27.
Freedman, V.A., and L.G. Martin
  1998 Understanding trends in functioning among older Americans. *American Journal of Public Health* 88:1457-1462.
Fried, L.P., K. Bandeen-Roche, J.D. Kasper, and J. Guralnik
  1999 Association of comorbidity with disability in older women. *Journal of Clinical Epidemiology* 52:27-37.

Glass, T.A., C.M. de Leon, R.A. Marottoli, and L.F. Berkman
    1999   Population based study of social and productive activities as predictors of sur-
           vival among elderly Americans. *British Medical Journal* 319(7208):478-483.
Grimshaw, J.M., and I.T. Russell
    1993   Effect of clinical guidelines on medical practice: A systematic review of rigourous
           evaluations. *Lancet* 342(8883):1317-1321.
Grob, G.
    1991   *From Asylum to Community.* Princeton: Princeton University Press.
Gudex, C., and G. Lafortune
    2000   An Inventory of Health and Disability-related Surveys in OECD Countries. Pa-
           per prepared for the Organization for Economic Co-operation and Development,
           Paris.
Gurland, B., P. Cross, and S. Katz
    1996   Epidemiological perspectives on opportunities for treatment of depression.
           American Journal of Geriatric Psychiatry 4:7-14.
Hupkens, C.
    1997   *Coverage of Health Topics by Surveys in the European Union.* EUROSTAT Working
           Papers, Population and Social Conditions 3/1998/E/No. 10. Luxembourg: Sta-
           tistical Office of the European Communities.
Idler, E.L., and Y. Benyamini
    1997   Self-rated health and mortality: A review of twenty-seven community studies.
           Journal of Health and Social Behavior 38:21-27.
Jacobzone, S., E. Cambois, E. Chaplain, and J.M. Robine
    1998   *The Health of Older Persons in OECD Countries: Is It Improving Fast Enough to Com-
           pensate for Population Ageing?* Labour Market and Social Policy Occasional Papers
           37. Paris: Organization for Economic Co-operation and Development.
Jorm, A.F., and D. Jolley
    1998   The incidence of dementia: A meta-analysis. *Neurology* 51(3):728-733.
Kane, R.A., R.L. Kane, and R.C. Ladd
    1998   *The Heart of Longterm Care.* New York: Oxford University Press.
Kannisto, V.
    1994   *Development of Oldest-Old Mortality, 1950-1990: Evidence from 28 Developed Coun-
           tries.* Monographs on Population Aging 1. Odense, Denmark: Odense University
           Press.
    1996   *The Advancing Frontier of Survival: Life Tables for Old Age.* Monographs on Popula-
           tion Aging 3. Odense, Denmark: Odense University Press.
Katz, J.N., L.C. Chang, O. Sangha, S.H. Fossel, and D.W. Bates
    1996   Can comorbidity be measured by questionnaire rather than by medical record
           review? *Medical Care* 34:73-94.
Kromhout, D.
    1999   Serum cholesterol in cross-cultural perspective. The Seven Countries Study. *Acta
           Cardiologica* 54:155-158.
Lussier, Y.A., D.J. Rothwell, and R.A. Cote
    1998   The SNOMED model: A knowledge source for the controlled terminology of the
           computerized patient record. *Methods of Information in Medicine* 37:161-164.
Manton, K.G., L. Corder, and E. Stallard
    1993   Estimates in the change in chronic disability and institutional incidence and
           prevalence rates in the U.S. elderly population from the 1982, 1984 and 1989
           National Long Term Care Survey. *Journal of Gerontology* 48:S153-S166.
    1997   Chronic disability trends in elderly United States populations. *Proceedings of the
           National Academy of Sciences, Medical Sciences* 94:2593-2598.

Mare, R.D.
  1990   Socio-economic careers and differential mortality among older men in the United
         States. In *Measurement and Analysis of Mortality*, J. Vallin, S. D'Souza, and A.
         Palloni, eds. Oxford: Clarendon Press.
Marmot M., G.D. Smith, S. Stansfeld, C. Patel, F. North, J. Head, I. White, E. Brunner, and A.
Feeney
  1991   Health inequalities among British civil servants: The Whitehall II study. *Lancet*
         337:1387-1393.
Marmot, M., and A. Feeney
  1996   Work and health: Implications for individuals and society. In *Health and Social
         Organisation*, D. Blane, E. Brunner, and R.G. Wilkinson, eds. London: Routledge.
Marmot, M., and M.J. Shipley
  1996   Do socioeconomic differences in mortality persist after retirement? 25 year fol-
         low-up of civil servants from the first Whitehall study. *British Medical Journal*
         313:1177-1180.
Marmot, M., and R.G. Wilkinson, eds.
  1999   *Social Determinants of Health*. Oxford: Oxford University Press.
Martelin, T.
  1995   Sociodemographic differential in mortality at older ages in Finland. In *Health and
         Mortality among Elderly Populations*, G. Caselli and A. Lopez, eds. Oxford:
         Clarendon Press.
Mechanic, D., and D.D. McAlpine
  2000   Use of nursing homes in the care of persons with severe mental illness: 1985 to
         1995. *Psychiatric Services* 51(3):354-358.
Mechanic, D., and D.A. Rochefort
  1992   A policy of inclusion for the mentally ill. *Health Affairs* 11:128-150.
  1996   Comparative medical systems. *Annual Review of Sociology* 22:39-70.
Moore, R., I. Brodsgaard, T.K. Mao, M.L. Miller, and S.F. Dworkin
  1998   Perceived need for local anesthesia in tooth drilling among Anglo-Americans,
         Chinese and Scandinavians. *Anesthesia Progress* 45:22-28.
Muir Gray, J.A.
  1997   *Evidence-based Healthcare: How to Make Health Policy and Management Decisions*.
         London: Churchill Livingstone.
Musick, M.A., A.R. Herzog, and J.S. House
  1999   Volunteering and mortality among older adults: Findings from a national sample.
         Journals of Gerontology. Series B, Psychological Sciences and Social Sciences 54(3):S173-
         180.
Nam, C.B.
  1990   Mortality differentials from a multiple-cause of death perspective. In *Measure-
         ment and Analysis of Mortality*, J. Vallin, S. D'Souza, and A. Palloni, eds. Oxford:
         Clarendon Press.
National Institute on Aging
  2000   *Databases on Aging. Survey Summaries*. Bethesda, MD: National Institute on Aging.
National Research Council
  1988   *The Aging Population in the Twenty-First Century. Statistics for Health Policy*. Com-
         mittee on National Statistics. P.M. Gilford, ed. Commission on Behavioral and
         Social Sciences and Education. Washington, DC: National Academy Press.
  1992   *Toward a National Health Care Survey: A Data System for the 21st Century*. Panel on
         the National Health Care Survey. G.S. Wunderlich, ed. Commission on Behav-
         ioral and Social Sciences and Education. Washington, DC: National Academy
         Press.

2001 *Cells and Surveys. Should Biological Measures Be Included in Social Science Research?* Committee on Population. C.E. Finch, J.W. Vaupel, and K. Kinsella, eds. Commission on Behavioral and Social Sciences and Education. Washington, DC: National Academy Press.

Organization for Economic Co-Operation and Development (OECD)
1996 *Caring for Frail Elderly People.* Social Policy Studies 19. Paris: Organization for Economic Co-Operation and Development.

Preston, S.H., I. Elo, and S. Quincy
1997 *Effect of Age Misreporting on Mortality Estimates at Older Ages.* Working Paper 98-01. Philadelphia: Population Aging Research Center, University of Pennsylvania.

Quinn, J.F., and R.V. Burkhauser
1994 Retirement and labor force behavior of the elderly. In *Demography of Aging.* Committee on Population. L.G. Martin and S.H. Preston, eds, pp. 50-101. Commission on Behavioral and Social Sciences and Education. Washington DC: National Academy Press.

Ribbe, M.W., G. Lunggren, K. Steel, E. Topinkova, C. Hawes, N. Ikegami, J-C. Henrard, and P.V. Jonnson
1997 Nursing homes in 10 countries: A comparison between countries and settings. *Age and Ageing* 26(S2):3-12.

Robine, J.M.
1999 Can We Hope for Both Long Life and Good Health? Paper prepared for the Panel on a Research Agenda and New Data for an Aging World, London, September, Committee on Population, National Research Council.

Robine, J.M., I. Romieu, and E. Cambois
1999 Health expectancy indicators. *Bulletin of the World Health Organization* 77:181-185.

Roe, C.J., E. Kulinskaya, N. Dodich, and W.R. Adams
1998 Comorbidities and prediction of length of hospital stay. *Australian and New Zealand Journal of Medicine* 28:811-815.

Salhi, M., G. Caselli, J. Duchene, V. Egidi, A. Santini, E. Thiltges, and G. Wunsch
1995 Assessing mortality differentials using life histories: a method and applications. In *Adult Mortality in Developed Countries: From Description to Explanation*, A. Lopez, G. Caselli, and T. Valkonen, eds., pp. 57-79. Oxford: Clarendon Press.

Smith, J.P.
1999 Healthy bodies and thick wallets: The dual relationship between health and economic status. *Journal of Economic Perspectives* 13:145-166.

Suvinen, T.I., P.C. Reade, B. Sunden, J.A. Gerschman, and E. Koukounas
1997 Temporomandibular disorders. Part I: A comparison of symptom profiles in Australian and Finnish patients. *Journal of Orofacial Pain* 11:58-66.

Thatcher, A.R., V. Kannisto, and J.W. Vaupel
1998 *The Force of Mortality at Ages 80 to 120.* Monographs on Population Aging 5. Odense, Denmark: Odense University Press.

Tunstall-Pedoe, H., D. Vanuzzo, M. Hobbs, M. Mahonen, C. Zygimantas, K Kuulasmaa, and U. Keil
2000 Estimation of the contribution of changes in coronary care to improving survival, event rates, and coronary heart disease mortality across the WHO MONICA Project Populations. *Lancet* 355:688-700.

United States Agency for International Development (USAID)
2000 Biological and Clinical Data Collection in Population Surveys in Less Developed Countries. Summary of a Meeting held January 24-25 by MEASURE Evaluation, Washington, DC.

Unutzer, J., W. Katon, M. Sullivan, and J. Miranda
  1999 Treating depressed older adults in primary care: Narrowing the gap between efficacy and effectiveness. *Milbank Quarterly* 77(2):225-256.
Vladeck, B.C.
  1980 *Unloving Care: The Nursing Home Tragedy*. New York: Basic Books.
Wells, K.B., A. Stewart, R. Hays, M. Burnam, W. Rogers, M. Daniels, S. Berry, S. Greenfield, and J. Ware
  1989 The functioning and well-being of depressed patients: Results from the Medical Outcomes Study. *Journal of the American Medical Association* 262:914-919.
Wilkinson, R., and M. Marmot, eds.
  1998 *Social Determinants of Health: The Solid Facts*. Geneva: World Health Organization.
World Health Organization
  1984 *The Uses of Epidemiology in the Study of the Elderly: Report of a WHO Scientific Group on the Epidemiology of Aging*. Technical Report Series 706. Geneva: World Health Organization.
Xuan, J., L.J. Kirchdoerfer, J.G. Boyer, and G.J. Norwood
  1999 Effects of co-morbidity on health-related quality-of-life scores: An analysis of clinical trial data. *Clinical Therapeutics* 21:383-403.

7

Well-Being: Concepts and Measures

It is an article of faith that the supreme criterion by which a government can be judged is the quality of life its citizens experience, including, of course, the duration of life itself. In life expectancy and in material standards, the 20th century was remarkable. Especially in the prosperous and industrialized sectors of the world—the United States, Scandinavia, Japan, and Western Europe—the magnitude of positive change was without precedent. Demographers estimate that increases in longevity during the past 100 years equal or exceed all previous gains from the Bronze Age to the end of the 19th century.

The causes of these gains are many, including public health and sanitation, improved nutrition and drinking water, and the achievements of medicine. Widespread use of vaccination and immunization, the development of antibiotics, pharmacological treatment of chronic diseases, surgical treatment of cardiovascular and orthopedic disease—all these belong in large part to the 20th century.

Even in countries that have been most advantaged in these ways, however, the gains have not been uniform in all life sectors. Gerontologists Matilda and John Riley (1994) have called the latter stages of the 20th century a time of *structural lag*, in which national policies and institutions have failed to keep pace with gains in longevity and health. The nature of employment and retirement, the place of education in the life course, and the structures for providing medical care have yet to catch up with the facts of octogenarian life expectancy, decades of life after usual retirement, and vigorous capability into genuine old age. Nor is the lag only institutional; public attitudes about aging and about older people—who they are, what they want, and what they can do—have the mark of the past about them. Lag in all these respects means that we have yet to achieve the quality of life made possible by the added years of life achieved.

Most people would agree that gains in life expectancy and material goods and services, important as they are, are not all we mean when we use terms such as *well-being* and *quality of life*. The idea of a more comprehensive set of measures—a complete and continuing index of national well-being—is not new. In the United States in 1929, then President Herbert Hoover created the President's Committee on Social Trends for the purpose of generating the necessary data and thus providing an improved basis for policy decisions. In the nature of such things, the committee's report, *Recent Social Trends*, appeared much later, in the midst of a great depression and the early years of the Roosevelt presidency. Forty years later, Wilbur Cohen, Secretary of Health, Education, and Welfare, submitted to President Lyndon Johnson an ambitious document with a modest title: *Toward a Social Report* (Cohen, 1969). This report provided some data and urged the collection of much more in seven main areas: health and illness, social mobility, physical environment, income and property, public order and safety, learning and science and art, and participation and alienation.

As these topics suggest, the 1969 report included some direct measures of well-being—health and illness, for example—and a number of economic and behavioral factors assumed to cause or enable well-being. Throughout the following decade, interest in the measurement of well-being ran high in many countries as part of a larger effort at creating "social indicators." The social indicators movement, as it was called, appears in retrospect to have been part of a larger international concern with well-being and the role of governments in its achievement. It was a time when such phrases as "welfare state" and "great society" were terms of aspiration rather than derision. In more recent years, interest in such measures has continued in the United States (e.g., as seen in the National Survey of Midlife Development in the United States), but with less visibility and with markedly less support from the major funding agencies.

Efforts at measuring quality of life continue in many other countries as well. For example, the multidisciplinary Berlin Aging Study looks at sources of well-being in very old age (see Baltes and Mayer, 1999, for an extended discussion). Some coordination and exchange of information is being accomplished through the MAPI Research Institute in Lyon, France, which publishes the *Quality of Life Newsletter*. Coordination and international exchange is also provided by the International Society for Quality of Life Research (ISOQOL). During the year 2000, the first National Quality of Life Symposium was held in China, and the Seventh Annual Symposium on Quality of Life Evaluation took place in the United States. Both of these symposia, like most of the research reported in the MAPI newsletter, focused on quality of life among people with specific diseases. The ACROSS Project of the European Union, for example, emphasizes outcome measures in rehabilitation in six European countries.

In 1995, the World Health Organization (WHO) reported the completion of pilot work on a 100-question form (WHOQOL) based on a broader conception of health as "a state of complete physical, mental, and social well-being, not merely the absence of disease." The aim is to assess "individuals' perceptions of their position in life in the context of the culture and value systems in which they live and in relation to their goals, expectations, standards and concerns" (Orley, 1995). WHOQOL-100 consists of six main sections: physical health, psychological health, level of independence, social relations, environment, and spirituality. Most of the questions within these sections ask for responses in terms of satisfaction or dissatisfaction on a five-point scale ranging from very satisfied to very dissatisfied. Some questions, however, ask about ability, confidence, or adequacy rather than satisfaction. The complete questionnaire, with its response scales, is available on the Internet, as well as from the WHO Division of Mental Health in Geneva, Switzerland.

In addition to these efforts that concentrate on the measurement of subjective well-being, many other survey-based datasets include some indicators of well-being, whether or not they are so labeled. Among them are measures of mortality and morbidity, measures of ability, and direct measures of life quality as experienced. Examples of ability are the ADL (Activities of Daily Living) scale; the IADL (Independent Activities of Daily Living) scale; and items intended to measure capacity to perform more strenuous activities, such as walking a half-mile or more or doing heavy housework. Direct measures of subjective well-being, as we shall see, take several forms. Unfortunately, relationships among the several conceptual levels represented by these various measures are seldom specified or fully examined.

The remainder of this chapter begins by examining various approaches to the measurement of well-being. We then summarize findings from research conducted to date on well-being among the elderly. The chapter ends with the panel's recommendations for future research in this domain.

THE MEASUREMENT OF WELL-BEING

Kahneman et al. (1999) propose five conceptual levels as relevant for research on well-being. In descending order, from molar to molecular, they are as follows:

- External ("objective") conditions (e.g., income, neighborhood, housing)
- Subjective well-being (e.g., self-reports of satisfaction/dissatisfaction)
- Persistent mood level (e.g., optimism/pessimism)
- Immediate pleasures/pains, transient emotional states (e.g., joy, anger)
- Biochemical, neural bases of behavior

The conceptual distinction that Kahneman and colleagues propose between objective (external) conditions and subjective well-being is familiar and important, although it is a methodological as well as a conceptual distinction. External conditions, such as neighborhood and housing, can be assessed by self-report (subjective) as well as by independent ("objective") observation. The distinction between the physiological or biochemical level and the others is also clear, although population-based research on well-being has yet to incorporate the biochemical level, and biochemical researchers show little interest in linking their work to more molar and subjective indicators of well-being. This linkage, nevertheless, has great scientific potential. Perhaps least obvious and most controversial is the distinction between persistent mood level and immediate pleasures or pains. We deal with this issue later in the section on stocks and flows in well-being analysis.

Kahneman et al. are critical of research on well-being in two main respects: the fact that most researchers concentrate on a single level without examining its relationship to the others, and that most rely on self-reported data without examining their biases. Kahneman et al. point out that measures of reported well-being were relatively stable during decades when income and other economic indicators were increasing substantially, citing this as but one example of the inappropriately modest relationships between objective conditions and subjective well-being. Their explanation for this lack of relationship emphasizes "construal processes"—biases in self-reported well-being that include the effects of temporary moods or associations, differing frames of reference and comparisons with others, and social acceptability bias (the wish to present oneself in favorable terms). They also discuss the phenomenon of the hedonic treadmill, proposed by Brickman and Campbell (1971) some 30 years ago in discussing theories of adaptation, which the panel believes is a more important explanation.

The Hedonic Treadmill

Diener (2000:36) summarizes the Brickman-Campbell theory as follows:

In a classic 1971 article, Brickman and Campbell suggest that all people labor on a 'hedonic treadmill.' As they rise in their accomplishments and possessions, their expectations also rise. Soon they habituate to the new level, and it no longer makes them happy. On the negative side, people are unhappy when they first encounter misfortune, but they soon adapt and it no longer makes them unhappy. On the basis of this reasoning, Brickman and Campbell proposed that people are destined to hedonic neutrality in the long run.

In the decades since its introduction, research on the hedonic treadmill has supported the concept in the main but added two qualifications: first, the process of hedonic adaptation may be toward a moderately positive rather than an absolutely neutral level of life satisfaction; second, after an experience of particular happiness or unhappiness, the tendency may be to return not to a universal level of satisfaction, but to a set point that reflects the temperament and personality of the individual. Recent analyses support both of these qualifications.

More than a million people responding to surveys in 45 countries have answered questions about their overall happiness or unhappiness with their lives. On a 10-point scale in which 10 represents maximum happiness, 1 maximum unhappiness, and 5 neutrality, the median response was slightly over 7 and the mean response not much lower (see Figure 7-1).

Explanations for the stability of well-being and happiness during periods of substantial improvement in objective circumstances emphasize adaptation processes and the distinction between transient moods and longer-term affective states. According to proponents of this distinction, an increase in wages, for example, creates a short-term elevation in mood but not a long-term alteration in level of well-being or happiness. Similarly, being turned down for a raise in pay creates an immediate reaction of unhappiness, often mixed with anger and resentment, but is not likely to alter significantly the individual's characteristic level of happiness or well-being. This adaptational dynamic explains the stability of happiness data in the United States over a period of 40 years during which real income more than doubled (see Figure 7-2).

While this and related evidence supports the hypothesis of the hedonic treadmill, other data clearly demonstrate the concept's limits. Cross-national comparisons (see Figure 7-3) indicate that countries high in gross national product (GNP) per capita also tend to be high in subjective well-being. Countries lowest in reported well-being were those in eastern Europe, in which many people were suffering both low income and recent severe reductions in income. Unaccustomed poverty adds to the fact of objective deprivation a sense of loss and the unavoidable comparison with an earlier and more prosperous time. In complementary

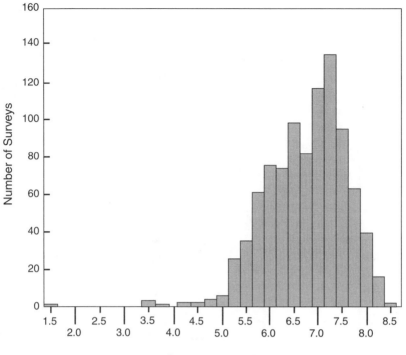

FIGURE 7-1 Subjective well-being scores in 45 nations.
NOTE: As self-reported in 916 surveys of 1.1 million people in 45 nations (with answers calibrated on a 0 to 10 scale, with 5 being neutral and 10 being the high extreme).
SOURCE: Myers and Diener (1996). Reprinted with permission.

fashion, countries in which GNP has been growing rapidly, even though they are still poor by international comparison, score relatively high in subjective well-being. In China, for example, self-reported well-being is almost as high as in Japan, although the two countries are almost as far apart in GNP per capita as the scale allows.

Comparative data on self-reported happiness, a concept perhaps more unambiguously "hedonic" than well-being, show a similar pattern. Veenhoven (1991) compared self-reported happiness and income (GNP) per capita for seven parts of the world. The results indicate a clear relationship between happiness and per capita GNP, with some tendency toward curvilinearity. Africa, while low in reported happiness, is not as low as the level of GNP would predict. And Latin America scores almost

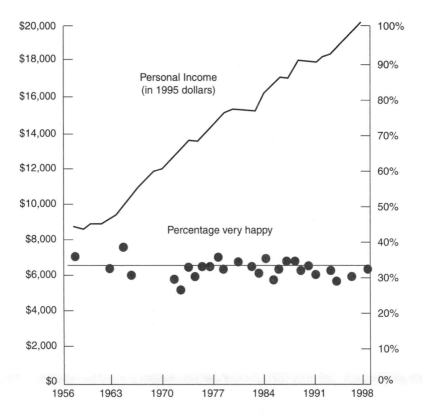

FIGURE 7-2 Economic growth and self-reported happiness in the United States: 1956 to 1998.
SOURCE: Myers and Diener (1996). Reprinted with permission.

as high in reported happiness as western Europe, which has more than double the Latin American GNP. The implication is that GNP is driving this relationship, but that cultural factors also play a significant role (see Figure 7-4).

Existing Research: The State of Play

A substantial amount of research has been conducted on the various types of well-being measures. Historically, much of this research has been concerned with two of the five categories proposed by Kahneman and colleagues.

First are the measures of external objective conditions, such as personal income growth, neighborhood characteristics, housing status, lon-

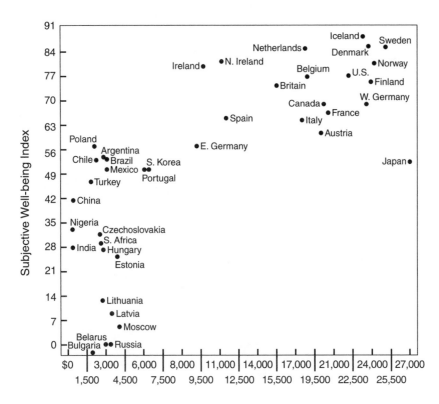

FIGURE 7-3 Relationship between per capita GNP and subjective well-being: Early 1990s.
NOTE: The subjective well-being index combines happiness and life satisfaction (average or percentage describing themselves as (a) "very happy" or "happy" minus percentage "not very happy" or "unhappy" and as (b) 7 or above minus 4 or below on a 10-point life satisfcation scale).
SOURCE: Inglehart (1997). Reprinted with permission.

gevity, health, and disability. These measures were originally designed to supplement the conventional measures of societal progress reflected by developments in the economic sphere—growth rate of GNP, level of investment and saving, distribution of income, level of consumption, and the like. To the extent that these supplemental objective conditions have an impact on well-being that is not reflected in the standard economic variables, they provide a richer and broader picture of societal well-being.

The second category of well-being measures on which research has focused—subjective self-reports of satisfaction/dissatisfaction—experienced a rapid development in the 1970s and 1980s. This research encom-

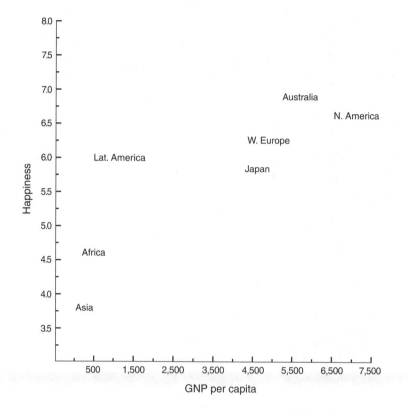

FIGURE 7-4 Relationship between per capita GNP and happiness in seven regions/countries: 1975.
SOURCE: Veenhoven (1991). Reprinted with permission.

passes much of what is usually characterized as the subjective well-being literature. Studies in this area include not only the global satisfaction measures associated with various aspects of people's lives—such as their income; their neighborhood; and their relationships with their children, their spouse, and other family members—but also research focused on human development and mental health. These latter measures, discussed below, focus on assessment of how people feel about themselves as indicated by scales of self-assessment, personal growth, and relationships with others.

Survey Approaches to Well-Being

Surveys of well-being use one or more of three definitions of well-being: (1) satisfaction with life, (2) health and ability/disability, and (3) composite indexes of positive functioning. This section provides examples of each of these approaches, along with an indication of their relative strengths and weaknesses.

Well-Being as Satisfaction with Life

"Now I want to ask you about your life as a whole. How satisfied are you with your life as a whole these days?" This question, from the 1976 national survey of the quality of American life (Campbell et al., 1976), is typical of those asked in many subsequent surveys. The scaling of responses, however, varies.

Campbell and colleagues used a seven-point scale, ranging from completely satisfied to completely dissatisfied. Andrews and Withey (1976) experimented with a number of different ways of scaling the global satisfaction question. They assumed that a person's assessment of life quality involves both a cognitive evaluation and some degree of positive or negative feeling. They attempted to capture both elements by presenting survey respondents with a seven-point scale anchored at one end by the word "delighted" and at the other by the word "terrible." Their D-T scale, as it was called, has not been widely used in spite of the considerable methodological evidence in its favor. It was used, however, by Headey and Wearing (1991) in their longitudinal study of well-being in Victoria, the most densely populated state in Australia. Their index of life satisfaction was based on six items, all scaled on nine points ranging from delighted to terrible. The question about "life as a whole" was asked twice, once at the beginning and once at the end of the interview. Other questions addressed "sense of meaning or purpose," "what you are accomplishing," "how exciting is your life," and "the extent to which you are succeeding and getting ahead."

Current survey usage favors direct questions about life satisfaction and a return to the familiar five-point scale. Typical is the study of Americans Changing Lives (House, 1998). The question is worded as follows: "Now please think of your life as a whole. How satisfied are you with it? Are you completely satisfied, very satisfied, somewhat satisfied, not very satisfied, or not at all satisfied?" The wording used reflects an attempt to spread the distribution and avoid the tendency for responses to cluster toward the satisfied end of the scale.

As Kahneman et al. (1999) point out and as Campbell (1981) had noted earlier, the use of such questions assumes that the varied experiences of a person's life somehow combine to produce a global state of well-being or its lack, that a person's sense and level of well-being are relatively stable rather than a labile response to transient events, that people are able to describe their state of well-being to an interviewer, and that they can be induced to do so. These assumptions have been challenged on two grounds. The first of these is the counterintuitive stability of well-being responses across cohorts and age groups, even during decades of substantial gains in material standard of living. Second is the sensitivity of subjective well-being responses to construal processes, that is, the cognitive and emotional factors that shape each respondent's assessment of his or her own life circumstances (Schwarz and Strack, 1999). The panel believes the latter criticism is the more valid.

Within the broad category of construal processes, Schwarz and Strack present evidence for five sources of bias in self-reported global assessments of subjective well-being. These include an assimilation effect, when some happy incident comes to mind and heightens the feeling of life satisfaction; and a contrast effect, when a happy event of the past is somehow used as a standard of comparison for present feelings and thus reduces the overall sense of well-being. Similar elevations or reductions in answering the well-being question may reflect transient moods, evoked by events of the moment. In addition, one's response about sense of well-being may be altered by silent comparison with others, a frame of reference that in most surveys is neither specified by the interviewer nor volunteered by the respondent. Finally, responses about well-being are subject to the bias of social acceptability, a tendency that varies among individuals and is itself measurable but seldom measured.

These methodological problems are serious and deserve more attention than they have received. The other criticism posed by Schwarz and Strack, which has to do with the stability of well-being levels across cohorts and age groups, can be countered more readily. The fact that reported levels of well-being did not show increases commensurate with gains in material indexes (e.g., income, automobile ownership) during the decades before 1980 does not necessarily indicate a problem in measurement. There are at least two plausible explanations. The first is the phenomenon of the hedonic treadmill described earlier—the tendency of expectations to rise (or fall) as life's objective circumstances and resources change. The second explanatory factor, a complement rather than an alternative to the hedonic treadmill, is that people are bringing other, nonmaterial criteria to bear upon the assessment of well-being. Allardt (1976) had proposed earlier that well-being depends on the satisfaction of three main categories of human needs—having, relating (loving), and being. The first of these, having, is gratified by the possession of material things, and income is an appropriate measure. The second, relating, can be met only by affectionate, supportive relationships with spouse or partner, family, and friends. Finally, the need for being or self-actualization can be met only by the actions of the individual, through the acquisition and exercise of valued traits and abilities. If one takes this view, the fact that well-being has not closely tracked increases in income, far from being a sign of measurement inadequacy, is an indication that well-being requires more than the satisfaction of material needs and thus is not measured sufficiently by income and other aspects of material satisfaction. Moreover, as we have seen, responses to global questions about life satisfaction and happiness, while not strongly related to objective economic data within countries, do show significant relationships in the expected direction when comparisons among countries are made.

Well-Being as Health

Virtually all studies that attempt to assess well-being include one or more questions about health. Self-reported health is an independent predictor of longevity, even after the major risk factors for early mortality have been statistically controlled (see Chapter 6).[1] A direct question about overall health, as asked in the SF-36 and its shorter version, the SF-12, is typical (Ware and Sherbourne, 1992). These widely used questionnaires, before entering into a more detailed inventory of health problems, begin by asking: "In general, would you say that your health is (Excellent, Very Good, Good, Fair, Poor)?" Campbell et al. (1976), in an attempt to avoid the biases of brief minor illnesses, asked: "Of course, most people get sick now and then, but overall, how satisfied are you with your health?"

When surveys of life quality have looked more intensively at health, the questions have usually addressed health-determined limitations on activities. The SF-12 questionnaire is typical. It begins with a question about overall health, on a five-point scale ranging from excellent to poor. This is followed by questions about health as limiting the performance of specific activities, about emotional problems as interfering with daily activities, and about mood and energy level.

Some age-related tendencies are common among the numerous surveys that have compared self-reports of life quality by different age groups. Overall satisfaction with life is not greatly different among age groups; indeed there is some evidence for slight increases in satisfaction (but not happiness) in older age groups. If this apparent tendency is confirmed by long-term longitudinal studies, one might conclude that it reflects a process of adaptation, of people's coming to terms with their lives.

Within the more specific life domains, only one—satisfaction with health—declines significantly with age. Given the increasing morbidity and comorbidity that often come with increasing age, reductions in health

---

[1]It should be noted, however, that prevalence figures derived from this measure may vary considerably, both within and across societies.

satisfaction are evidence of people's actual experience and of the validity of self-reporting.

Composite Indexes of Well-Being

Various indexes of overall well-being or positive functioning have been used in different surveys. Some are simple summations or averages of domain-specific satisfaction scores. Others use weighting procedures in which responses to the direct question about overall life satisfaction are dominant, or in which satisfaction responses are combined with measures of happiness or positive and negative affect.

Critics of these approaches point out that they have in common an emphasis on gratification and a neglect of other aspects of what might be considered a "good life." Adler (1987:52) argues that Western philosophy includes two distinct conceptions of happiness. One is gratification of an individual's desires, whatever they may be; the other is "the ancient ethical conception of happiness as a whole life well-lived because it is enriched by the cumulative possession of all the goods that a morally virtuous human being ought to desire." The key word in this long definition is "ought"; an external standard of values is thus imposed on an individual's experience of happiness. If his or her gratification derives from sources that would not be desired by "a morally virtuous human being," one is instructed not to count this as happiness, or at least to distinguish between two kinds of happiness on the basis of their sources, moral and amoral.

This argument has value, but the panel does not accept Adler's conclusion. The value comes from the reminder that research on satisfaction, gratification, happiness, and other such hedonic responses becomes much more meaningful when we also investigate their sources—the events, conditions, and relationships that evoke them. But the panel believes that to incorporate this kind of source information into the definition of happiness, as Adler does, is counterproductive.

A different and more constructive criticism is found in the work of Ryff (1989; 1995; see also Singer and Ryff, 1999). She argues that three rather separate lines of research and theory have been concerned with definitions of well-being: theories of human development; of clinical psychology; and of mental health, especially positive mental health. From these sources, she proposes six defining components of well-being: self-acceptance, purpose in life, environmental mastery, autonomy, personal growth, and positive relationships with others.

In the MacArthur studies of midlife (MIDUS, 2000), each of these six components was measured by three items. These items were presented to respondents as statements, and agreement or disagreement was measured on a seven-point scale ranging from "strongly agree" to "strongly disagree." Sample items from the scale are shown below, each identified by the dimension it is intended to measure:

- "In many ways, I feel disappointed about my achievements in life." (self-acceptance)
- "Some people wander aimlessly through life, but I am not one of them." (purpose in life)
- "The demands of everyday life often get me down." (environmental mastery)
- "Maintaining close relationships has been difficult and frustrating for me." (personal relationships with others)
- "For me, life has been a continuous process of learning, changing, and growth." (personal growth)
- "I tend to be influenced by people with strong opinions." (autonomy)

In a national sample, cross-sectional comparisons of three broad age groups (young adult, midlife, and older adult) show differing patterns for the six components of well-being. Environmental mastery and autonomy increase between young adulthood and midlife. Purpose in life and personal growth show decreases with age, especially between midlife and older age. Positive relationships with others increase steadily and significantly from the young to the oldest age group. Self-acceptance shows no significant differences with age (Ryff, 1995).

All of the survey approaches reviewed thus far measure well-being either as a present state or a retrospective judgment over an extended time period. Self-reports of this kind are valuable, but they do not reflect the variability of health, happiness, and well-being over time that all people experience in varying degrees. The moment-to-moment reports that Kahneman and colleagues obtained from people undergoing stressful procedures demonstrate short-term variability, and studies of time-use samples (discussed later in this chapter) provide further insight into the variability experienced by individuals under the conditions of everyday life. The latter variations and the accompanying differences among individuals in their magnitude and duration imply the need for an additional criterion of well-being. This criterion might be termed *resilience*, and would measure the ability of an individual to deal effectively with stressful life events. Relevant conceptual dimensions would include the magnitude of deflection from the individual's characteristic set point of well-being, the duration of that reduction, and the rapidity and completeness of his or her return to the set point. These issues are of special importance for the well-being of older men and women because of their increased exposure to bereavement and illness (comorbidity). The concept of resilience is discussed in greater detail in a later section of this chapter.

Work and Well-Being

To understand the meaning of a person's overall satisfaction with life requires breaking down the broad concept of life satisfaction and looking separately at the major life sectors—marriage, family, work, income, housing, neighborhood, community, and others. Of these, work has a special significance. It is a source of income, which in turn determines housing, neighborhood, and the many other aspects of life that are in some degree monetarized. But a person's employment also demands a significant part of his or her time and energy. For most people it is a source of friendships, and for many it provides a means of utilizing valued skills and abilities. For all these reasons, work (employment) ranks high among the determinants of overall life satisfaction. Only family life, income, and all nonwork activities in combination rank higher, and work is the major determinant of income, which in turn determines access to many nonwork activities.

Thousands of studies have been conducted on work-related subjects, including worker motivation, job stress and its effects, satisfaction and dissatisfaction with job content, working conditions, supervision, rewards, and many others. Despite differences in terminology and theoretical orientation, there is substantial consensus on the job characteristics that determine work satisfaction. They include the following:

- Task content, especially variety and the opportunity to use valued skills
- Autonomy, especially regarding the methods and pace of work
- Supervision, especially supportive behavior by supervisors
- Resources, including information, as well as appropriate tools and equipment
- Coworker relations and the opportunity for informal contact and conversation
- Working conditions, including physical surroundings, noise level, and security
- Rewards, wages, and fringe benefits
- Promotion and prospects for advancement for outstanding performance

To understand the place of work in people's lives, all these aspects should be encompassed by the inquiry. At a minimum, studies of well-

being should include two questions about a person's job—his or her satisfaction with the work, and his or her rating of the job on a scale from
excellent or highly desirable to poor or very undesirable. Evidence is that
the adaptation process figures prominently in people's responses on satisfaction. In thinking about their own satisfaction or dissatisfaction with
their jobs, individuals take into account their education and experience,
their age, and the state of the labor market (Kahn, 1981; Warr, 1999).
These processes are not apparent in their responses to the short-answer,
fixed-alternative questions by which satisfaction with work is typically
measured. They may be revealed, however, when interviews are less
structured and responses are recorded verbatim. For example, consider
the following excerpt from an interview with a blue-collar worker whose
first response to the question of satisfaction with work was: "I got a
pretty good job." The interview then asked: "What makes it such a good
job? The answer was instructive: "Don't get me wrong. I didn't say it is
a *good* job. It's an OK job, about as good as a guy like me can expect. The
foreman leaves me alone and it pays well. But I would never call it a good
job. It doesn't amount to much, but it's not bad" (Strauss, 1972:55).

Emotional States

Some recent innovative but controversial work on well-being explores
a set of concepts involving emotional states—both persistent moods and
immediate pleasures and pains. Research on emotional states as immediate pleasures and pains is the focus of a substantial effort undertaken
recently by psychologists (Kahneman et al., 1999; Seligman and
Czikszentmihaly, 2000). This work starts with the proposition that conventional measures of well-being derived from retrospective self-reports
of satisfaction or dissatisfaction have serious biases that cannot easily be
controlled. Proponents of this view assert that a more valid assessment of
subjective well-being requires a model in which the immediate pleasures
and pains associated with people's circumstances are monitored continu-
ously. In this literature, the instantaneous record of pleasures and pains
is called *direct utility*; the integral of direct utility over an episode is called
total utility or *objective well-being*. Retrospective recollection of the global
satisfaction or dissatisfaction associated with the immediate pleasures or
pains of a previous time is called *remembered utility*, and is essentially
equivalent to subjective well-being as described earlier. The basic idea
behind this model is that a subject's instantaneous report of the pleasures
or pains associated with a particular activity or episode is the least biased
of any of the subjective well-being measures, and therefore should constitute the core data for scientific understanding of human happiness and its
correlates.

Research along these lines has required experimental subjects to report successive levels of pleasure or pain during brief episodes of an acute or dramatic nature. In the most widely cited case, respondents were asked to report every 60 seconds, on a scale ranging from no pain at all to excruciating pain, the level of pain associated with a colonoscopy, an unpleasant and painful medical diagnostic procedure that lasts between 10 and 20 minutes. But if one is thinking of using instantaneous pleasure and pain as a way to measure utility, the method of measurement should be applicable to routine activities. That is, the measures should be obtained for a sampling of activities that represent what individuals typically do during the course of a day—talking to a spouse, lunching with a friend, walking through the park, commuting to work, using a word processor, and so on. Use of the instantaneous pleasure/pain response as a measure of well-being thus turns out to be operationally equivalent to asking respondents about the level of pleasure and pain associated with a random sampling of the activities on which they spent time during some recent period of days or weeks.

The notion that instantaneously recorded pleasure and pain is a valid representation of objective well-being (because it is less vulnerable to the biases associated with self-reports of global recollections of satisfaction with various aspects of life) depends critically on the premise that meaningful distinctions in levels of pleasure and pain can be measured not only for dramatic events such as colonoscopies, but also for the events that together constitute everyday life. Moreover, the notion that the summing of pleasures and pains yields a good index of well-being depends on the premise that the only source of utility from an activity is the integral of the instantaneous pleasures/pains associated with that activity.

But what if the activity is seen as an unpleasant experience that produces a desirable outcome later in life? That is, suppose the activity is cleaning the house. Most subjects regard this as a dull activity. But having spent time on producing a clean house, they will derive more enjoyment from entertaining friends than if the house were untidy. Thus the utility from the activity of cleaning house is derived in part from the instantaneous pleasures/pains associated with that activity, but may also encompass the future utility obtained when the clean house is used for social entertainment. In economic terminology, one might think of cleaning the house as an investment in a future benefit derived from using a clean and orderly house for social entertainment. The same is true for many monotonous and physically demanding jobs, whose rewards and satisfactions are often extrinsic rather than intrinsic to the activity itself.

Analysis of the instantaneous pleasures or pains associated with episodes as a way to measure well-being has a close counterpart in studies of time use, which sometimes measure the satisfaction derived from activities as well as the hours devoted to them. While almost all countries have some information on the use of time among their populations, in two cases (Sweden and the United States), information about the level of enjoyment associated with various activities has been collected along with the time-allocation data (see Juster and Stafford, 1986; Klevmarken, 1999). Such data are available for the United States in 1975-1976 and 1981-1982 and for Sweden in 1984-1991. In these studies, data on satisfaction with activities are obtained from responses to a question of the following type, asked for each of a set of daily activities: "Think about a scale from 10 to 0. If you enjoy doing an activity a great deal, rank it as a 10; if you dislike doing it a great deal, rank it as a zero; if you don't care about it one way or the other, rank it in the middle as a 5. For example, if you like it some you might rank it 6 or 7. Keep in mind that we're interested in whether you like doing something, not whether you think it's important to do. How much do you enjoy (activity 1, 2, . . .) ?"

Although the enjoyment scale is not necessarily identical to the instantaneous utility associated with the pleasures or pains of an activity, there is clearly a close correspondence. The most important difference is probably that the enjoyment scale data are a recollection based on a (typical) past event, while the instantaneous pleasure/pain data are for an event currently under way.

Interestingly enough, questions about the satisfaction derived from specific activities produce results that are apparently inconsistent with conventional economic views of utility maximization. Economists tend to think of work as an activity producing a major extrinsic reward (income) but having, especially at the margin, negative intrinsic rewards. That is, economists think of people as working up to the point at which the income produces utility that is just equal to the disutility attached to the work itself—otherwise people would do more work (if they could) than they do. Data on satisfaction with activities, according to this model, ought to show that work ranks poorly on the scale of intrinsic satisfaction or enjoyment. But in fact work is the second or third most highly rated activity, just behind playing with children and socializing with friends, and it outranks all other leisure activities except for these two. The activity associated with the least intrinsic benefits or satisfaction is clearly housework.

Stocks and Flows in Well-Being Analysis

Before examining the state of knowledge relative to the well-being measures discussed above, we may note another analytically useful distinction among the measures: whether they can be thought of as representing the degree of satisfaction with stable features of the social and economic landscape, or as behaviors that produce well-being directly and may also do so indirectly by changing the environment. The first could be labeled a stock, the second a flow. The conceptual framework here tends to reflect the way economists think about the world, while much of the well-being literature reflects the perceptual schemes of psychologists.

The basic idea of stocks is that they represent a state of being that reflects the cumulative impact of past history on current state. With regard to financial variables, for example, total assets would represent the stock since they show the cumulative impact of lifetime saving behavior, along with any return to that saving. And if assets represent the stock, the change in assets, or current-period saving plus or minus capital gains, represents the flow.

A similar framework can be applied to noneconomic sources of well-being. For example, the current state of one's relationship with a spouse, children, or friends can be thought of as reflecting a past history of inter-action that has produced a characteristic level of satisfaction with those relationships. Thus the stock of associations can be thought of as an assessment of the overall degree of satisfaction with the relationship, while the flow can be thought of as the transient emotional states (joy, anger, and the like) evoked by some specific event, interaction, or activity. The cumulative effect of such events, of course, is to change the stock. For example, discussing a family problem with one's spouse is an activity that almost certainly generates immediate affect or flow (e.g., anger, pleasure, relief, guilt) but also may, and often will, have a persisting impact on satisfaction with the marriage (stock) and perhaps other family relation-ships as well.

As this example suggests, a concern for measuring well-being leads to an interest in activities that affect well-being temporarily or enduringly—that is, affect both the flow and the stock. A useful way to think about the relationship between satisfaction and activities is to recognize that all human activities can be thought of as producing two kinds of satisfaction or reward. One is *intrinsic* satisfaction, reflecting the degree of enjoyment associated with performing the activity. The other is the *extrinsic* satisfac-tion, associated with a product or outcome of the activity. Activities typically generate both intrinsic and extrinsic satisfaction or dissatisfac-tion. For example, cleaning the house can be thought of as yielding the extrinsic rewards associated with a clean and orderly house, which en-hance the satisfaction associated with living in the house, plus any intrin-sic satisfaction (or minus any intrinsic dissatisfaction) associated with the activity.

The panel regards conceptualizing satisfaction along stock and flow dimensions as a useful way of linking the concepts of activity and satis-faction. For the most part, the measures of well-being reported in the existing literature are stocks rather than flows; respondents are asked to sum up their satisfaction with life as a whole or with certain of its domains—neighborhood, family relationships, housing, and so on. Similarly, aspects of well-being associated with human development and mental health (e.g., self-acceptance, purpose in life, environmental mastery) can be conceptualized usefully as stocks. In some unspecified way, however, these summations are the result of the continuous flow of life experiences and the activities that create those experiences or expose the individual to them.

Moreover, the activities in which people engage during the course of the day, week, month, or year have immediate effects on flows of satisfaction or dissatisfaction (intrinsic rewards or their lack), short-term effects through their products (extrinsic satisfaction or dissatisfaction), and potential effects on the persisting level of life satisfaction or well-being (stocks). To continue an earlier example, cleaning one's house not only generates intrinsic satisfaction or dissatisfaction with the activity itself and immediate extrinsic satisfaction with the result, both of which are flows, but may also add to one's self-esteem, which is a stock.

Satisfaction effects are measurable as both stocks and flows, at least in principle. Conventional measurements of satisfaction as stocks are the standard fare of well-being analysis. Yet the immediate satisfaction associated with activities has also been measured, although less often, by eliciting subjective judgments from respondents about the level of enjoyment derived from a specific list of activities or the instantaneous pleasure/pain associated with the activities. Data on satisfaction with activities tend to be used in analyses of time use or time allocation, in which the objective is to understand the choice of activities in terms of both satisfaction with the activities themselves (the flows) and satisfaction associated with the enhancements of the stock that result from the activities.

Time-Use Data

Among the important information needed to provide an adequate basis for assessing changes in life satisfaction in older people is data on the way older people use their time, combined with data on the satisfaction obtained from those activities. A good deal of methodological work has explored the reliability and bias associated with various types of time-use measures (Juster and Stafford, 1986). It has been found that the most unbiased measures of time use consist of a 24-hour diary of events, with the optimum survey design involving the use of multiple time diaries reflecting different days of the week and seasons of the year. The major problem with using time diaries to document changes in activity patterns as people age is that the diaries are extremely expensive relative to other survey methods. Measuring activities during a 24-hour period takes between 20 and 25 minutes of survey time, and if multiple diary days are needed to provide a good representation of activities for different days of the week, that amount of time must be multiplied by a factor of at least two and probably more.

Alternative methods of measuring patterns of time use include "stylized" questions. For example, "During the past week, about how much time did you spend doing x, y, z, where x, y, z?" represents activities such as watching television, doing the dishes, working in the garden, working for pay, and reading. The evidence indicates that these types of time-use measures will typically yield underestimates, and for some activities, very serious underestimates. It is also clear from the methodological literature that social desirability biases are substantial for some of the stylized measures of time use. For example, parents are likely to seriously overreport the amount of time they spend reading to their children when asked about that activity in a stylized mode, and similarly to underreport the amount of time their children spend watching television.

One of the attractive features of assessing changes in life satisfaction over time by analyzing time diary data is that it is a relatively simple matter to attach satisfaction measures to the activities. As noted earlier, both U.S. and Swedish time-use data provide measures of the satisfaction associated with different activities. The data on satisfaction with specific activities—called process benefits—turn out to be quite illuminating about the sources of life satisfaction and associated measures of well-being.

FINDINGS ON WELL-BEING AMONG THE ELDERLY

Subjective Well-Being and Aging

As noted earlier, most studies find that overall subjective well-being, measured as satisfaction, is about the same for different age groups, or even slightly higher among older people than among middle-aged and younger adults. Satisfaction with health, however, is an exception; consistent with data on morbidity and comorbidity, satisfaction with health is lower among older people. The finding of overall stability in life satisfaction, while based almost entirely on cross-sectional research, is consistent with theories of adaptation, which argue essentially that people come to terms with their lives as they grow older. When well-being is measured on a scale of happiness and unhappiness, however, older people tend to give fewer responses of either extreme happiness or unhappiness. This apparent dampening of affect or emotion with increasing age has been interpreted as one aspect of a more general "slowing down" and reduction in intensity of response (Campbell, 1981).

Age-related changes in patterns of activity are in sharp contrast with the relative stability of satisfaction responses, and the most conspicuous of such changes in activity is retirement from paid employment. In the United States, national surveys show that hours of paid work decline after age 50 and drop sharply after age 60; hours of unpaid productive activities, on the other hand, begin to decline later in life and persist in a significant amount beyond age 75. Volunteering does not, however, show a significant increase after retirement, even though many people report expectations of becoming more active as volunteers after retirement; participation in voluntary organizations varies as a function of health and degree of connectedness with others. Time spent with other family members shows a substantial increase as people leave paid work and as work-related social interactions tend to diminish over time. Finally, leisure activities, such as watching television, traveling, and visiting, are all likely to rise on average.

Resilience

The ability to recover from negative (stressful, threatening, damaging) life events is an important attribute at any age, but acquires additional importance as people age. Even older people who describe themselves as very happy or as high on a scale of well-being are unlikely to have been in that state at all times. A few may have avoided, by design or fortuitously, the stressful life events and challenges that threaten well-being. Some may have been born with the kind of genetic endowment that confers relative immunity from the infirmities and chronic diseases common in old age. Still others, in old age, may be reaping the benefits of a lifetime of health-promoting habits of diet and exercise. All these factors, especially in combination, may enable people to go through later life in a state of good physical health, sustained cognitive function, and unvarying sense of well-being. The more common experience of aging, however, involves some number of accidents and illnesses, losses and bereavements, crises of adult children, involuntary retirement, moves from a longtime home, and the like. The high incidence of such events in later life raises the question of how successfully people deal with them, that is, how such events affect well-being in both the short term and beyond.

For research in this area, the panel proposes the concept of *resilience* noted earlier, defined as the ability to recover quickly and completely from such misfortunes and challenges. Holmes and Rahe (1967) developed a broad inventory of such negative events in a questionnaire form that has been widely used. Cross-sectional comparisons of people reporting different levels of stressful life events do not always show consistent differences in well-being, nor do such comparisons reveal the speed and completeness of recovery. Only bereavement over the loss of a child or spouse has been studied more intensively and with attention to the magnitude and duration of negative impact (see, for example, Wortman et al., 1993). Findings of this research show frequent prolonged grief effects in such cases. Wortman et al. (1993) found that, on a measure of life satisfaction, widows and widowers scored significantly lower than a control group for 10 years, and that they scored higher on depression for almost 20 years. Of the potential moderators of adaptation to negative events, social support has been most studied and has been shown to have a significant buffering effect. Advance notice or warning of an impending negative event also moderates its effects (Berenbaum et al., 1999).

Resilience can be inferred from cross-sectional comparisons and retrospective accounts. Stronger, although more difficult, research designs would require longitudinal study of specific event sequences that would include assessment of well-being before the stressing challenge is encountered and subsequent monitoring to observe the initial decremental effect, the time required to regain stability of well-being, and the level of well-being regained.

RECOMMENDATIONS

7-1. Cross-national research on aging should include an overall measure of subjective well-being (life satisfaction), with comparable questions for major life domains. Cross-national comparisons should also include the experience of major life events, especially the stressful events that are increasingly likely in old age, such as illness, bereavement, retirement (complete or partial), and changes in activity patterns. The range of methods for assessing well-being has increased greatly in recent years. Scales of satisfaction-dissatisfaction and happiness-unhappiness still predominate, although the work of some researchers (e.g., Ryff and colleagues) goes beyond that approach. The debate between objective and subjective definitions of well-being persists. That debate, we believe, is mistaken: neither objective conditions nor subjective responses are sufficient; both are needed to understand the quality of life. The environment, neighborhood, and community in which people live; the work they do; the income they receive—all are essential determinants of the life they lead. But these objective measures are not sufficient to reveal whether people find their lives satisfying or dissatisfying, fulfilling or frustrating. Conversely, to know only subjective responses, with their inevitable processes of adaptation and compromise and their limitations in perspective, is inadequate for both science and public policy.

7-2. Standardized and validated measures of subjective well-being (physical, cognitive, happiness) should be developed for continuing use in ongoing national surveys. National policies differ in the benefits and services provided to older men and women, and cultures differ in the opportunities and demands presented to people as they age. These differences do much to define the quality of life experienced by older people. Cross-national data are available on GNP and other economic indicators. But the ultimate criterion by which nations should be compared and by which governments should be judged is the quality of life they provide to their citizens and residents. Data on well-being are an essential element in assessing quality of life.

7-3. Cross-national research should include documenting, at appropriate intervals, the changes in time use and lifestyle that characterize the adult life course, especially the transition from full-time employment to retirement. Complementary to data on subjective well-being (i.e., how people feel) is the question of what they do. Especially important are data on the various forms of productive activity (paid and unpaid, formal and informal) and the satisfaction or dissatisfaction these activities generate.

7-4. Data on self-perceived health—people's sense of their own health on a scale from excellent to poor—should be obtained for all countries. Long life is a prime value in all countries, and it is therefore a criterion for assessing the relative success of nations. Moreover, countries differ greatly in life expectancy, and these differences are not entirely explained by economic factors. Research shows that an individual's rating of his or her own health is a strong predictor of mortality or survival. Such ratings are easily obtained, and they can be considered as leading indicators of things to come. They are therefore of great potential value to policy makers.

7-5. In those countries that have the necessary technical and fiscal resources, data should be collected that link specific activities (work and nonwork) to the pleasure or pain they generate. Most measures of well-being are linked to life events and activities by means of recollection; past events are then analyzed to explain present well-being or its lack. Such retrospective efforts, however carefully undertaken, are vulnerable to the biases and limitations of individual memory. Much of this vulnerability can be avoided if people are asked to rate the pleasure or pain and/or satisfaction or dissatisfaction associated with specific activities at the time those activities are being performed. The methods used for such research, already available through studies of time use in a few countries, need both wider utilization and further development.

REFERENCES

Adler, M.J.
   1987   *We Hold These Truths.* New York: Macmillan.
Allardt, E.
   1976   Dimensions of welfare in a comparative Scandinavian study. *Acta Sociologica* 19:227-239.
Andrews, F.M., and S.B. Withey
   1976   *Social Indicators of Well-Being.* New York: Plenum.
Baltes, P.B., and K.U. Mayer
   1999   *The Berlin Aging Study. Aging from 70 to 100.* Cambridge: Cambridge University Press.
Berenbaum, H., C. Raghavan, H.-N. Le, L. Vernon, and J. Gomez
   1999   Disturbances in emotion. In *Well-Being: The Foundations of Hedonic Psychology*, D. Kahneman et al., eds. New York: Russell Sage.
Brickman, P., and D.T. Campbell
   1971   Hedonic relativism and planning the good society. In *Adaptation-Level Theory: A Symposium*, M.H. Apley, ed., pp. 287-302. New York: Academic Press.
Campbell, A.
   1981   *The Sense of Well-Being in America.* New York: McGraw Hill.
Campbell, A., P.E. Converse, and W. Rodgers
   1976   *The Quality of American Life.* New York: Russell Sage.
Cohen, W.J.
   1969   *Toward a Social Report.* Ann Arbor: University of Michigan Press.
Diener, E.
   2000   Subjective well-being: The science of happiness and a proposal for a national index. *American Psychologist* 55(1):34-43.
Headey, B., and A. Wearing
   1991   Subjective well-being: A stocks and flows framework. In *Subjective Well-Being: An Interdisciplinary Perspective*, F. Strack, M. Argyle, and N. Schwarz, eds. Oxford: Pergamon Press.
Holmes, T.H., and R.H. Rahe
   1967   The social readjustment scale. *Journal of Psychosomatic Research* 11:213-218.
House, J.S.
   1998   Age, work, and well-being: Toward a broader view. In *Impact of Work on Older Adults*, K.W. Schaie and C. Schooler, eds. New York: Springer.
Inglehart, R.
   1997   *Culture Shift in Advanced Industrial Society.* Princeton, NJ: Princeton University Press.
Juster, F.T., and F. Stafford, eds.
   1986   *Time, Goods, and Well-Being.* Ann Arbor, MI: Institute for Social Research.
Kahn, R.L.
   1981   *Work and Health.* New York: Wiley.
Kahneman, D., E. Diener, and N. Schwarz, eds.
   1999   *Well-Being: The Foundations of Hedonic Psychology.* New York: Russell Sage.
Klevmarken, N.A.
   1999   Measuring investment in young children with time diaries. In *Wealth, Work, and Health: Innovations in Measurement in the Social Sciences*, J.P. Smith and R.J. Willis, eds., pp. 34-63. Ann Arbor, MI: University of Michigan Press.

MIDUS (National Survey of Midlife Development in the United States)
 2000 Available: http://www.icpsr.umich.edu/cgi/ab.prl?file=2760 [February 28, 2001].
Myers, D.G., and E. Diener
 1996 The pursuit of happiness: New research uncovers some anti-intuitive insights into how many people are happy—and why. *Scientific American* 274(5):70-72.
Orley, J.
 1995 The WHOQOL Measure: Production of the WHOQOL-100 Field Trial Form. *Quality of Life Newsletter* 12:3 (April).
Riley, M.W., and J.W. Riley
 1994 Generational relations: A future perspective. In *Aging and Generational Relations over the Life Course: A Historical and Cross-Cultural Perspective*, T.K. Hareven, ed. Berlin: De Gruyter.
Ryff, C.
 1989 Happiness is everything—or is it? Explorations on the meaning of psychological well-being. *Journal of Personality and Social Psychology* 57:1069-1081.
 1995 Psychological well-being in adult life. *Current Directions in Psychological Science* 4:99-104.
Schwarz, N., and F. Strack
 1999 Reports of subjective well-being: Judgmental processes and their methodological implications. In *Well-Being: The Foundations of Hedonic Psychology*, D. Kahneman et al., eds., pp. 61-84. New York: Russell Sage.
Seligman, M.E.P., and M. Czikszentmihaly
 2000 Positive psychology: An introduction. *American Psychologist* 55(1):5-14.
Singer, B., and C.D. Ryff
 1999 Hierarchies of life histories and associated health risks. *Annals of the New York Academy of Sciences* 896:96-115.
Strauss, G.
 1972 Is there a blue-collar revolt against work? In *Work and the Quality of Life*, J. O'Toole, ed. Cambridge: Massachusetts Institute of Technology Press.
Veenhoven, R.
 1991 Questions on happiness: Classical topics, modern answers, blind spots. In *Subjective Well-Being: An Interdisciplinary Perspective*, F. Strack, M. Argyle, and N. Schwarz, eds., p. 13. Oxford: Pergamon Press.
Ware, J.E., and C.D. Sherbourne
 1992 The MoS 36-item, short form health survey (SF-36): Conceptual framework and item selection. *Medical Care* 30:473-483.
Warr, P.
 1999 Well-being and the work place. In *Well-Being: The Foundations of Hedonic Psychology*, D. Kahneman et al., eds. New York: Russell Sage.
Wortman, C.B., R.C. Silver, and R.C. Kessler
 1993 The meaning of loss and adjustment to bereavement. In *Handbook of Bereavement: Theory, Research, and Interventions*, M. Stroebe, W. Stroebe, and R. Hansson, eds., pp. 349-366. Cambridge: Cambridge University Press.

8

Conclusion and Major
Recommendations

The inexorable momentum toward increasingly aged populations around the world may well become the most significant demographic process of the 21st century. Sustained shifts in population age structure will require innovative national and international policy responses. For these responses to be effective in optimizing societal well-being, they must be based on an enhanced scientific understanding of the critical dynamics associated with population aging, such as the determinants of retirement decisions; the links among labor force participation, health status, and economic status; the relationship between retirement decisions and the specific features of both public and private pension plans; the impact of changes in public transfer systems on private transfers; the relationships among aging, income, and private savings; and the impact of medical technology on health, disability, and longevity. The preceding chapters have focused in turn on these domains and their important inter-relationships and offered recommendations for data and research in each area. Beyond those domain-specific recommendations, the panel developed six major, overarching recommendations that we believe are essential to effective cross-national research and to the generation of policy-relevant data for an aging world.

I. The development and use of multidisciplinary research designs are crucial to the production of data on aging populations that can best inform public policy.

The range of topics covered by the preceding chapters illustrates the need for a multidisciplinary approach that cuts across research domains. Recent demonstrations of the importance of cross-domain relationships—between health and retirement decisions, between economic status and health, between family structure and well-being in older age—support the contention that public policy must be guided by an understanding of the interplay among multiple factors. Initiatives in the United States, Europe, and Asia that integrate several salient domains of people's lives into single survey instruments have proven to be successful prototype data collection efforts. Examples of such endeavors include the Berlin Aging Study, the U.S. Health and Retirement Study (HRS), the Taiwan Study of the Elderly, the National Survey of Midlife Development in the United States, and the German Socio-Economic Panel. From their inception, these studies have included some or all of the following domains: income and wealth, labor force activity and retirement, health status (including biologic measurement) and utilization of health care facilities, cognition, and intergenerational transfers. The panel believes these models can be (and in some cases have been) successively adapted and used in many countries, both more and less industrialized.

It is the panel's conviction that the optimum way to develop both the research agenda and the data needed to address the economic and social issues associated with an aging world is through ongoing interaction among multidisciplinary national scientific communities. We believe extended interaction among sociologists, economists, demographers, epidemiologists, social psychologists, and statisticians is essential to (1) the creation and refinement of harmonized measures (conceptually comparable across societies) needed to understand outcomes such as labor force participation, health and disability status, complex family relationships, and economic status; and (2) the development of databases that can maximize the potential of cross-country and cross-time research for identifying the determinants of critical outcome variables. To deal effectively with differences among countries in policies, institutions, and incentive structures, it is equally essential that the multidisciplinary dialogue be driven by appropriate theories and models and that the data requirements of these theories and models be the main criteria used to select the empirical content of studies on aging populations.

It is important to stress that potential gains will not be realized unless there is a continuing and effective dialogue between the policy community and researchers, leading to the design of a program of data collection that can properly inform policy makers. This dialogue must be ongoing since many of the key dimensions of population aging can be expected to shift as socioeconomic circumstances change.

II. Longitudinal research should be undertaken to disentangle and illuminate the complex interrelationships among work, health, economic status, and family structure.

There is a pressing need in most countries for longitudinal microdata that include extensive measures of economic status, financial incentives to retire, various aspects of health status, and intergenerational relations and transfers. Such data are needed to better understand patterns of age-related transition along these dimensions, interrelationships among the dimensions, and ultimately the ways in which these domains contribute to overall well-being. One can anticipate with some degree of certainty the demographic parameters and trends that give rise to broad policy issues. Much less is known about individual responses to policy interventions, for example, the labor supply response of 60-year-old men and women to a restructuring of public pension benefits that raises the early retirement age from 62 to 65. Ultimately, policy options are grounded in understanding individual and family behaviors and their responsiveness to changing life circumstances.

From a research standpoint, the variation in response patterns associated with changing circumstances implies the need for panel studies that trace cohorts over time. Studies can be repeated cross sections, single cohort panel studies, or panel studies that continue to add new cohorts at the bottom end of the age range and are thus continually representative of the study population. If affordable, panel studies that add new cohorts are clearly best, since they not only capture the dynamics of change over time for individuals, but also continue to describe the broader population and not just a single cohort. Because the world is dealing with a phenomenon (population aging) that is likely to require the careful attention of policy makers for at least the next five decades, neither repeated cross sections nor single-cohort designs are very attractive. Interestingly, panel studies that add new cohorts may be less expensive than repeated cross sections with the same frequency and sample size simply because the cost of reinterviews is much lower than that of initial interviews.

It is crucial to note that the focus of panel studies of aging should not be restricted to the upper ends of the age spectrum. We know that the characteristics of tomorrow's cohorts of elderly will be very different from those of today and will be determined by lifelong experiences. Within the bounds of practicality, surveys need to capture as much of the life course experience as possible.

III. National and international funding agencies should establish mechanisms that facilitate the harmonization (and in some cases standardization) of data collected in different countries.

The panel believes major scientific and policy gains would be possible if a number of countries could be induced to embark on data design and collection activities that would provide a rich set of comparable (i.e., harmonized) data. Advantages would arise from the confluence of several factors: the differential rates of population aging throughout the world that result from differences in fertility and mortality histories, and thus provide a unique opportunity for countries to learn from each other's experiences; the concomitant economic and social changes (e.g., in pension reform, marriage and divorce rates, schooling levels, adoption of innovative medical technology) that are occurring differentially throughout the world; and the growing awareness among policy makers that problems resulting from global aging pose what are arguably the most important set of economic and social challenges they will face over the next half-century. To benefit from the possibility of exploiting institutional differences to understand the effects of policy measures, data collection efforts in different countries must be harmonized in the sense that conceptually comparable information is collected, and procedures (e.g., for sampling and quality control) are synchronized to the extent possible. Much of this harmonization can probably be achieved through extensive exchange of information among scientific groups working on new data collection efforts.

This emphasis on harmonization does not imply that survey protocols need to be identical in all countries. Each country has unique institutional features and policy priorities that should help shape data collection and research. To illustrate, while all countries are likely to regard estimates of household wealth as an important element of their data collection activity, they are unlikely to measure the same components; for example, only the United States has 401(k) plans in household wealth portfolios. On the other hand, disability, disease, and functional health need to be measured in a standardized way if useful cross-national analysis is to be possible.

The track record of prior attempts to impose standardized data collection approaches across countries is mixed at best. Thus, the goal can accurately be described as harmonization rather than standardization (although, as noted, standardization is essential in some cases). The objective is to enable researchers to estimate accurate models of the incentives to work, to retire, and to save, and make it possible to link these patterns to other important domains of older peoples' lives.

IV. Cross-national research, organized as a cooperative venture, should be emphasized as a powerful tool that can enhance the ability of policy makers to evaluate institutional and programmatic features of policy related to aging in light of international experience,

**and to assess more accurately the impact of potential modifications
to existing programs.**

Cross-national studies conducted within a framework of comparable
measurement can be a substantially more useful tool for the analysis of
policy impact than studies of single countries. A cross-national perspective provides a broader and richer set of institutional arrangements within
which to understand policy initiatives, and offers opportunities to relate
variations in institutional arrangements to the distribution of attributes
that determine program eligibility, benefit levels, and ultimately individual and household behaviors.

Sophisticated comparative analyses can exploit differences and
changes in policy rules across countries by isolating their impacts from
those of other macroeconomic and social changes. One penetrating example of cross-national research on 11 developed countries, as described
in Chapter 3, revealed three important features that could not easily have
been discerned from single-country studies. First, the data showed a
strong correspondence between early and normal retirement ages and the
probability of departure from the labor force. Second, public pension
provisions in many countries were found to place a heavy tax burden on
work past the age of early retirement eligibility, and therefore to provide
a strong incentive for early withdrawal from the labor force. Third, this
implicit tax—and hence the incentive to leave the labor force—varied
substantially among countries, as did retirement behavior. Thus considering comparisons across the countries made it possible to draw several
general conclusions about the relationship between retirement incentives
and retirement behavior.

More generally, at least three conditions must be met to provide an
accurate assessment of policy impacts on behavior. Thinking of the policy
as a treatment, (1) there must be a sizable comparison (untreated) group
with observable characteristics similar to those of the treatment group; (2)
the comparison group must be unaffected by the policy (no spillover
effects); and (3) the treatment and comparison groups must be subject to
the same socioeconomic trends over time. Cross-national comparisons
can help on all three counts. Policy interventions typically occur in one
country but not elsewhere, meaning that valid comparison groups generally exist across but not within countries. Comparison groups in other
countries are unlikely to be affected by a policy intervention in one country, so that spillover effects within countries do not necessarily distort the
estimated impact of the intervention. Finally, comparison groups can be
selected on the basis of characteristics that suggest relatively similar life
experiences; for example, individuals with high incomes and education
levels can be compared across countries. And even when within-country

variation is informative, cross-country comparisons can add substantially to the variability in the data and thereby improve the precision of a policy intervention's estimated impact.

V. Countries should aggressively pursue the consolidation of information from multiple sources to generate linked databases.

The integration of different types of information (e.g., survey, census, administrative, medical) produces a dataset whose depth and explanatory power exceed what is possible for any single source. The advantage of linking survey data with administrative records is that the latter are likely to contain extended histories that could not be obtained from a survey, or if obtainable, would be associated with significantly higher measurement error. Under ideal conditions, therefore, administrative records can provide unbiased measures of change over time for a standard set of concepts. The ability to merge data of this sort with data tailored to the analytic issues addressed by surveys clearly has major advantages.

Beyond the scientific advantages, the linking of administrative and other information with survey data reduces respondent burden, a not-insignificant factor given the complexities of survey research instruments and the sometimes strong cultural reluctance to participate in survey endeavors. And finally, close attention must be paid to novel and potentially revolutionary ways of gathering data. The likelihood that a large majority of households in many countries will soon be connected to the Internet, for example, opens up promising new methods of data collection, similar to those noted in Chapter 4 with regard to the Netherlands CentER panel.

VI. The scientific community, broadly construed, should have widespread and unconstrained access to the data obtained through the methods and activities recommended in this report.

Good data are public goods for both policy and research. Scientific advances and policy insights that may emerge from the development of a dataset are greatly enhanced if a broad community of scientific users with different interests, theoretical perspectives, and models have ready access to the information. Moreover, the best way to identify errors in data is through the user community. The HRS in the United States, begun in the early 1990s and soon to be entering its second decade, is a prominent example of how data should be made available to the research community at large. Perhaps the most important reason for the widespread use of HRS data is that they are made available in a timely fashion on the Internet to scientists and policy makers alike. More than 300 scientific papers, many by non-U.S. researchers, have been written using these data.

The track record and protocols for access to data in many countries tend to discourage use of the data. In various European and Asian countries, researchers' access to data is severely limited or unnecessarily costly in terms of time and/or money. Because of restricted access and the limited role of scientists in the design of surveys, scientific innovation in the collection of data is hampered. Moreover, many of the best scientists in these countries often choose to use data from other countries to test their ideas since it is too difficult to use their own national data.

The panel recognizes that all surveys involve legitimate and thorny issues of privacy and confidentiality that must be explicitly addressed and resolved. There are, however, statistical and legal methods for preserving confidentiality that can be used without unduly limiting scientific access to the data.

In summary, the enhanced scientific understanding needed to provide effective guidance for public policy in many countries will depend on the generation of longitudinal databases that contain representations of the critical sets of variables needed to model aging processes. The beginnings of such rich longitudinal and multidisciplinary data systems are available in the designs of various surveys mentioned throughout this report. While these are good models from which to start, what is clearly needed is a multinational version(s) of these models that takes account of differences in the nature and structure of institutions in both developed and developing countries.

Appendix A

Learning from Cross-National Research

Suppose we are interested in the impact of a particular policy or treatment 'x' on a specific outcome 'y'. As an example we might think of y as an active health index and x as a particular diagnostic treatment, say, screening for some symptom. In any national data set we observe x, y, and a set of covariates z. The covariates z include individual and local variables (for example, age, education, local unemployment).

Ignoring, for a moment, the observable covariates, without loss of generality we may write

(1) $y(i,j,t) = b(i,j,t) \times (i,j,t) + u(i,j,t)$ for individual i, in country j and time period t

where $b(i,j,t)$ measures the response by individual i in country j at time t to the policy intervention x. If the effect of the policy given by $b(i,j,t)$ varies across countries and time periods, there is little to be gained from cross-country, longitudinal, cross-cohort, or repeated cross-section analyses. Thus, one of the basic hypotheses underlying a call for cross-national longitudinal data collection or cross-national analysis of repeated cross-sections is the assumption that basic behavioral responses are stable across countries and time.

Making this assumption, we rewrite equation (1) as

(2) $y(i,j,t) = b(i) \times (i,j,t) + u(i,j,t)$

where b(i) is the individual response coefficient to the policy or treatment x.

An extreme version of equation (2) assumes a common response effect across all individuals, i.e., a "homogeneous effects" model. An intermediate specification might allow the response parameters to vary according to observed covariates (the z variables defined above). In general, however, the "heterogeneous effects" model of equation (2) has become the standard reference model for evaluating policy interventions.

PARAMETERS OF INTEREST

To fully understand the impact of a policy intervention or treatment 'x' on the outcome measure 'y', the best-case situation would be to know the full distribution of the response parameters b(i). For example, although the mean or median response may be positive, the lower quartile of the response distribution could still show a negative impact. However, we do not see the same individual with and without the treatment at the same time and in the same country. Typically, therefore, we must settle for the average effect.

A properly designed experiment measures the expected impact of the treatment on individuals drawn at random from the population. Again, this can usually be broken down into the average response for subgroups according to observed covariates 'z'.

For nonexperimental data, a popular alternative parameter of interest is the average impact of the intervention on those who are included in the program, that is, the average treatment effect on the treated. Suppose we divide a particular group according to the observed variables z; for example, we might choose women who are between 50 and 60 years of age who live in a high-unemployment area. Among these women, let some subsample be subject to the treatment, and the average response for this subsample is the impact of the treatment on the treated.

When the treated and comparison groups are chosen randomly as in an experiment, the average treatment of the treated measures the average treatment effect. But when the treatment group occurs by self-selection or by some other nonrandom mechanism, we are simply measuring the average treatment effect among the treated. This is a much less interesting parameter but one that is used regularly in the ex-post evaluation of policy interventions.

METHODS

One simple measure of the average response parameter is to take the difference in the outcomes between the treated group and the comparison group. Suppose x(i,j,t) = 1 for those who are treated and = 0 for the comparison group. Also, suppose y(1) and y(0) represent the average outcome measures for each of these groups, respectively. Then we have

(3) $y(1) - y(0) = b(1) + u(1) - u(0)$

Provided the bias term [u(1) – u(0)] is zero in the subpopulation, equation (3) consistently estimates the average treatment effect on the treated b(1) for this subpopulation. But how do we guarantee that this bias term is zero?

(A): If the comparison group (x(i,j,t) = 0) is chosen by randomized control, then for large enough samples, the bias term u(1) – u(0) is identically zero by design.

(B): If the bias term [u(1) – u(0)] is constant before and after the treatment, then comparing the difference in the outcome variable *before* the reform [y'(1) – y'(0)] with the difference *after* the reform [y*(1) – y*(0)] again consistently estimates b(1).

(4) $[y^*(1) - y^*(0)] - [y'(1) - y'(0)] = b(1)$

Unfortunately, the conditions for equation (4) are difficult to satisfy in a nonexperimental setting. Three conditions are required:

• There is a sizable comparison group with similar observable characteristics.
• The comparison group is completely unaffected by the reform.
• The treatment group and the comparison group are subject to the exact same trends over time.

Within-Country Comparisons

Suppose all that is available are national samples. Where treatments are global for a particular subpopulation, such as the introduction of national screening (or a universal pension provision), the first condition fails immediately; no suitable comparison group exists. When there are spillover effects on the rest of the community, the second condition fails. Finally, the comparison group can be chosen within a country but the two groups are sufficiently different that they have systematically different health experiences over time, the final condition fails.

Cross-National Comparisons

Cross-national comparisons can help in all three of the above cases. Interventions or policies—for example, a universal health insurance scheme—often occur in one country and not another. So even if they are global within a country, there is variation across countries. The before and after contrasts can then be drawn across countries. Alternatively different countries may introduce similar interventions or treatments but with different timings, so that the contrast in equation (4) can still be made. Second, spillover effects are typically limited to within national boundaries, so that the contrast across countries is still valid. Finally, similar comparison groups can be chosen across countries, e.g., high-income and well-educated individuals who are likely to experience the same overall trends. Note also that even where within-country variation is informative, cross-country comparisons can add substantially to the informative variability in the data, and therefore considerably improve the precision of estimates of the impact of such interventions.

Measurement Issues

The hypothesized stability of responses that allows us to move from the general but vacuous equation (1) to the stable form of equation (2) assumes that the measurements of the variables $y(i,j,t)$ and $x(i,j,t)$ are comparable across time and space. Again restricting attention to linear relations, the general relationship between measurements in two countries, j and j', and two time periods, t and t', may be written as

(3) $x(i,j',t') = d(j,t) + c(j,t) \times (i,j,t)$

Substituting equation (3) into equation (1), we obtain

(4) $y(i) = b(i)(d(j,t) + c(j,t)) \times (i) + u(i) = d(j,t) + b(i)c(j,t) \times (i) + u(i)$

Ideally, if we could measure $x(i,j,t)$ comparably across countries and time, we could assume that $d = 0$ and $c = 1$ for all j and t and thus (potentially) test the hypothesis of behavioral stability using approaches described in the preceding section (e.g., test the hypothesis that $b(i,j) = b(i,j')$). If we cannot make this assumption, it is easy to see that the estimated effect of x on y in country j' may differ from its estimated effect in country j even if behavior is the same in both countries, simply because the measurement of x differs ($b(i)$ is not equal to $b(i)c(j)$). Failure to have comparable measures of important variables can severely reduce the possibility of exploiting cross-national variations in policies and other variables to enhance scientific knowledge of behavioral responses.

In some cases, these measurement problems are trivially easy to correct. For instance, temperature measured in Fahrenheit in the United States can be converted to centigrade to conform to European measurements. In other cases, the theoretical idea is well understood but not trivial to implement. An example is the conversion of monetary measures into a common value. Here, observed foreign exchange rates may convert francs into dollars, but this conversion may not conform to a purchasing power parity rate that could be used to equate the true purchasing power of given incomes in France and the United States. For many variables used in studies of health, psychology, and economics, methods for obtaining common measurements are not well understood, in part because they have received inadequate systematic attention from the scientific community. Progress is currently being made on a number of fronts. For example, there is a continuing large-scale, cross-national effort to create instruments that can produce valid measures of depression that are comparable across countries, cultures, and language groups. To continue making progress along these lines, the active collaboration of scientists from different disciplines and countries is imperative.

Biographical Sketches of Committee Members and Staff

F. Thomas Juster *(Chair)* is professor emeritus of economics at the University of Michigan, and a fellow of the American Statistical Association and of the National Association of Business Economists. He was director of the University of Michigan Institute for Social Research (ISR) from 1976 to 1986 and is currently a research scientist at ISR. He spent most of his prior professional career in New York with the National Bureau of Economic Research. He has chaired the Committee on the Quality of Economic Statistics of the American Economics Association, been a member of several committees of the National Academy of Sciences, served on the Brookings Panel as a senior advisor, and been a member of various advisory committees of the American Statistical Association. Dr. Juster's research interests include savings and wealth accumulation among U.S. households; time allocation within households; the determinants of retirement; and the interrelationships among health status, labor force status, and economic status.

Richard Blundell is professor of economics at University College, London, and also holds appointments as research director of the Institute for Fiscal Studies and research director of the ESRC Centre for Micro-Economics Analysis of Fiscal Policy. He has held visiting professor positions at the University of British Columbia, the Massachusetts Institute of Technology, and the University of California at Berkeley. He was elected fellow of the Econometric Society in 1991 and fellow of the British Academy in 1996. In 1995 he was awarded the Jahnsson Prize for his work in microeconometrics, labor supply, and consumer behavior. Dr. Blundell was editor of the *Journal of Econometrics* from 1992 to 1997, and in 1997 became coeditor of *Econometrica*. His published papers have appeared in *Econometrica*, *Review of Economic Studies*, *American Economic Review*, *Journal of Econometrics*, *Journal of Applied Econometrics*, and *Economic Journal*.

Richard V. Burkhauser, an economist, is Sarah Gibson Blandings Professor and chair of the Department of Policy Analysis and Management at Cornell University. He has published widely in the area of U.S. and European social policy. He is on the editorial boards of *The Gerontologist*, *The Journal of Disability Policy Studies*, *The Review of Income and Wealth*, and *Labour Economics*. Dr. Burkhauser is also a member of the Panel Study of Income Dynamics board of overseers. He is currently editing a special issue of *Labour Economics on the Health, Wealth, and Work of Older Persons* using international dynamic data. Dr. Burkhauser received his Ph.D. in economics from the University of Chicago.

Graziella Caselli is professor of demography and director of the Dipartimento di Scienze Demografiche at the University of Rome "La Sapienza." She also is honorary president of the European Association for Population Studies. Dr. Caselli has written extensively on the demography of Italy, health and mortality transitions in Europe, and health and mortality among elderly populations.

Linda P. Fried is professor of internal medicine at the Johns Hopkins School of Medicine, with a joint appointment in epidemiology in the Johns Hopkins University School of Public Health. Her research concerns the development of preventive health care for older adults. She is principal investigator of the Cardiovascular Health Study (CHS) and of the Women's Health and Aging Studies (WHAS I and II). These studies focus on the risk factors for cardiovascular diseases and atherosclerosis in men and women aged 65 and older (CHS) and on defining the roles of major chronic diseases in causing physical disability and frailty in older adults (WHAS I and II). Dr. Fried also is research director of a multicenter initiative to evaluate the import of enhanced activity through productive social roles on health promotion in older adults, and the director of a training grant on the epidemiology and biostatistics of aging.

Albert I. Hermalin is professor emeritus of sociology and research scientist at the Population Studies Center, University of Michigan. He has served as chair of the Committee on Population of the National Academy of Sciences and as president of the Population Association of America. He currently is working on a comparative study of aging in Asia, a multiyear collaborative project with the Philippines, Taiwan, Thailand, and Singapore. The focus of the study is on the rapid social, economic, and demographic changes under way and their impact on the health and socioeconomic well-being of the elderly, as well as on intergenerational relations more broadly.

Robert L. Kahn is professor emeritus of psychology and public health at the University of Michigan, where he is also a research scientist emeritus in the Institute for Social Research, of which he was a founder. His research has concentrated for many years on two main subjects: organizational behavior and aging. His books and articles on organizations have analyzed their overall effectiveness, their impact on the health of their members, and their relevance for international relations. Dr. Kahn is a fellow of the American Academy of Arts and Sciences, the American Association for the Advancement of Science, and numerous professional organizations.

Arie Kapteyn is professor of econometrics and director of CentER at Tilburg University, the Netherlands. He is the author of more than 100 scientific papers on applied welfare economics, preference formation, household decision making, leisure and labor supply, econometrics of panel data, latent variables, variance components, consumer demand, and savings. Dr. Kapteyn's recent papers have appeared in the *American Economic Review*, the *Journal of Public Economics*, *De Economist*, and *Labour Economics*.

Kevin Kinsella is a Special Assistant with the International Programs Center, Population Division, U.S. Census Bureau, where he has been employed since 1979. During the period 1999-2001, he worked with the Committee on Population of the National Research Council as Study Director for this panel report as well as another project that assessed the pros and cons of collecting biological indicators in population-based surveys. Prior to his assignment with the National Research Council, Kinsella was Chief of the Census Bureau's Aging Studies Branch. His professional activities have focused on the role of women in development, population projections for developing countries (particularly in Latin America), and the demography of aging internationally.

Michael Marmot is professor of epidemiology and public health at University College, London (UCL). He is best known as the principal investigator of the Whitehall II Study on socioeconomic differences in health and disease among British civil servants. He became director of the International Centre for Health and Society at UCL in 1994, was appointed a member of the Royal Commission on Environmental Pollution, and awarded an MRC Professorship in 1995. Dr. Marmot was elected fellow of the Royal College of Physicians in 1996 and fellow of the Academy of Medical Sciences in 1998, and was knighted by the Queen in 2000 in recognition of his broad-ranging contributions to the fields of epidemiology and public health.

Linda G. Martin has been president of the Population Council in New York since 1999. Previously, she was RAND's vice president for research development, and from 1993 to 1995 was vice president and director of RAND's Domestic Research Division, which conducted research on health, education, labor and population, and criminal and civil justice. Prior to joining RAND, Dr. Martin held positions at the National Research Council, the East-West Center, the University of Hawaii, and the U.S. House of Representatives. Her past research has focused on demographic change in Asia and Africa, and she has published extensively on aging issues. Currently she is working on trends in disability in the United States. Dr. Martin received an A.B. in mathematics from Harvard University and an M.P.A. and Ph.D. in economics from Princeton University.

David Mechanic is René Dubos Professor of Behavioral Sciences and director of the Institute for Health at Rutgers University, where he was formerly dean of the Faculty of Arts and Sciences. He also directs the Institute's Center for Research on the Organization and Financing of Services for the Severely Mentally Ill and a postdoctoral training program in mental health services research funded by the National Institute on Mental Health. He is the author of numerous books and other publications on health policy and health services research. His current research interests include trust relationships between clients and physicians, the effects of managed care on mental health services, and patterns of inpatient treatment for patients with schizophrenia. Dr. Mechanic is a member of the National Academy of Sciences and its affiliate, the Institute of Medicine, and has served on many national commissions and advisory boards. He is a recipient of the Distinguished Investigator Award from the Association for Health Services Research; the Lifetime Achievement Award from the Mental Health Section of the American Sociological Association; the Carl Taube Award for Mental Health Services Research from the American Public Health Association; and the Health Services Research Prize awarded by the Association of University Programs in Health Administration and the Baxter Allegiance Foundation, the highest honor in the health services research field.

James P. Smith holds the RAND chair in Labor Markets and Demographic Studies and was the director of RAND's Labor and Population Studies Program from 1977 to 1994. He has directed numerous projects and written extensively in the areas of immigration, the economics of aging, black-white wages and employment in the United States, the effects of economic development on labor markets, wealth accumulation and savings behavior, and the interrelationships between health and economic status among the elderly. He chaired the National Institute on Aging's (NIA) Ad Hoc Advisory Panel on Extramural Priorities for Data Collection in Health and Retirement Economics, and currently serves on NIA's Data Monitoring Committee for both the Health and Retirement Survey and the Asset and Health Dynamics Among the Oldest-Old Survey. He is a member of the National Science Foundation Advisory Committee for the Panel Study of Income Dynamics and is the public representative of California's Occupational Safety and Health Board, appointed by the governor. He has received the National Institutes of Health (NIH) MERIT Award, the most distinguished honor granted to a researcher by NIH. Dr. Smith received his Ph.D. in economics in 1972 from the University of Chicago.

Beth J. Soldo is the Joseph E. and Ruth E. Boettner Professor of Financial Gerontology and director of the Boettner Center at the University of Pennsylvania School of Social Work. Previously, she was professor of demography at Georgetown University. She has done extensive research on various aspects of aging, including family structure, social support, mobility, intergenerational transfers, and health dynamics of the oldest old. She is a collaborator on two national surveys of the elderly: the Health and Retirement Survey and the Survey of Asset and Health Dynamics Among the Oldest Old. Dr. Soldo received her B.A. in sociology from Fordham University and her M.A. and Ph.D. in sociology from Duke University.

Robert Wallace is professor of preventive medicine and internal medicine at the University of Iowa College of Medicine. He has been a member of the U.S. Preventive Services Task Force (USPSTF) and the National Advisory Council on Aging of the National Institutes of Health. He currently is a member of the Health Promotion and Disease Prevention Board of the Institute of Medicine and a senior advisor to USPSTF. Dr. Wallace's research focuses on the causes and prevention of disability among older persons in the United States and internationally. He has substantial experience in the conduct of both observational cohort studies of older persons and clinical trials, including preventive interventions related to osteoporotic fracture and coronary disease prevention. He is the site principal investigator for the U.S. Women's Health Initiative (WHI), a national intervention trial exploring the prevention of breast and colon cancer and coronary disease, and is the deputy chair of WHI's Executive Committee.

Robert J. Willis, a professor of economics, joined the University of Michigan in 1995 and holds joint appointments with the Survey Research Center at the Institute for Social Research and the Population Studies Center. Before coming to Michigan, Dr. Willis held appointments at the University of Chicago, the State University of New York at Stony Brook, and Stanford University. He has been elected to the Board of Directors of the Population Association of America; has served on advisory boards for a number of surveys, including the Panel Study of Income Dynamics, the High School and Beyond Survey, and the Health and Retirement Survey; and was recently appointed as representative to the Census Advisory Board by the American Economic Association. Dr. Willis received his Ph.D. from the University of Washington in 1971.

David Wise is John F. Stambaugh Professor of Political Economy at the John F. Kennedy School of Government, Harvard University, and the director for Health and Retirement Programs at the National Bureau of Economic Research. He has written extensively on individual savings, pensions, and assets in later life, and has authored or edited numerous books and papers on the economics of aging. Dr. Wise recently finished a multiyear 11-country collaborative study of social security programs and retirement around the world.

Zeng Yi currently is senior research scientist at the Center for Demographic Studies of Duke University, with joint appointments as professor of demography at the Institute of Population Research, Peking University, and as distinguished research scholar at the Max Planck Institute for Demographic Research, Rostok, Germany. Previously, he was director of the Institute of Population Research at Peking University. His primary research fields are population aging and family household dynamics. Dr. Zeng has authored or edited nine books and nearly 100 professional papers, about half of which are in English and published in academic journals or series in the United States, England, the Netherlands, Belgium, Austria, Denmark, and Italy. He received his Ph.D. from Brussels Free University in 1986 and conducted postdoctoral research at Princeton University.

Index

committee methodology, 3
community supports, 204, 207-208, 211, 213, 217
contraception, 16
cost of health care, 2, 17, 155, 158-159, 166, 168-169, 181, 200, 201, 203, 208, 210, 217, 220
cultural factors, 204, 211, 217, 220
defined, 225-226, 230, 252
educational attainment and, 203, 205, 222
education of public, 207
elderly, definition of, 30
employment and, general, 24-25, 201-202, 204, 205, 222-223, 224
family factors, 203, 220, 221; *see also* *"care of..."* under Family factors
funding, 208, 211; *see also* Medicaid; Medicare
gender factors, 220, 223, 228
home care, 158, 175, 181, 211, 213, 220, 232
income security, 102
institutional care, 42, 121, 181, 209, 210, 218-219
intergenerational transfers, 13, 17, 155, 158-159, 166, 168-169
longitudinal research, general, 4, 206-207, 214, 220-221, 224
nutrition, 47, 202, 203, 205, 207, 224, 250, 271
oldest old, 37
pain and pain management, 225, 253, 265, 266, 267, 269, 273
preventive care, 12, 201, 202, 203, 207-208, 209, 210, 213, 220, 227, 228, 230, 231, 238, 240, 244
professional training, 201, 202
public health services, 1, 47, 202, 205, 207, 208, 209, 211, 250
retirement, 9, 67, 69, 77, 86, 91, 93, 94-95, 98, 203
self-care, 209, 211, 212, 213, 220, 231, 232, 233, 237
self-rated health status, 129, 206, 207, 225, 229-230, 232, 253, 260, 261-262, 263, 265, 266, 273
social factors, general, 200, 201, 203, 204, 206, 212, 220, 221, 224
socioeconomic status, 26, 110-111, 203, 208, 220, 221-225

standards, 207, 213, 215-216
technology, 201, 202, 208
wealth and income security, 10, 110-111, 128, 129, 203
Heart disease, *see* Cardiovascular disease
Historical perspectives, *ix*, 1, 15-16, 18, 30
capital gains and savings, 110
employer-provided pensions, 102
employment, 66
fertility, 15-16, 30, 39, 44-45
life expectancy, 47, 48, 49, 52, 53, 55, 56, 205-206, 250
living standards, 102
OECD labor force, 8
oldest old, 59
pensions/retirement income, 66, 102
savings, 102, 110, 116
speed of population aging, 38-39
wealth, 114-116, 123
Home health care, 158, 175, 181, 211, 213, 218, 220, 232
self-care, 209, 211, 212, 213, 220, 231, 232, 233, 237
Housing, 155, 158, 202, 203, 205, 256-257
coresidence of elderly and children, 19, 166, 174, 177, 180, 183, 184
institutional care, 42, 121, 181, 209, 210, 218-219
living arrangements of elderly persons, 180, 188, 212, 253
wealth, home ownership as, 111-112, 121, 128, 131, 132, 140-141, 142, 158, 175
HRS, *see* Health and Retirement Survey
Hungary, 38, 48

I

Immigration and emigration, 15, 44-45
Income, 16, 23, 91, 98, 102-151 (passim)
see also Pensions; Socioeconomic status
consumption and, 105
health status, 222
intergenerational transfers, 166, 178
multidisciplinary approaches, 3
replacement income, 19, 78, 80, 81, 85, 104, 142, 146, 148
well-being, 253, 254-256, 258, 260-261, 264
Income Panel Survey (IPS), 129, 130